THE ARCHITECTURE OF McKIM, MEAD & WHITE 1870–1920

GARLAND REFERENCE LIBRARY
OF THE HUMANITIES
(VOL. 114)

THE ARCHITECTURE OF MCKIM, MEAD & WHITE
1870–1920
A Building List

Leland M. Roth

GARLAND PUBLISHING, INC. • NEW YORK & LONDON
1978

Library of Congress Cataloging in Publication Data

Roth, Leland M
  The architecture of McKim, Mead & White,
1870–1920.

  (Garland reference library of the humanities; v. 114)
  Bibliography: p.
  Includes index.
  1. McKim, Mead & White—Catalogs.
2. Architecture, Modern—19th century—Catalogs.
3. Architecture, Modern—20th century—Catalogs.
I. Title.
NA737.M4A4   1978   720'.6'57471   77-83368
ISBN 0-8240-9850-1

Printed on acid-free, 250-year-life paper
Manufactured in the United States of America

To Carol
a constant help

and Amanda
who arrived
as this was born

Contents

Preface

For more than a quarter of a century, McKim, Mead & White was the largest architectural firm in the world, producing buildings of a quality and at a rate that impressed colleagues and the public both in the United States and in England. Some were small undertakings, renovations or additions, while others were major commissions that entailed years of study and even longer periods of construction. Indeed, some of the firm's plans for groups of buildings or for large museums were never fully realized, so extensive were they.

Because of the profusion and dissemination of the firm's work, because of its widespread publication, and because of the firm's influence on the hundreds of young architects who passed through the office, McKim, Mead, and White had a pronounced effect on the architecture of their own generation and on that which followed. Most especially, they focused their attention on urban and public buildings and so played a large part in shaping the character of urban architecture during the very years when the city became the dominant element in American life.

Some of their best work, such as Columbia University or the ill-fated Pennsylvania Station, has always been well known, but even in their own time the wide range of the firm's activity was not fully understood. Then, after 1930, when all historicist and traditional architecture became suspect, even more of their work was forgotten. This building list attempts to correct this by cataloguing all of the firm's important work, from the moment the partners started their separate practices up through the formal withdrawal of Mead from office affairs in 1919. The object was to be as complete as possible, but omissions and errors in so large a body of material are perhaps inevitable. Nearly all of the urban work was examined *in situ* by the author and addresses checked, but as yet this is not feasible for all of the more scattered domestic work, much of which has been studied by my colleague Richard Guy Wilson, who graciously supplied several photographs reproduced here. Although conflicting schedules prevented incorporation of more information on the domestic work, we look forward to more expanded collaborative ventures in the future.

The list is divided into several separate sections that correspond to the phases of formation of the partnership. Part IA gives the individual work of the young architects from 1870 to 1877; IB gives the work of the first partnership, McKim, Mead & Bigelow, from 1877 to 1879; and IC gives the work of McKim, Mead & White from 1879 through 1919. A fourth section, ID, gives miscellaneous nonarchitectural work of Stanford White from 1879 through 1906. Based largely on the Bill Books in the McKim, Mead & White Archive (see the Bibliography), the preserved bills sent out to all clients, these lists give the location, address, present condition, dates (date started and dates of construction), partner in charge, contractor, cost, and location of extant working drawings. Each commission or project is given a number, and all are presented in alphabetical order according to the name of the client or the proper name of the building. There is cross-listing within the list between client and building name.

The building list is followed by Part II, a year-by-year summary of annual construction contract amounts. These figures can be most accurately compared by using the figures in Part III, an index of building costs from 1870 through 1977. Each of these sections—the building list, the summary of contracts, the building cost index—is preceded by brief introductory and explanatory comments in which the sources for each are cited. The building lists and tables are followed by an extensive bibliography. Since the commissions and projects are listed alphabetically by name and client, a short index is provided giving geographical locations and the names of artists with whom the firm worked.

Important examples of the firm's work have been reproduced in the large *Monograph of the Work of McKim, Mead & White, 1879–1915*, 4 vols. (New York, 1915–1920), but the four hundred plates of that folio presented only 170 commissions. The list presented here attempts to illustrate as many of the firm's 945 commissions as possible, drawing from a wide range of sources. Some of the illustrations are taken from the *Monograph*, some from publication in contemporary journals, some from the large collections of photographs of the firm's work in the New-York Historical Society and the Museum of the City of New York, some from the scrapbooks deposited in the Avery Library, Columbia University. Many of the photographs were taken by the author on field surveys made from 1968 to 1977. Several views have been supplied by Richard Guy Wilson.

Although the firm's own records have served as the basis of this list, there are significant omissions in the official documents themselves; for instance, much of White's collaborative work with Augustus Saint-Gaudens does not appear at all in the Bill Books. The well-known Adams Memorial is one example. Because of these lacunae, it is altogether possible that continuing research may add to this list.

In compiling this information I have been greatly aided by many individuals and institutions. In particular I would like to thank Richard Guy Wilson; the members of the White family and especially Laura Chanler White, the wife of Lawrence Grant White, Stanford White's son; the New-York Historical Society, particularly Dr. James J. Heslin, Director, and Wilson Duprey, former Curator of Maps and Prints, and Wendy Shadwell, who succeeded him; the Avery Library, Columbia University, particularly Adolf Placzek, Librarian; the Museum of the City of New York; the Manuscript Division of the Library of Congress; and Walker O. Cain.

Evanston, Illinois
December, 1977

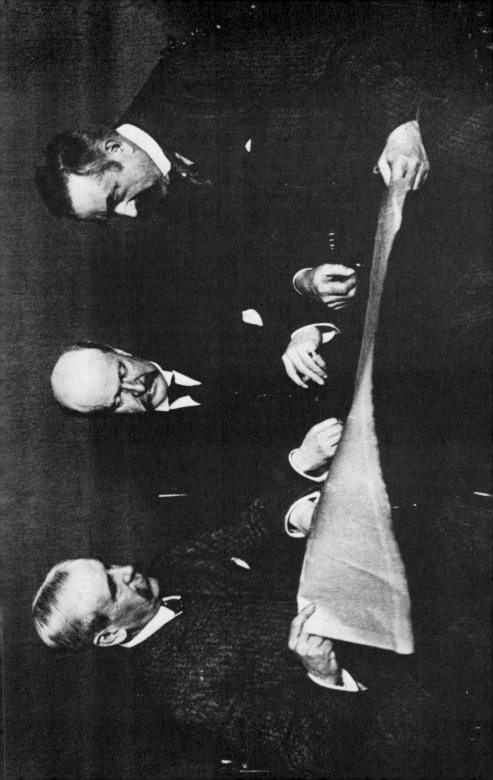

Agreement

57 Broadway — June 21 - 1880 —

The following articles of copartnership have this day been entered into by the undersigned —

1 — This agreement to hold good for one year from July 1st 1880 —

2 — The firm to be known under the name of McKim Mead & White —

3 — All receipts to be banked —

4 — All expenses to be paid by the firm from the gross receipts —

5 — The net receipts to be divided in the following proportion —
Charles F. McKim to draw 42/100 —
Wm. R. Mead " " 33/100 —
Stanford White " " 25/100 —

6 — Collections on all bills rendered between July 1st 1880 and July 1st 1881 to be considered as receipts —

7 — In case of dissolution of this

2. Original agreement of the partnership of McKim, Mead, and White, dated June 21, 1880. Courtesy of Laura Chanler White.

Opposite: 1. (left to right) Mead, McKim, and White, formal portrait, examining a drawing, c. 1905. (From C. Baldwin, *Stanford White*).

partnership – or failure to renew
at the end of the year – the
business will be settled in the
same ratio of division –

Charles F. McKim

Wm R. Mead

Stanford White

McKim, Mead, and White:
Their Office and Its Influence

It was esteemed by students of architecture a great privilege to be admitted to the office of these architects, which seemed to breathe the spirit of the fifteenth century.

William A. Boring to Charles Moore, 1927.

The agreement reproduced on the preceding pages (Fig. 2), written in longhand on yellow foolscap, documents the beginning of what was, at the turn of the century, the most famous American architectural partnership—McKim, Mead & White. Other architects of their generation, such as Sullivan and Wright of Chicago, or Otto Wagner of Vienna, may be better known for their having grappled with the problems of a modern industrialized architecture, but McKim, Mead, and White, because of their insistence on high standards of workmanship, their use of sumptuous and colorful building materials, their expansive public spaces, and their celebration of local tradition, are again being appreciated and studied much as they were at the beginning of this century.

The three began their individual careers during the 1870's and came together in 1879. They conducted an increasingly bustling practice; altogether they received somewhat more than 940 commissions during the half-century in which they were active, a few executed before the forming of the partnership, but most from 1879 to 1908 under the direct supervision of either McKim or White. Still others were carried out by younger partners who continued the office using the same name, first under Mead's supervision and then, after his death, well into the twentieth century.

McKim, Mead & White came to have a profound and far-reaching influence, largely through the impact of the firm's hundreds of buildings from Maine to Oregon, North Dakota to Texas, and through the extensive publication of a great majority of these in both the architectural and popular press. Beyond the physical presence of the buildings, the firm exerted a strong influence through the great number of architects it trained who then established their own offices across the United States. In his biography of McKim, Charles Moore gives the names of 513 office employees, a significant number of whom later became prominent architects in their own right and who held executive offices in local and national professional organizations.[1] Nor was this transience in the office viewed with disapproval. McKim's earliest biographer, Alfred Hoyt Granger, noted that McKim took particular interest in his assistants, encouraged them to enter important competitions, and even secured commissions for them when he felt they were ready to start their own careers.[2] What made the effect of the McKim, Mead & White office *atelier* particularly strong was that the firm devoted its greatest energy to urban and public buildings, and the young men who passed through it began their careers at precisely that moment when the city became the dominant force in American life. As a result, McKim, Mead, and White and their many assistants and students played an important part in giving shape to the modern American city.

The success of the firm arose from many fortunate coincidences, beginning with the happy coming together of three radically different and yet perfectly complementary personalities— McKim, a sober, Quaker-bred perfectionist Pennsylvanian; Mead, a good-humored, levelheaded, taciturn Yankee; and White, a redheaded ebullient New Yorker. The oldest was William Rutherford Mead (August 20, 1846, to June 20, 1928; Fig. 3), born in Brattleboro, Vermont, his father a prosperous lawyer and his mother the sister of utopian-socialist reformer John Humphrey Noyes.[3] Young Mead received the normal elementary education in Brattleboro, supplemented by a keen appreciation of the arts at home; his sister Elinor was a painter and his older brother, Larkin Goldsmith, became an important sculptor. When William was seven his brother was already working in the studio of Henry Kirke Brown in New York. Later, in the company of his brother, William visited the state capitol at Montpelier, recalling in later years that he must have been disposed towards classical architecture by seeing the impressive domed Doric capitol building by Ammi B. Young.[4]

Mead entered Norwich University in Northfield, Vermont, but finished his education at Amherst College in 1867. He then went to New York where for a short time he worked for an engineer and then entered the office of architect Russell Sturgis, one of the most vociferous champions of Ruskin's principles in the United States. He was in Sturgis's office as a paying student and was put in the care of George Fletcher Babb, a young assistant. About a year after Mead arrived, the office of Sturgis and Peter B. Wight was moved from 98 Broadway down to number 57, across from the Trinity churchyard, to a building where a number of the younger architects were setting up, among them George B. Post and Gambrill & Richardson. Mead remained with Sturgis another two years, leaving in 1871 to go to Florence, where his brother had established a studio; there he studied rather informally at the Accademia delle Belle Arti before returning to New York sometime during 1872–1873.

Charles Follen McKim (August 27, 1847, to September 14, 1909; Fig. 4) was the son of widely dissimilar parents. His father was one of the leading and most active abolitionists, his mother a quiet Quaker also active in the antislavery movement.[5] McKim's father frequently traveled collecting funds for the movement and later, following emancipation, for freedmen's education. During one such trip, while his mother was staying with relatives in rural Chester County, Charles was born. The boy was named after Karl Follen, the professor of German at Harvard who had been summarily dismissed because of his outspoken abolitionist sentiments. As a child Charles lived in Philadelphia and then Germantown, just outside the city, but for his education he was sent to Eagleswood School, run by Theodore Weld, the former abolitionist leader, in what remained of the disbanded utopian communities of the North American Phalanx and the Raritan Bay Union, near Perth Amboy, New Jersey.[6] While Charles completed his high school work in Philadelphia, the family moved to a new home in the carefully planned and landscaped Llewellyn Park, Orange, New Jersey, when his father took a new position in New York City after the

Civil War. At first intent on going to Harvard College, Charles modified his views, deciding instead to enter the Harvard Lawrence Scientific School, where he could train as a mining engineer. Once there, however, in 1866, McKim felt it imperative that he finish his education at the École des Mines, Paris, France. As the year progressed and he experienced difficulty with the more technical subjects and mathematics, he discovered that his classes in French and mechanical drawing gave him much more satisfaction. He decided to become an architect, but for this too he had to go to France. In an effort to force Charles to examine his plans more realistically, McKim's father placed him in the office of a friend, Russell Sturgis, during the summer of 1867 (this was before Mead arrived). Meanwhile, McKim's father asked advice of many friends, among them Henry Villard and William Howard Furness (father of the Philadelphia architect). The result of the inquiries was that Charles went to Paris and in the fall of 1878 was admitted to the École des Beaux-Arts.

In Paris McKim entered the *atelier* of Pierre-Gérôme-Honoré Daumet, remaining nearly three years. He submitted several *projets,* though he did not win any prizes, and returned to the United States just before the outbreak of the Franco-Prussian War in 1870. When McKim came back, he brought with him not the Parisian styles, as did Ernest Flagg, for example, but rather the spirit of the École, with its insistence on broadly and clearly conceived conceptual order as represented in the *parti* and on the direct expression of this order in a rationally articulated exterior. To the Beaux-Arts concepts of processional, ceremonial space and visual enrichment scaled to the human eye and frame, McKim added Ruskinian precepts he had absorbed during his brief stay in Sturgis's office— expressive massing, solid and straightforward construction with openly expressed materials, natural colors, symbolic meaning enhanced by mural painting and decorative sculpture, and adherence to national traditions.

As soon as he returned from France, McKim went to New York and was employed by Gambrill & Richardson, preferring the challenge of that city to Philadelphia, where he had been offered a position by Frank Furness.[7] In the office of H. H. Richardson, also a

3. William Rutherford Mead, 1846–1928. (From C. Moore, *The Life and Times of Charles Follen McKim*).

4. Charles Follen McKim, 1847–1909. Drawing by Jane Emmett, April, 1906. (From A. H. Granger, *Charles Follen McKim, A Study of His Life and Work*).

5b. Stanford White, c. 1906. Courtesy of Laura Chanler White.

5a. Stanford White, 1853–1906. Photograph of c. 1878. Courtesy of Laura Chanler White.

Harvard alumnus and a student of the École, McKim became a principal assistant, working on the Brattle Square Church, the Hampden County Courthouse, and, in the spring of 1872, on the early studies for Trinity Church. Meanwhile, however, McKim had begun to obtain his own commissions, and while the Trinity drawings were studied and modified during 1872–1874, McKim gradually withdrew from Richardson's office, spending more and more time in his own rooms at 57 Broadway.

In large part McKim's place was filled by a young man admitted to Richardson's office in the spring of 1872—this was Stanford White (November 9, 1853, to June 25, 1906; Figs. 5a and 5b), who was then only nineteen.[8] White was the son of a prominent writer and critic of music and literature in New York who in 1865 became involved in the founding of the new liberal journal, the *Nation*. Through this venture the father met Frederick Law Olmsted, another of the founders. Stanny, as he was known to the family, developed quite early an absorbing interest in the visual arts and wished to become a painter. When John La Farge, another of his father's acquaintances, discouraged the idea, advice was solicited from Olmsted, who suggested that the youngster be placed in the office of his friend Richardson, for the profession of an architect was much more reliable.[9] In this way White came under Richardson's tutelage, but within two years, so quick was the young man's grasp and so marked his ability (and so conscientious was Richardson's training), White became a major assistant, in charge of much of the interior detailing of the residential work. He was also made field representative and building superintendent, as Richardson's worsening Bright's disease increasingly kept him bedridden.[10] White and Richardson learned much from each other and together developed a drafting style which makes it difficult to determine who did certain drawings. Devoted to "The Great Mogul," as he called Richardson, White for a time even wore a full beard resembling that of his mentor (Fig. 5a). A good example of White's best work is his study of 1874 for the tower of Trinity Church, based on the lantern of the Cathedral of Salamanca, Spain, as suggested by Richardson. In the next four years White supervised construction of the Cheney Building, Hartford, and the changes made by Richardson to the New York State Capitol, Albany, while designing almost wholly the various Cheney house projects that came out of the Gambrill & Richardson office. After Richardson moved his own practice to Brookline, Massachusetts, in 1874, White became the liaison between Boston and New York, where until 1878 Richardson maintained the formal association with Gambrill.

In the meantime White had met Augustus Saint-Gaudens, a struggling young sculptor in New York, and the two became close, lifelong friends. In 1877 they were at work on three collaborative designs—the Edwin Dennison Morgan tomb, the David Glasgow Farragut Memorial, and the Robert Richard Randall Memorial—the first of their many and highly successful joint creations. Concerning these, as well as the many collaborative works that followed in the next thirty-five years, there was a constant exchange of advice, from sculptor to architect about something in the pedestal or base that needed correction, or from architect to sculptor about a leg or arm that needed repositioning. There was little jealousy over authorship between the two, and this collaborative spirit was to spread to others, helping to spark the so-called Renaissance in the American visual arts after 1887.

In 1878 White left Richardson for a trip to France, heading for Paris in the company of his friend Charles McKim, whom he had come to know well while in Richardson's office. Indeed, once Richardson had relocated in Brookline, White seems to have spent a great deal of time in McKim's small office at 57 Broadway, perhaps helping out at the drafting table. In 1874 Mead had set himself up at 57 Broadway as well, and shortly thereafter he and McKim began to split expenses and to aid each other *en charette* during those long nights when piles of drawings had to be finished as a job neared completion. They submitted a joint entry in the competition for the Providence City Hall in 1874, but were unsuccessful (see Building List No. 16). Neither was especially skilled in making the engaging presentation drawings such as White was doing for Richardson, so during 1876 or 1877 they added a third member to their company, William B. Bigelow, a highly gifted draftsman whom McKim had known at the École and whose sister, Annie, McKim had married in 1874. During the summer of 1877 all four—McKim, Mead, Bigelow, and White—had made an extended sketching trip along the Atlantic coast north of Boston in search of examples of the Colonial architecture then beginning to attract so much attention in the wake of the nation's centennial. About the same time, McKim, Mead, and Bigelow formed a partnership since their office affairs had become so intertwined. Neither McKim's marriage nor the partnership with Bigelow fared well, however, and by mid-1878 Annie had left McKim, taking their infant daughter, Margaret, and the partnership began to come apart. Hence McKim sought a quieter, safer, more congenial place—he went to Paris with White.

For about a year and a half White remained in Europe, camping out with the Saint-Gaudens family, who had settled in Paris while Augustus put the finishing touches on the Farragut and made it ready for casting in bronze. McKim, in the meantime, had returned to New York and resumed work. Finally, having made rapid tours of France and Italy, his money exhausted, his sketch books brimming, White was making ready to return to New York, perhaps to Richardson's office again, when McKim and Mead wrote asking if he would like to join them. They may not have expressed it directly, but they sorely needed someone like White now that Bigelow had withdrawn—someone deft with a pencil, with an eye for sensitive, delicate interior detailing. On August 23, 1879, White departed Liverpool, bound for New York. On Monday, September 8, 1879, he came into the office, and the partnership of McKim, Mead & White was started. Perhaps after the debacle with Bigelow, Mead urged caution, but after nearly ten months had passed the seal was given to what had already existed in fact; on June 21, 1880, the partnership was made official.

Had the partnership started ten or fifteen years earlier, the story would have been radically different, but McKim, Mead, and White had the good fortune to start their practice at the moment when the United States emerged from a deep business depression during the 1870's. The resultant need for a great volume of building was coupled with an unexpressed desire for something better than the High Victorian Gothic or Second Empire Baroque styles that had been popular following the Civil War through the 1870's.

McKim, Mead, and White were young, alert, knowledgeable in the wide range of styles of contemporary and historic Europe, and they were especially sensitive to the classic heritage of native Georgian and Federalist architecture, which they helped "rediscover." To clients they seemed eager to take on new problems and new building types—large frame summer houses, casinos and country clubs, apartment buildings, public lending libraries. Because of their varied backgrounds and personal interests, they had contacts in many disparate parts of society. Commissions came quickly, and buildings were finished just as rapidly. Between 1879, when they started, and 1887, when the Boston Public Library marked the emergence of their mature work, the partners had 215 significant commissions; compare this to the 100 or so commissions that Mrs. Van Rensselaer listed for Richardson during his entire career.[11] The amount of construction contracts for this first period was about $4,550,000.[12] The subsequent period, from 1887 to 1894, from the Boston Public Library up to the depression of the 1890's, saw a reduced number of commissions: about 176. These, however, were larger, more important works, so that the amount of contracts rose to $15,005,465. The years 1894 through 1899, marked by the depression and the Spanish-American War, saw a further reduction of the number of commissions to about 126, forcing a reduction in the office staff. Ironically, continuing inflation of the dollar caused the amount of contracts to increase during this period to $21,788,000. The turn of the century witnessed renewed prosperity, and for McKim, Mead & White it was a reprise of the halcyon days of the mid-1880's; the firm received 210 commissions from 1900 to 1910, with contract amounts totaling $36,379,768. Again the office grew and hummed with incessant activity.

The firm was doubly fortunate that these two periods of intense business and building activity—from 1879 to 1892 and again from 1899 to 1911—occurred before the enactment of the graduated income tax by Congress. Within a decade after its passage in 1913, the sources of private munificence that had been such an important part of the firm's patronage began to dry up.

The offices at 57 Broadway occupied the top, fifth floor of a narrow cast-iron-fronted commercial building running along Exchange Alley. Across the front, with a view down on Broadway and along the alley, were a small reception room and three small chambers, each six feet square, intended as the private offices of the partners. In each of the three cells there was just enough room for a small rolltop desk and a chair. Behind this section (known among the draftsmen as the "Holy of Holies," according to Egerton Swartwout) was a large single drafting room with about a dozen long tables.[13] It was hung about with pieces of wrought iron, plaster casts of ornament, and a disparate collection of drawings. Passage from the offices to the drafting room was through a single leather-covered swinging door with an oval glass pane at the top through which one peered cautiously since White was likely to come bursting through at any moment. Since space, especially in the front offices, was so limited, the partners tended to spend a great deal of their time in the drafting room, with the result that the early work of the firm, up to the removal of the offices to larger quarters in 1891, is marked by a fusion of personal styles; quite literally, a building was designed not by one but by all three in concert. After moving to larger rooms the partners spent less time in the drafting room. Preliminary designs were then worked out privately with a senior assistant, and as a result the personal characteristics of the partners are more easily discernible after 1891.

Architects who had been draftsmen with the firm during this early period later described the camaraderie that grew up not only among the younger men, but with the partners as well. At noon, the partners in the office, and any assistants and draftsmen who wished to, lunched together at an accustomed table in an Italian restaurant around the corner, followed by a walk through Bowling Green and around the Battery before returning to the office. Mead organized office baseball teams for which there were frequent warm-up sessions in the drafting room using wads of tracing paper—when the partners were out.[14]

For several years during the mid-1880's the office had what might be described as an "adjunct partner." This was Sidney V. Stratton, another highly skilled draftsman who had become acquainted with McKim while the two were in Daumet's *atelier* in Paris. They both returned in 1870 and shortly afterward Stratton became friendly with Mead and White as well. He had a separate practice, though he sublet rooms from the firm and his name appeared for a few years on the office stationery, below the names of the partners and separated from them by a line. Moreover, the Bill Books indicate that fees for a few commissions were to be sent directly to Stratton, suggesting that he was fully responsible for their design. The arrangement had ended by 1886 when Stratton went his own way, though he remained close to the partners thereafter.

By 1891 the original offices were hopelessly overcrowded, so new rooms were found at 1 West 20th Street, somewhat to the north. These proved to be temporary, for in the spring of 1894 the office was moved one block north to the fifth floor of a new nine-story fireproof building of brick and stone. This was the Mohawk Building, 160 Fifth Avenue, built by Van Ingen and Company, wool importers, which had just opened in 1892 (Figs. 6, 7). Here larger private offices were laid out, and later, separate offices were created for William Mitchell Kendall, William Symmes Richardson, and Burt L. Fenner, the principal assistants of each of the partners. Unfortunately, during these successive moves, quantities of correspondence and drawings for commissions long since finished were discarded in an effort to keep the size of the fireproof vault reasonable.

From the beginning both McKim and White were the major designers, with White having the special responsibility for interior detailing. Mead did little preliminary design, though he did offer timely criticism on his partners' plan arrangements, and indeed, for several large public buildings such as the Rhode Island State Capitol, the plan was almost entirely Mead's. McKim studied a design slowly and with utmost patience, sitting at a draftsman's side indicating verbally changes that were then carried out by the draftsman. Such a procedure might consume one or two hours, only to be repeated later in the day, for several days, until just the right proportions had been arrived at.[15] White, on the other hand, would explode through the swinging door, rush up to a draftsman, any draftsman, push him off his stool, grab tracing paper, dash off a dozen sketches in rapid succession, slap his hand on one, say "Do that!," and disappear. The whole process might just fill five min-

6. Mohawk Building, 160 Fifth Avenue, New York, N.Y., 1892. The McKim, Mead & White offices filled the fifth floor. (From *King's New York*).

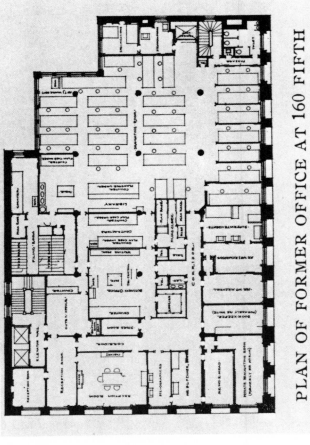

PLAN OF FORMER OFFICE AT 160 FIFTH AVENUE.

7. Plan of the McKim, Mead & White offices at 160 Fifth Avenue, as arranged c. 1911. *Brickbuilder* 22 (December, 1913).

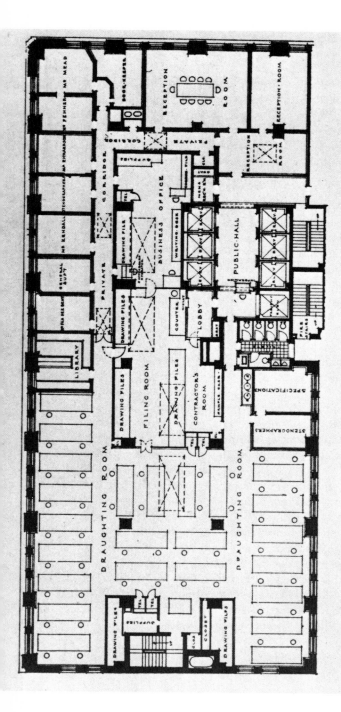

PLAN OF NEW OFFICE IN THE ARCHITECTS' BUILDING.

11. Plan of the McKim, Mead & White offices at 101 Park Avenue, as arranged in 1913. Reproduced at the same scale as Fig. 7. *Brickbuilder* 22 (December, 1913).

utes.[16] This difference showed itself too in the number of jobs each partner brought into the office. Sometime in the mid-1890's a count was taken: Mead had two commissions, McKim about seven or eight, and White was working on more than ninety.[17] Nor did White hold to conventional working hours. Several of the more advanced assistants worked on competition entries after hours in the office, and they discovered just how much time White spent there. He might appear pounding at the door before seven in the morning, his arms full of rolled drawings, or he might bound in after the opera, in full dress, throw his cloak aside, and set to work; when draftsmen arrived in the morning the room might be festooned with garlands of tracing paper filled with White's rapid sketches and cryptic notes.[18]

Many said that White never seemed to stop, and yet there were quiet times. Often, on short winter days, after the light had failed and the lamps were lit, the partners would quietly puff cigars while studying each other's work, commenting and making suggestions (Figs. 1, 8).[19]

Compared to White, McKim was a strict traditionalist, sending his assistants to scour the large office library (perhaps as many as 2,500 volumes at its peak) for precedents to corroborate a detail under study. Conversely, White would use any arrangement, material, or detail that seemed to suit the situation; once, when an assistant could not maintain the axis in a complicated plan, White's impatient response was, "Damn it all, *bend* the axis."[20] If he swept by a draftsman's table, grabbed a drawing, and said, "this is the goddamnedest thing I ever saw," or "this looks like hell," it was high praise. White might never say it directly, but if he called to Mead, waving a drawing, and said, "Look at this, Dummy, swell isn't it," the draftsman knew he was making real progress.

To his partners, and to the assistants (behind his back), Mead was known affectionately as "Dummy" because he said so little. Yet his quiet masked a shrewd mind, and when he spoke up about his partners' work they took strict notice for he was seldom wrong. He used to joke that his main function in the office was to keep his partners from making fools of themselves. Stanford's son, Lawrence Grant White, who became a partner in the firm himself several years after his father's death, said that if McKim was the hull of the ship of the firm and White was the sail, then Mead was the anchor; and Saint-Gaudens is said to have drawn a cartoon showing Mead holding the strings of kites labeled McKim and White flying in opposite directions.[21] Mead managed the office and supervised the hiring of the draftsmen; in many ways he had the closest personal contact with the staff for it was he who distributed the pay envelopes Saturday afternoon. To the outsider he may have seemed to do little, and yet he was the linchpin of the organization, the governor on White's enthusiasm and the spur to McKim's caution.

Although their approaches to preliminary studies were radically different, beyond this McKim's and White's methods were rather similar and reflected the strong influence of Richardson. Neither viewed working drawings as finished documents. Details and even proportions were restudied long after drawings had gone off to the contractor, and it was not uncommon for completed sections of a building to be dismantled and rebuilt at the architects' expense.[22] If the process of initial design was rapid, especially for White, the period of refinement and construction might be excruciatingly slow, as when the architects insisted building cease while they waited for just the right color marble to be procured and cut to the exact size needed. Expediency at the building site was not condoned, for the architects believed that their work would stand as commendation or reproach long after both the designer and builder had ceased to exist. In this they echoed the sentiments of Jefferson, who urged his countrymen to build well, for as he wrote in his *Notes on the State of Virginia*, "every new edifice is an actual and permanent acquisition to the State, adding to its value as well as to its ornament." Accordingly, except where mandated by law, the firm felt little obligation always to take the lowest bid on construction. Rather, they urged their clients to employ the most reputable and responsible builders, and indeed their major contractor was Norcross Brothers of Worcester, Massachusetts, the best-known and most experienced builder of their generation. In fact, according to one former assistant, the only room on the fifth floor of 160 Fifth Avenue not occupied by the firm when he was there was the New York branch office of Norcross Brothers, manned by Thomas

Dolan   Vander Bent   Farmer   Mead &   L.G.W.   Rowling   J.K.Smith.
                                    Adams

Office Staff. McKim Mead & White - 1924.

Above: 8. *(left to right)* White, Mead, and McKim on the grounds of "Box Hill," the home of Stanford White at St. James, Long Island, New York, c. 1900. Lawrence Grant White is shown approaching from the left. Courtesy of Laura Chanler White.

Below: 9. McKim, Mead & White office staff, 1924. Courtesy of Laura Chanler White.

Reilly, whom the firm consulted incessantly.[23] Though Mead was in charge of engineering design and construction supervision, he was greatly assisted by Teunis J. Van der Bent and Burt Fenner, who took up these fields as their respective specialties.

Too much cannot be made of the contribution of the builder to the firm's work. To modern eyes the working drawings prepared by the office seem to lack information now considered standard and essential. The reason for this is that much was left to the judgment of the builder, so that quite literally the best work of McKim, Mead & White is a collaborative effort of enlightened client, sensitive architect, and conscientious master builder, and the final result owes much to the selfless contributions of each of these three parties.

The office organization was rather loose. Because of the sharp differences in temperament between McKim and White, the draftsmen tended to align themselves with one or the other. Not surprisingly, descriptions of McKim and White can differ widely depending on the camp to which the writer belonged. Those gifted and industrious men who had been in the office longest or who had the best formal training became the major assistants: Henry Bacon and Kendall for McKim; Philip Sawyer and Richardson for White; Fenner and Van der Bent for Mead. Bacon, Sawyer, and scores of others eventually set off on their own, but Kendall, Richardson, and Fenner stayed and were made partners themselves in 1906 only months before White's sudden death; Van der Bent's elevation was delayed until 1909.

When a project came into the office the partner in charge would make initial sketches himself or with one of his principal assistants. Once the preliminary designs were developed, other draftsmen would be drawn in by the assistant, or perhaps by the partner himself, and all of these would constitute the "project team" that would remain with the project while working drawings were completed and as construction progressed. The hierarchy was not purely pyramidal, and certainly was not strictly stratified, but resembled more the camaraderie of the École *ateliers*. H. Van Buren Magonigle remembered no division heads or squad bosses. "'Efficiency' was unknown," he wrote; "when we had to work overtime, we got a dollar for dinner—nothing for our time—and broke our backs to get the work done; everything was rather happy-go-lucky; but what a place, what an atmosphere for the formation of artists."[24] Even after the office was moved for the third and last time in 1913, Mead jokingly ribbed that "We never had any system and haven't now—have we Fenner?"[25]

The size of the office staff varied according to the state of the economy and, as a result, the number of commissions underway. When White joined in September, 1879, there were already four draftsmen, one of whom was Joseph Morrill Wells. By this time Sturgis had begun to close his practice, turning instead to writing, so George Fletcher Babb left him to join his friends McKim and White at the start of 1880. Soon after, however, he left to form his own partnership with Cook and Willard. Wells was extremely gifted, not so much in plan organization as in the study of detail and ornament, and his contribution was so significant that in 1889 he was offered a partnership that, enigmatically, he refused. He died of pneumonia the following year.[26]

As the firm prospered during the 1880's the staff grew steadily to about seventy-five or eighty, reaching a high of about 110 during 1891–1893 when there was so much extra work connected with the Columbian Exposition. As the depression reduced the number of commissions, however, the staff had to be cut back to about fifty-five. By 1902, as the business of the office prospered, the staff was increased to nearly its full complement of one hundred, though it dropped after McKim's death and was further reduced by exigencies of war during 1916–1918.[27] When a formal photograph of the office personnel was taken in 1924, there were fifty-two present (Fig. 9). In 1900 McKim, Mead & White was the largest architectural office in the world, though a decade later it was surpassed by Burnham & Company of Chicago in size and degree of hierarchical organization. Nonetheless, because of its proximity to Europe, McKim, Mead & White continued to be the focus of particular attention, especially for the British, among whom an office supervised by a single architect was still the rule.

In spite of White's assassination in 1906 and McKim's death in 1909, the character of the office changed very little at first. In part this was due to Mead's continuing supervision of the office and also because the junior partners had been in the office so long. Kendall (1865–1951) had entered the office in 1882, having graduated from Harvard, studied architecture two years at MIT, and spent two years at the École in Paris. His character was much like that of McKim, with whom he became associated quite early; during McKim's absences from the office, as when he traveled to Chicago during 1892–1893 or with the Senate Park Commission in 1902, his work was turned over to Kendall. Richardson (1873–1931) studied at the University of California and at MIT before traveling in Europe with a short stay at the École in 1894; the following year he entered the office and in a short time was White's principal assistant. Fenner (1869–1926) was also a student at MIT, after a period of study at the University of Rochester; he entered the office in 1891, coming directly from Cambridge, Massachusetts. Van der Bent (1863–1936) was a native of the Netherlands; a graduate of the University of Delft in 1885, he entered the office in 1887.[28]

As early as 1904 a few commissions were placed entirely in the hands of the younger men; and by 1906 Richardson was almost entirely in charge of as important an undertaking as Pennsylvania Station, New York. In 1920 Kendall drew up a list of the firm's most important buildings and, with the advice of all the partners (presumably including Mead), indicated for each who was the designer and who was the principal assistant. Kendall's attributions, incorporated into the building list given here, show that many of the important buildings between 1904 and 1910 were actually the work of the junior partners.

Perhaps as early as 1915 or 1916 Mead began to curtail his office work, supervising only three projects; when he formally retired in 1919 his influence on office design was marginal. Nevertheless, he maintained an office in the new quarters on the sixteenth floor of the Architects' Building, 101 Park Avenue, to which the firm moved in 1913 (Figs. 10, 11, 12, 13). In fact, Mead had been one of the instigators behind the construction of the new building devoted to architects' offices and the building trades where many of the important New York firms, such as George B. Post & Sons, relocated. Here too were offices of many of the young men who

10. The Architects' Building, 101 Park Avenue, New York, N.Y. The McKim, Mead & White offices filled the sixteenth floor. *Brickbuilder* 22 (December, 1913).

12. Conference Room, offices of McKim, Mead & White, 101 Park Avenue, in 1913. *Brickbuilder* 22 (December, 1913).

13. Filing Room, offices of McKim, Mead & White, 101 Park Avenue, in 1913. *Brickbuilder* 22 (December, 1913).

had once been with the firm or with Post. In 1914 Lawrence Grant White came into the office, following his graduation from Harvard and six years spent at the École; he was made a partner in 1920. Four years later James Kellum Smith entered the office, becoming a partner in 1929. He and the younger White became the senior partners and continued the office under the same name until 1961, when the practice passed to Milton B. Steinman and Walker O. Cain on Smith's death. The offices at 101 Park Avenue have changed somewhat over the years, but there Walker O. Cain & Associates, the lineal descendent of McKim, Mead & White, continues to practice.[29]

The founding partners were dedicated to building good public architecture, and they were equally concerned for the education of future architects. This concern took many forms, especially in the many activities of McKim. In 1887 McKim's second wife, Julia Appleton, died, leaving him a house on Beacon Street in Boston and a summer house that he had designed only a few years before for Miss Appleton and her sister in Lenox, Massachusetts. McKim sold the Lenox property, using one-third of the proceeds to support a lying-in hospital in Boston and another third to establish a traveling scholarship for architecture students at Columbia University. The remainder he held in reserve, using it during the 1890's to help sustain the fledgling American Academy in Rome, another of his architectural education efforts. McKim was instrumental in starting the Academy in 1895, and he nurtured it for years as he attempted to build a permanent endowment. Once the endowment was assured, McKim used what was left of the Appleton estate money to establish the Julia Appleton McKim Traveling Fellowship in architecture at Harvard.[30] Beyond this, when McKim observed an assistant in the office who was ready for study in Europe, he would underwrite the cost of the journey, disguising what was an outright grant as a loan; if the money was repaid, it went towards helping another office assistant to see Europe.[31]

For a time during the 1890's McKim conducted a formal *atelier* as an adjunct to the architectural program at Columbia University. His assistant in this was John Russell Pope, then an advanced student in architecture at Columbia. At the same time a second *atelier* was conducted by Thomas Hastings, once a principal assistant to McKim in the office, who was aided by William Adams Delano.[32] More informally, the firm participated in other educational programs, as in the early 1880's when they helped form the Architectural League and served on its juries, examining entries submitted by architectural students throughout the city.[33] Once the reputation of the firm was established by the Boston Public Library, McKim received many letters from aspiring architects, asking what was the best course of study. McKim invariably answered by saying that the inquirer should attend a good college, then work in an office for a few years for practical experience, and then travel in Europe, preferably with a period of study at the École des Beaux-Arts.[34]

The founding partners took very seriously this obligation to train young architects, and if there were fewer students in the office after McKim's death, the junior partners nonetheless played an important part in training yet another generation of architects by publishing *A Monograph of the Work of McKim, Mead & White, 1879–1915*, in installments of twenty plates that began to appear in 1914. By 1920 the last group of plates had been published, making a total of four hundred plates in four volumes. Special photographs were taken of the buildings and hundreds of new drawings were prepared by office draftsmen. Ink on linen, some of these measured as much as thirty by forty inches, though they were all reduced as much as 3,000% to fit the elephantine *Monograph* plates, thereby gaining great sharpness of detail. Through the *Monograph*, some of the most important work of the firm was made available in considerable detail, and so marked was the reception of the volumes that a smaller Student's Edition, consisting of all of the line drawings from the original, was brought out after the First World War.

The four volumes of the *Monograph*, by themselves, would have exerted a noticeable influence on a profession already greatly interested in the firm's work, but even greater than this, perhaps, was the effect which the founding partners had on the many young architects who passed through the office. Among the most important were Cass Gilbert, Henry Bacon, and John Merven Carrère and Thomas Hastings, the last of whom met in the office and then left to form their own partnership. Others did likewise. Edward

York and Philip Sawyer; William A. Boring and Edward L. Tilton; Walter D. Bliss and William B. Faville; Francis L. V. Hoppin and Terence A. Koen; James Brown Lord and J. Monroe Hewlett; Evarts Tracy and Egerton Swartwout—all met in the office and then launched their own practices. Frank J. Helme worked in the office before forming a partnership with Harvey Wiley Corbett, as did Thomas M. Kellogg before joining with John H. Rankin, and Will S. Aldrich before joining with Edmund J. Eckel. Other prominent former assistants included John Mead Howells (nephew of Mead and architect of the Tribune Tower in Chicago), John Galen Howard, Edward Pearce Casey (who completed Smithmeyer & Pelz's Congressional Library, Washington, D.C.), Harry C. Lindeberg, Lionel Moses, and H. Van Buren Magonigle. Other assistants went into teaching or related fields, such as A. D. F. Hamlin who succeeded William R. Ware at Columbia and taught there many years, himself succeeded by William A. Boring who left private practice, and Warren P. Laird who taught for an extended period at the University of Pennsylvania. Gorham Phillips Stevens devoted himself quite early to classical archaeology and for many years served as the director of the American Academy in Athens, carrying out important studies on the development of the Acropolis. Royal Cortissoz, who had begun as an office boy and general assistant, became a prominent art and architecture critic, though he became rather rigidly orthodox in later years.

Many of these offshoot offices established themselves in New York, while others became important in cities across the country. Rankin & Kellogg practiced in Philadelphia, Eckel & Aldrich in St. Joseph, Missouri, while Bliss & Faville carried the classicizing influence of McKim, Mead & White to San Francisco where the firm set up practice in 1898. To the north the influence of the firm was already evident in the work of Whidden & Lewis in Portland, Oregon. William H. Whidden had been McKim's assistant, and having traveled to Portland in 1882 with McKim to inspect sites for buildings of the Northern Pacific Railroad, he returned and formed a partnership with Ion Lewis in 1890. Many of these firms then trained yet another generation of architects who carried the sensitivity to symbolic functional expression and to materials, site, and local tradition that had come to mark the work of McKim, Mead & White. An example is Alfred E. Doyle, trained by Whidden & Lewis, who built some of the best work in the Pacific Northwest, and who, in his turn, trained Pietro Belluschi.

McKim, Mead, and White left an imprint also on the firms with whom they worked on buildings too far from New York for direct supervision. When possible they associated with former assistants, as with Bliss & Faville for the Mackay School of Mines at Nevada State University, but in other instances they worked with firms previously not familiar to them. On the Robert W. Patterson house, Chicago, they worked with Holabird & Roche, supervisory architects. For the State Savings Bank, Detroit, their associated architects were Donaldson & Meier; and the successive phases of the Bank of Montreal were supervised by Montreal architect Andrew T. Taylor, who later wrote an obituary article on McKim.

Though the firm designed one hotel for Louis Sherry to be built in London, England (see No. 781), it remained a project. The firm never built in England, but its influence there can be seen in Bush House, London, by Helme & Corbett, and even more in Devonshire House, Piccadilly, London, by Carrère & Hastings, 1924–1926, designed in collaboration with and supervised by Charles Herbert Reilly, one of the most ardent British admirers of McKim, Mead & White.[35] The firm had been approached, as early as 1893, by a British client who wanted a hotel near the Royal Opera House, but nothing was done. Soon afterward English architectural students began to appear at 160 Fifth Avenue asking to be added to the office staff.[36] Banister Fletcher visited the office in 1893, hoping to work there for a short time to see how a large American office was run, but reductions in the staff because of the depression made that impossible.[37] Meanwhile, English architects and critics began to study the firm's work closely, with the result that in 1903 McKim was awarded the King's Gold Medal by the Royal Institute of British Architects.[38] Coincident with the award and McKim's trip to England to accept it, a large exhibit of the firm's work was mounted in London. After this McKim kept up correspondence with Aston Webb, the prominent London architect, and they exchanged designs and comments.[39] It was in 1909 that Reilly first contacted the office asking for photographs of their work for use as examples for his students in the School of Architecture, University of Liverpool.[40] Even before Mead had a chance to ship them, Reilly crossed the Atlantic to see American architecture for himself and to visit large American firms. On his return he spoke of his reactions before the Architectural Association of Ireland, describing in some detail the office of McKim, Mead & White and praising their work.[41] His students were as enthusiastic as he, so that when the first portions of the *Monograph* reached England they were well received and eagerly studied. Eventually, in 1924, Reilly published a small book on the firm, and in many ways his concise and perceptive assessment has not been surpassed. To a large extent it is accurate to say that through Reilly's constant proselytizing and his contact with scores of students in Liverpool, he helped spread the influence of McKim, Mead & White to the far corners of the British Empire. And by means of the *Monograph* it went even beyond; one Japanese architect from Osaka wrote to the firm in 1923, saying that a few plates from his copy were missing and could he please be sent replacements.[42]

Why was it that contemporaries reacted so strongly in favor of the architecture of McKim, Mead, and White, and why is it beginning to enjoy renewed approbation today? Surely it is more than the love of columns or a fixation on the past. Perhaps it is because the forces that motivated McKim, Mead & White then were widely appreciated and because they are again being accepted. McKim, Mead, and White held fast to a fervent Ruskinian and Vitruvian idealism to build well. They wished to bring a measure of order and harmony to the urban American environment at a time when it seemed their entire culture was in flux. They wanted to reinvigorate the native classic American building tradition. They looked upon architecture and urban design as a concert of all the arts celebrating function. They attempted to mold plans that had an inner inevitability so that people moved from space to space as though drawn by an internal gravitational force. They believed that every site, rural and urban, was different, and that though one might use a universal and national classicism, it was always to be shaped and conditioned by the traditions of the place. They believed that to provide merely the most economical solution demeaned first the client and then all of the building's users; it was the architect's responsibility to shape the best design in the best way. They repudiated "minimum standards," knowing all too well that such rapidly become the only standards and because they viewed architecture as a commitment to the future. They believed that a building was far more than an efficient package; building was an expressive art, the creation and manipulation of forms and spaces that shape human experience, amidst which people play out their lives, and that at every moment affect human activity physically, psychologically, and emotionally. Like Vitruvius, they believed it the architect's mandate to accommodate use, to build solidly, and especially to bring pleasure.

> *And when they observed that nature had been lavish in providing building materials of great use, they carefully employed each to its fullest, thus giving grace to the refinements of life, embellishing them with luxuries.*

Vitruvius, *De Architectura*, 1.2.

Notes

1. Charles Moore, *The Life and Times of Charles Follen McKim* (Boston, 1929), 327–337. The roster of employees from which Moore obtained his list is still maintained by Walker O. Cain & Associates, New York; Moore's transcription is accurate up to 1910.

2. Alfred Hoyt Granger, *Charles Follen McKim, A Study of His Life and Work* (Boston, 1913), 5, 108. While still in the office, young assistants William Boring and Edward Tilton entered and won the competition for the new U.S. Immigration Station at Ellis Island. Likewise, York and Sawyer started their career together while still in the office. See Egerton Swartwout, "An Architectural Decade," manuscript written c. 1930 (?), copy in the office of Walker O. Cain

& Associates; see also Philip Sawyer, *Edward Palmer York: Personal Reminiscences* (Stonington, Ct., 1951).

3. Sources on the life of William Rutherford Mead are cited in the bibliography.

4. William Rutherford Mead, untitled manuscript of reminiscences written c. 1918, copy in the McKim, Mead & White Archive, New-York Historical Society, New York, reprinted in Moore, *McKim*, 40–42.

5. Sources on the life of Charles Follen McKim are cited in the bibliography; the primary source remains Moore, *McKim*.

6. See Benjamin P. Thomas, *Theodore Weld, Crusader for Freedom* (New Brunswick, N.J., 1950), and Dolores Hayden, *Seven American Utopias: The Architecture of Communitarian Socialism, 1790–1975* (Cambridge, Mass., 1976).

7. From a letter, James Miller McKim to Charles F. McKim, September 21, 1869, in the Charles Follen McKim Collection, Manuscript Division, Library of Congress.

8. Sources on the life of Stanford White are cited in the bibliography. The primary source remains Charles C. Baldwin, *Stanford White* (New York, 1930).

9. Letter, Frederick Law Olmsted to Stanford White, April 9, 1885, in the Stanford White Papers, Manuscript Division, New-York Historical Society, New York.

10. White's extensive travels on behalf of Richardson are evident from his letters back to his family; some of these are in the possession of Robert White, Saint James, L.I., N.Y.; others are in the Stanford White Papers, New-York Historical Society. The most important of these are reprinted in Baldwin, *White*.

11. Maria Griswold Van Rensselaer, *Henry Hobson Richardson and His Works* (Boston, 1888).

12. Figures concerning contract amounts are from data maintained by the office and now kept by Walker O. Cain & Associates. The

figures on commissions are from a count of entries in the firm's Bill Books, McKim, Mead & White Archive.

13. The original office as it was c. 1887 is described in Sawyer, *York*, 17–27.

14. Sawyer, *York*, 17–27; H. Van Buren Magonigle, "A Half Century of Architecture," *Pencil Points* 15 (May, 1934), 226; Swartwout, "Architectural Decade," 126.

15. McKim's methods are described by Henry Bacon, "Charles Follen McKim—A Character Sketch," *Brickbuilder* 19 (February, 1910), 38–44, and Magonigle, "Half Century" (March, 1934), 116.

16. White's methods are described in Magonigle, "Half Century" (March, 1934), 116–118; and in Swartwout, "Architectural Decade."

17. Magonigle, "Half Century" (March, 1934), 116.

18. Philip Sawyer, "Stanford White as those trained in his office knew him," *Brickbuilder* 15 (December, 1906), 247; and Albert Randolph Ross, "Stanford White as those trained in his office knew him," *Brickbuilder* 15 (December, 1906), 246.

19. Ross, "Stanford White," 246.

20. Lawrence Grant White, *Sketches and Designs by Stanford White* (New York, 1920), 15.

21. L. G. White, *Sketches & Designs*, 17.

22. Bacon, "Character Sketch," 44; J. Monroe Hewlett, "Stanford White as those trained in his office knew him," *Brickbuilder* 15 (December, 1906), 245.

23. Noted in Swartwout, "Architectural Decade," 72. For Norcross Brothers see James F. O'Gorman, "O. W. Norcross, Richardson's 'Master Builder': A Preliminary Report," *Journal—Society of Architectural Historians* 32 (May, 1973), 104–113.

24. Magonigle, "Half Century" (March, 1934), 116; and Swartwout, "Architectural Decade," 95.

25. Quoted in D. Everett Waid, "The Business Side of an Architect's Office: The Office of Messrs. McKim, Mead & White," *Brickbuilder* 22 (December, 1913), 267.

26. For Joseph Morrill Wells see Moore, *McKim*, 48–49; and Baldwin, *White*, passim, and miscellaneous materials in the Correspondence Files, McKim, Mead & White Archive.

27. Figures derived from office staff roster, Walker O. Cain & Associates.

28. For the junior partners see a memorandum on Kendall's life, McKim, Mead & White Archive. For Kendall see: *Bulletin of the Michigan Society of Architects* 15 (October 7, 1941), 3; *Pencil Points* 22 (September, 1941), 65; *National Cyclopedia of American Biography*, Current Volume A (1930), 551. For Richardson see the New York *Times*, March 27, 1931, 27. For Fenner see: *American Architect* 129 (February 5, 1926), 226; *Architectural Record* 59 (March, 1926), 274–275; *Journal — American Institute of Architects* 14 (March, 1926), 129; and "Burt Leslie Fenner," *Dictionary of American Biography*, 6:323, by Talbot F. Hamlin.

29. See *Brickbuilder* 22 (December, 1913), entire issue, for the Architects' Building, 101 Park Avenue. Information on the later partners of McKim, Mead & White (1925–1961) is from McKim, Mead & White, *Recent Work of the Present Partners of McKim, Mead & White* (New York, 1952), 7–8, and from records in the office of Walker O. Cain & Associates.

30. Moore, *McKim*, 52–53. For the role of McKim in founding the American Academy in Rome see Moore, *McKim*, 128–181, 246–254, 273–274, 308–314; and Lucia and Alan Valentine, *The American Academy in Rome, 1894–1969* (Charlottesville, Va., 1973).

31. Frederick P. Hill, *Charles F. McKim: the Man* (Francestown, N.H., 1950), 24–25.

32. Letter, John Russell Pope to C. Moore, September 20, 1926, reprinted in Moore, *McKim*, 150–151, in the Charles Moore Collection, Manuscript Division, Library of Congress.

33. See *Critic* 1 (January 29, 1881), 8; *American Architect and Building News* 9 (April 16, 1881), 184; Roger Riordan, "The Architectural League of New York," *Century* 25 (March, 1883), 698–708.

34. There are a number of such letters in the McKim Collection, Library of Congress; see, for example, his responses to Wendell Garrison, March 11, 1893; to Prescott Hall Butler, July 13, 1893; and to Eugene Bigler, December 2, 1895.

35. See Henry-Russell Hitchcock, *Architecture: Nineteenth and Twentieth Centuries*, 3rd ed. (Baltimore, 1968), 402.

36. Letter, James Crowdy, London, to McKim, Mead & White, July 24, 1893, McKim, Mead & White Archive. Letter, Richard Harding Davis to S. White, n.d., Stanford White Papers, New-York Historical Society.

37. Letter, C. F. McKim to Banister Fletcher, c/o Barr Ferree, New York, July 12, 1893, McKim Collection, Library of Congress.

38. Moore, *McKim,* 223–241.

39. Letter, Aston Webb, London, to C. F. McKim, January 30, 1907, Charles Moore Collection, Manuscript Division, Library of Congress.

40. Letters, C. H. Reilly, Liverpool, to McKim, Mead & White, May, 1909, McKim, Mead & White Archive.

41. C. H. Reilly, "The Modern Renaissance in American Architecture," *Journal—Royal Institute of British Architects* 17 (June 25, 1910), 630–635.

42. Letters, Uchida Trading Company, on behalf of R. Baba of Osaka, Japan, to McKim, Mead & White, March 5 and 6, 1923, McKim, Mead & White Archive. There are also letters in the Archive relating to the shipment of each volume of the *Monograph* to the library of McGill University, Montreal, Quebec.

THE ARCHITECTURE OF
McKIM, MEAD & WHITE
1870–1920

I   BUILDING   LIST

The data given here are based on the Bill Books in the McKim,
Mead & White Archive, New-York Historical Society, New York. Bills
sent to clients for services rendered were copied as they went out by
wet letterpress onto the tissue pages of volumes specially bound for
this purpose; in each book there were 400 numbered pages. These Bill
Books, the most complete of the firm's financial records, continue
uninterrupted in seventeen volumes from July 22, 1878, through December 31, 1947.

Since the Bill Books were started about a year after McKim,
Mead & Bigelow was organized, information for earlier work is derived
from published sources, fragmentary evidence in the firm's Archive,
the biographies of the partners, and the files of the Newport Historical Society. The dissertation on the early work of McKim by Richard
Guy Wilson is also helpful. Even for the later years, the Bill Books
are not absolutely complete, for many pages have been cut out, some
by Charles Moore when working on his biography of McKim; moreover,
little of White's work for Augustus Saint-Gaudens, Daniel Chester
French, or Frederick MacMonnies appears in them. For information on
the sculptural work John Dryfhout, Michael Richman, and Robert Judson
Clark have been most helpful.

If a strict count were taken from the Bill Books, a greater number of commissions would be found than given here, but most of these
added items would be very minor commissions—fireplace mantelpieces,
dining room wallpaper, and other lesser alterations. In compiling
this list a minimum qualifying contract amount was used: $200 for
1878-1879, increased roughly parallel with inflation to about $1000
in 1919.

This list is in some ways like that prepared by Moore for his
biography of McKim, but where Moore noted 505 commissions from 1880
through 1910, this list presents 945 works, covering the period 1870
through 1919. Curiously Moore chose to give only the date each work

1

was finished rather than begun; in this list, wherever possible, the date a design was started is given as well as the dates of construction. This building list is presented in three sections, IA, IB, and IC, each section corresponding to a change in office organization— the individuals, the first short-lived partnership, and the second partnership. A fourth section, ID, comprises various designs by White which, because of their nature or the lack of information, cannot be catalogued in the same way as the commissions in the preceding sections.

Information for each commission is given in as standardized a form as possible:

NAME: All commissions are listed alphabetically by the name of the client or, in the case of colleges or institutions, by the name of the institution. For large building groups, such as Columbia University, the preliminary planning is cited first and then each building is listed alphabetically. In some instances a business building known by a proper name is cross-indexed by client. The sculptural works and memorials are listed alphabetically according to the official name for each. In the index all sculptural work is cross-indexed by sculptor.

DESCRIPTION: The nature of each commission is described if it is not evident in the name or title, but "competition" signifies an unsuccessful entry in an open or invitational competition. For sculpture, "base" means a pedestal or support for a figure; "setting" means an enclosure incorporating benches, fountains, plants, among other elements; "funerary monument" means a stone of varying size but excludes a building meant for above-ground interment. All such funerary monuments are listed by client. It is not always possible to give a clear description of every commission, for much has disappeared and the Bill Books themselves are not always definitive. There was no need to tell the client what a bill was for, and hundreds of entries read simply: "on a/c commission. . . ." Moreover, before 1881 entries were written in longhand (initially by Mead himself); if too much moisture was used in making the copy, it became hopelessly blurred. By 1881, however, bills were being typed, making much clearer copies.

DATES: The month and year begun are taken from Bill Book entries when available, or from notices in local newspapers as kept in
a scrapbook in the McKim, Mead & White Archive, New-York Historical
Society. Entries in the Bill Books often indicate when charges were
started for travel expenses, site inspection, and preliminary designs.
Construction dates show the year started and when finished. In cases
in which the exact date cannot be precisely determined, the closest
approximation is given, indicated by "c."

DESIGNER: In many cases the partner in charge of a major commission can be determined from a list drawn up by William Mitchell
Kendall in 1920 (in the McKim, Mead & White Archive) which bears a
note saying that the attributions had been checked by each partner,
presumably including Mead. For White's work there is a list prepared
by his son, Lawrence Grant White, in *Sketches and Designs by Stanford
White* (New York, 1920), and subsequently used in Charles C. Baldwin,
Stanford White (New York, 1931). These attributions are identified
"[LGW, B, K]"; other attributions are my own suggested by internal or
external evidence. For a few designs the name Sidney V. Stratton is
noted in the Bill Books and payment was to be sent directly to him.

The partners themselves were most strenuous in their objections
to any such attribution to a single partner. In December, 1885, *Art
Age* noted, in commenting on the Edgar house in Newport, that White was
the architect, to which he immediately responded in a letter, reprinted
in *Art Age* in January, 1886, that "no member of our firm is ever indi-
vidually responsible for any design which goes out from it."

CONTRACTOR: The builder is sometimes indicated in the Bill
Books, but in some cases the name is taken from correspondence or
from newspaper clippings in the scrapbook, McKim, Mead & White Archive.

COST: The figures are taken from the Bill Books and from financial records in the office of Walker O. Cain, New York, and are those
from which fees were computed. Two figures are often cited here; the
first is for the building itself while the second is for interior finishing. The standard fee was 5% of the first figure and 10% of the second. In those instances where there is no description of the nature of
the work, but where the second figure is significantly larger than the
first figure, this is interpreted as alterations and additions to an

3

existing building. In some cases the firm prepared drawings for one of the major speculator-builders in New York (David H. King, jr., the Goelet brothers, or Michael Reid) and the work was carried out by them, unsupervised by the firm; for these commissions the fee was a flat 3½% of the estimated cost ("est."). In those instances in which a job never proceeded beyond preliminary designs, the approximate cost of the building, as noted in the Bill Books, has the prefix "c."

Costs are given only as a relative index so that one commission may be compared with another. This works best, however, only within a given year. To compare between years, adjust building costs using Section III. Furthermore, the Building Cost Index of Section III does not accurately reflect replacement costs of buildings erected at the turn of the century. Rare marbles and other materials have been exhausted, and the skill to work them has virtually disappeared, so that the cost of duplication is far greater than the Index suggests.

EXTANT DRAWINGS: Because of the culling of material when the office was twice moved (1891 and 1894), few drawings of the earliest work survive. The great bulk of the remaining material is in the McKim, Mead & White Archive, New-York Historical Society, where it was deposited in two lots in 1953 and 1968. Each group of drawings was accompanied by a general catalogue prepared by the successor firm. Of the more than 500 tubes of drawings, it has been possible to open and inspect only about a tenth, and of these, errors in the original catalogues have been uncovered for about one tube in eight.

ASTERISKS: A number preceded by an asterisk (*) indicates that the building or design is illustrated in the following section.

4

IA   INDIVIDUAL   WORK
1870 – 1877

CHARLES   FOLLEN   McKIM
WILLIAM   RUTHERFORD   MEAD
STANFORD   WHITE

This section covers the earliest work of the founding partners
prior to the formation of the first, short-lived partnership. Unfortunately, few of these buildings survive. There are several incom-
plete sets of drawings for houses, c. 1870 to c. 1874, by McKim in
the firm's Archive, New-York Historical Society. Because the clients
for these cannot yet be identified as the drawings are not fully labeled, they are tentatively called Houses A, B, C, D, E, and F. For
House A there is only an attic plan, but it bears the round office
stamp of Gambrill & Richardson with the date, December 28, 1870,
around which is neatly penciled "Charles F. McKim, Architect, Office
of. . . ." House B is a box-like masonry building with a Mansard roof.
Houses C, D, and E are all closely related in style and appear to be
predecessors of McKim's Francis Blake, jr., house (see Building List
No. 1). House F is a chalet-like remodeling of a seventeenth-century
(?) Dutch colonial house; the drawings are not signed and may not be
McKim's work. There are other drawings, some on McKim's office stationery, for perhaps four additional houses, stair-halls, and furniture. There appear to be no drawings in the Archive by Mead for
this period.

In his short reminiscence essay [reprinted in Charles Moore,
The Life and Times of Charles Follen McKim (Boston, 1929), 40-42],
Mead remembers that McKim left Richardson in 1872 on the strength
of "a commission for designing several small country houses in
Orange, N.J." No drawings or correspondence have been found in the
McKim, Mead & White Archive which fit this description.

McKim, along with several other architects, is reported to have prepared designs for stations for the Gilbert Elevated Railroad Company, New York, but since he seems to have done nothing beyond preliminary sketches (which have not survived), this is not listed here; see the *American Architect and Building News* 3 (January 26, 1876), 33.

*1.   Blake, Francis, jr.
      house
      Newton Lower Falls, Mass.
         condition: demolished
         begun: 1875   built: 1875
         designer: McKim

*2.   Cayuga Lake Hotel
      near Interlaken, N.Y.
      on Lake Cayuga
         begun: 1875   built: 1875 (first section)
         designer: Mead

*3.   Child, William S.
      school
      Second and Chestnut Streets
      Newport, R.I.
         condition: extant
         begun: 1875   built: 1875
         designer: McKim

*4.   "Dennis, John, house" (built c. 1745)
      additions and alterations to house
      65 Poplar Street
      Newport, R.I.
         condition: extant
         begun: 1876   built: 1876
         designer: McKim
         cost: $2,000

*5.   Dunn, Thomas
      preliminary design for house
      Newport, R.I.
         not built
         begun: 1877
         designer: McKim
         extant drawings: New-York Historical Society

*6.   Elberon Hotel
      renovation of existing Charles G. Francklyn house
         for L. B. Brown
      Ocean Avenue
      Elberon, N.J.
         condition: demolished
         begun: 1876   built: 1876-1877
         designer: McKim

*7.   Elberon Hotel
      cottages adjacent to hotel
      Ocean Avenue
      Elberon, N.J.
         condition: several extant
         begun: 1877   built: 1877-1880
         cost: c. $ 40,000

*8.   Fairchild, Charles F.
       stable and barn
       79 Second Street
       Newport, R.I.
          condition: extant
          begun: 1876   built: 1876
          designer: McKim

*9.   Farragut, Admiral David Glasgow, Memorial
       base for bronze figure (by Augustus Saint-Gaudens)
       Madison Square
       New York, N.Y.
          condition: extant, moved to new location
          begun: 1876-1877   built: 1880-1881
          designer: White with Augustus Saint-Gaudens [LGW, B]
          cost: c. $ 2,500, for base alone

*10.   Francklyn, Charles G.
       house
       Ocean and Lincoln Avenues
       Elberon, N.J.
          condition: demolished
          begun: 1876   built: 1876
          designer: McKim

*11.   Herrick, Dwight S.
       house
       Peekskill-on-Hudson, N.Y.
          begun: 1877   built: 1877
          designer: Mead

*12.   Howells, William Dean
       house, "Redtop"
       Belmont, Mass.
          condition: extant
          begun: 1877   built: 1877-1878
          designer: McKim with Mead

*13.   Livermore, John
       stairwell (alteration to existing house)
       Montclair, N.J.
          begun: 1874   built: 1874 (?)
          designer: McKim

14.   Morgan, Edward Dennison, sr.
       mausoleum
       Cedar Hill Cemetery
       Hartford, Conn.
          condition: destroyed by fire, August 21, 1884
          begun: 1877   built: 1883-1884
          designer: White with Augustus Saint-Gaudens [LGW, B]
          cost: $ 14,682, for tomb and sculpture

*15.   Page, Henry A.
           library, addition to existing house
           Montrose, N.J.
               begun: 1875?   built: 1876
               designer: McKim

*16.   Providence City Hall
           competition entry
           Providence, R.I.
               not built
               begun: 1874
               designers: McKim and Mead

 17.   Randall, Robert Richard, Memorial
           base and setting for bronze figure (by Augustus Saint-Gaudens)
           Sailors' Snug Harbor
           Staten Island, N.Y.
               condition: extant
               begun: 1878 (figure started 1876)   built: 1884
               designers: White with Augustus Saint-Gaudens [LGW]

*18.   "Robinson, Thomas, house" (built c. 1725)
           additions and alteration to house
           64 Washington Street
           Newport, R.I.
               condition: extant
               begun: 1874   built: 1874
               designer: McKim

*19.   Sargent, Joseph
           house
           Worcester, Mass.
               begun: 1872   built: 1872
               designer: McKim
               extant drawings: New-York Historical Society

*20.   Simpson, John
           house
           Peekskill-on-Hudson, N.Y.
               begun: 1873-1874   built: 1874
               designer: Mead

*21.   school house
           project
           location unspecified
               begun: 1873-1874
               designer: McKim

*22.　Taylor, Moses
　　　　house
　　　　Ocean and Park Avenues
　　　　Elberon, N.J.
　　　　　condition: extant
　　　　　begun: 1876-1877　　　　built: 1877
　　　　　designer: McKim
　　　　　cost: $ 60,000

*23.　Ward, Samuel Gray
　　　　house, "Oakswood"
　　　　Lenox, Mass.
　　　　　condition: demolished
　　　　　begun: 1877　　built: 1877-1878
　　　　　designer: McKim [K], with Bigelow (?)
　　　　　cost: $ 33,204

* 24.　Wormley, Katherine Prescott
　　　　house
　　　　2 Red Cross Avenue
　　　　Newport, R.I.
　　　　　condition: extant
　　　　　begun: 1876　　built: 1876-1877
　　　　　designer: McKim
　　　　　cost: $ 4,000

IB   MᶜKIM, MEAD & BIGELOW
1877 — 1879

In 1874 McKim and Mead began to collaborate in a formal way
and during the next three years they both began to rely on the help
of William B. Bigelow. The son of John William Bigelow, a cotton
merchant in New York, the young architect resided there and at "Bay-
side," the family summer home in the old section of Newport. Here
he may have first met McKim who was then beginning to work in Newport. It is likely that here too McKim met Annie, William's sister,
to whom he became engaged. Bigelow had gone to Paris in the spring
of 1873, had spent some time at the École des Beaux-Arts, and had returned in 1874 about the time McKim married Annie. While in France
Bigelow had made a series of elaborate and richly textured sketches
of rural buildings and houses which McKim, as de facto editor, published in the *New York Sketch Book of Architecture* late in 1874 and
in 1876. These show Bigelow to have been a highly gifted draftsman.
In May, 1877, Bigelow had not yet been formally added to the partnership, judging from entries in a diary kept by Mrs. Thomas Dunn for
whom McKim was then designing a summer house in Newport (the Dunn
Diary is now in the collections of the Newport Historical Society).
By November, 1877, however, Bigelow had been officially added, for
the rendering of the Christ Church Rectory, Rye, New York, published
that month in the *American Architect and Building News*, is inscribed
"McKim, Mead & Bigelow, Architects, 57 Broadway, New York."

Although some kind of accounting must have been practiced in
1877, it was not until July 22, 1878, that the Bill Books were started.
The first entry is for a final bill, summarizing all costs, sent to
Samuel Gray Ward for "Oakswood," a shingled summer house near Lenox,
Massachusetts. Although the starting date for the house is not noted,
Ward was billed for expenses incurred in thirty-three trips to Lenox,
indicating that work commenced sometime in 1877.

The house for Anna C. Alden at Fort Hill, Lloyd's Neck, Long Island, New York, begun in May, 1879, appears to have been the last joint commission of McKim, Mead & Bigelow. During the year the partnership had begun to come apart and Bigelow had taken on independent work. According to George W. Sheldon, *Artistic Country Seats*, 2 vols. (New York, 1886-1887), Bigelow designed two seaside summer houses in New Jersey on his own and he is cited as the sole architect of the J. M. Cornell house in Monmouth Beach, New Jersey. This house is also entered in the Bill Books, with a note of Bigelow's name, suggesting that he was particularly involved in its design. On August 4, 1879, he signed a receipt for payment of the fee for the Cornell house plans, duly recorded in the Bill Books. It was the last time his name appeared there.

After leaving the firm, Bigelow retained his own rooms at 57 Broadway until 1881 when he moved his office to 18 East 18th Street. He maintained a separate practice until the turn of the century.

*25.   Alden, Mrs. Anna C.
            house, "Fort Hill" or "Tower Hill"
            Lloyd's Neck
            Long Island, New York
                begun: May, 1879   built: 1879-1880
                designer: McKim
                cost: $ 47,787

26.   Amherst College Library
            library, preliminary design
            Amherst, Mass.
                not built
                begun: 1879
                cost: c. $ 10,000

27.   Beaman, Charles Cotesworth
            alterations to existing townhouse
            27 E. 21st Street
            New York, N.Y.
                condition: demolished
                begun: January, 1879   built: 1880-1881
                cost: $ 9,500

28.   Butler, Charles Edwards
            unspecified work
            no location given
                begun: 1879
                cost: c. $20,000

*29.   Butler, Prescott Hall
            house, "Bytharbor"
            Moriches Road
            St. James, N.Y.
                condition: extant, remodeled
                begun: 1878   built: 1879-1880
                designer: McKim
                cost: $ 5,182

30.   Casey and others
            house
            Lenox, Mass.
                begun: August, 1878   built: 1878-1879
                cost: $ 9,785

*31.   Christ Church Rectory
            house
            Rectory Street
            Rye, N.Y.
                condition: extant, remodeled
                begun: October (?), 1877   built: 1878-1879
                cost: $ 12,000
                contractor: Mead & Tufft

32. Cooper, William
       alterations to existing house
       no location given
           begun: 1878   built: 1879
           cost: $ 5,800

*33. Cornell, J. M.
       house
       Monmouth Beach, N.J.
           begun: January, 1879   built: 1879
           designer: Bigelow (?)
           cost: $ 6,500

*34. Dickerson, Edward Nicoll
       townhouse
       64 E. 34th Street
       New York, N.Y.
           condition: extant, greatly remodeled
           begun: November, 1877   built: 1878-1879
           designer: McKim (?)
           cost: c. $ 45,000

35. Fearing, Henry B.
       house (?)
       no location given
           begun: 1879   built: 1879
           cost: $ 6,000

36. Furniss, C.
       alterations to existing house
       Lenox, Mass.
           begun: December, 1878   built: 1879
           cost: $ 11,400

*37. Hartshorn, Stewart
       model house
       Short Hills, N.J.
           condition: extant
           begun: June or July, 1879   built: 1880
           cost: $ 5,350

38. Havemeyer, James
       alterations to existing house
       no location given
           begun: August, 1878   built: 1879

39. Hewitt, Mrs. Abram S.
       interior decorating
       no location given
           begun: January, 1879   built: 1879
           cost: $ 40 ("Japanese paper for ceiling in small room")

14

40. Higginson, F. L.
 house
 Beverly Farms, Mass.
  begun: May, 1879   built: 1879
  cost: $ 876

41. Packer, C. M.
 house ("cottage")
 Elberon, N.J.
  begun: October, 1878 built: 1878
  cost: $ 4,700

42. Roosevelt, Frederick
 house
 Skaneateles, N.Y.
  begun: March, 1879   built: 1880-1881
  designer: Mead, with interiors by White
  cost: $ 12,340

43. Talbot, Richmond
 house
 Lincoln Avenue
 Elberon, N.J.
  begun: March, 1878   built: 1878
  cost: $ 7,000

44. Taylor, Henry Augustus Coit
 house
 Lincoln Avenue
 Elberon, N.J.
  condition: demolished
  begun: March, 1878   built: 1878
  designer: McKim (?)
  cost: $ 13,931

*45. Thompson, Frederick Ferris
 townhouse
 283 Madison Avenue
 New York, N.Y.
  condition: demolished
  begun: July (?), 1879 built: 1879-1881
  cost: $ 59,552
       + 6,409
        65,961

46. Thurston, L. B.
 unspecified interior decoration work
 no location given
  begun: 1878   built: 1879-1880 (?)

15

*47. Tuckerman, Lucius
       "The Benedict" Apartment Building
       80 Washington Square
       New York, N.Y.
          condition: extant, remodeled
          begun: March, 1879   built: 1879-1882
          cost: $ 102,074

*48. Union League Club
       competition entry
       New York, N.Y.
          not built
          begun: April (?), 1879

 49. White, J. M.
       additions and alterations to existing house
       Lenox, Mass.
          begun: August, 1878   built: 1879
          cost: $ 6,000

*50. Williams, Clement W.
       duplex house
       4914 Greene
       Philadelphia (Germantown), Penna.
          condition: demolished
          begun: September, 1878   built: 1878-1879
          designer: McKim
          cost: $ 10,200

Ic   MᶜKIM, MEAD & WHITE
1879 — 1919

While White was staying with the Saint-Gaudens family in Paris
during the summer of 1879, he received a letter from Mead offering
him the position in the office being vacated by Bigelow. He had
known McKim for some time, having met him in Richardson's office
seven years earlier. He also knew Mead, perhaps less well, and he
had spent part of the summer of 1877 with them both touring the Massachusetts and New Hampshire coasts looking for picturesque colonial
architecture. Although he must have frequented the drafting room
of McKim, Mead & Bigelow at 57 Broadway, and perhaps even assisted
in some small way as suggested in the renderings of McKim, Mead &
Bigelow designs, he appears not to have been an employee. White
remained a part of the Gambrill & Richardson firm, with his base of
operations in the Gambrill office at 57 Broadway, though he made frequent trips to Brookline. His only official work outside of the Gambrill & Richardson office was with Augustus Saint-Gaudens and a few
of his preliminary sketches for the Farragut Memorial are still among
the Richardson drawings in the Houghton Library, Harvard University
(see, for instance, drawing MON-B3).

It is possible that White considered returning to Richardson's
office, settling in Brookline, but when he boarded ship in Liverpool
on August 23, 1879, bound for New York, Mead's letter must have decided the matter. White reached New York on Saturday, September 6,
and the following Monday entered the office, thereafter known as
McKim, Mead & White. The next day he wrote to Saint-Gaudens from
57 Broadway, "I have gone into partnership with McKim and Mead on the
same proposition made to me in Mead's letter. It really, after all,
was quite as liberal as I could expect for the first year." [Letter
reprinted in the *Architectural Record* 30 (September, 1911), 287.]

Whether any new work came into the McKim, Mead & White office
during September, 1879, is uncertain, but the first appearance of

White's name in the Bill Books occurs October 1, on a bill for alterations to the James J. Higginson house, 16 E. 41st Street, New York. It is significant that White's first appearance in the records is in connection with interior finishing, his major responsibility in Richardson's office. Among White's immediate jobs were the interiors of several houses already started by McKim, Mead & Bigelow, among them the Anna C. Alden house, the Frederick Roosevelt house, and the Frederick F. Thompson house.

A

51.   Abbey, Captain Thomas
monument
Enfield, Conn.
condition: extant
begun: November, 1914   built: 1915-1916
cost: $ 17,002

*52.   Adams Memorial   (for Henry Adams)
base and setting for bronze figure
(by Augustus Saint-Gaudens)
Rock Creek Cemetery
Washington, D.C.
condition: extant
begun: 1886   built: 1891-1892
designer: White with Saint-Gaudens [LGW, B]
cost: unrecorded for base
contractor: Norcross Brothers
extant drawings: New-York Historical Society

53.   Adams, Edward Dean
townhouse (part of the Villard house group)
455 Madison Avenue
New York, N.Y.
condition: extant
begun: September, 1883   built: 1884-1885
cost: c. $ 50,000
extant drawings: New-York Historical Society

*54.   Adams, Edward Dean
house, "Rohallion"
Rumson Neck
Seabright, N.J.
condition: extant
begun: December, 1886   built: 1887-1888
designer: White [LGW, B, K]
cost: $ 133,076
contractor: R. V. Breese

*55.   Adams, Edward Dean
additions to "Rohallion"
Seabright, N.J.
condition: extant
begun: April, 1890   built: 1890
designer: White
cost: $ 32,998

56.   Adams, Edward Dean
gardener's cottage at "Rohallion"
Seabright, N.J.
begun: May, 1898   built: 1899
cost: $ 3,380

57. Agnew, Dr. Cornelius Rea
   house
   deForest Road
   Montauk Point, N.Y.
      condition: extant
      begun: May, 1882   built: 1883
      cost: $ 9,950

*58. Alden, Robert Percy
   house
   Cornwall, Penna.
      condition: extant
      begun: October, 1880   built: 1881-1884
      cost: $ 22,399
            + 9,326
            31,725

59. Alexandre, Mrs. John J. (Nathalie)
   house, "Nirvana"
   Stamford, Conn.
      begun: March, 1894   built: 1895-1897
      cost: $ 31,357

*60. Algonquin Club
   217 Commonwealth Avenue
   Boston, Mass.
      condition: extant
      begun: October, 1886   built: 1887-1889
      designer: McKim [K]
      cost: $ 197,121
      contractor: Norcross Brothers

61. Altman and Company
   alterations to front of building, project
   Sixth Avenue and 19th Street
   New York, N.Y.
      not built
      begun: December, 1886
      cost: c. $ 53,400

*62. American Academy in Rome
   Villa Aurelia
   Janiculum Hill
   Rome, Italy
      condition: extant
      begun: c. 1910   built: 1912-1914
      designer: Kendall [K]
      cost: unrecorded

*63.   American Safe Deposit Company and Columbia Bank
        two-story banking facility with offices above
        Fifth Avenue and 42nd Street
        New York, N.Y.
            condition: demolished
            begun: October, 1882   built: 1883-1884
            designer: White
            cost: $ 202,189

*64.   American Surety Company
        competition entry
        Broadway and Pine Street
        New York, N.Y.
            not built
            begun: November, 1893

*65.   American Tobacco Company (Havana Tobacco Company)
        alterations for salesroom
        1137 Broadway
        New York, N.Y.
            condition: demolished
            begun: July, 1902   built: 1902-1903
            designer: White [LGW, B]
            cost: c. $ 100,000

*66.   Amherst College
        Biology and Geology Building
        Amherst, Mass.
            condition: extant
            begun: January, 1906   built: 1908-1909
            designer: Mead
            cost: $ 90,401

*67.   Amherst College
        (Biology and Geology Building) Porticoes added to
        Amherst, Mass.
            condition: extant
            begun: 1912   built: 1912
            cost: $ 2,006

*68.   Amherst College
        Converse Memorial Library
        Amherst, Mass.
            condition: extant
            begun: March, 1915   built: 1916-1917
            designer: Mead (?) with Kendall (?)
            cost: $ 230,826

*69.   Amherst College
        Fayerweather Hall   (Physics Laboratory)
        Amherst, Mass.
            condition: extant
            begun: January, 1892   built: 1892-1894
            designer: Mead [K]
            cost: $ 87,039
            contractor: Norcross Brothers

*70.   Amherst College
        Observatory
        Amherst, Mass.
            condition: extant
            begun: c. 1902   built: 1903-1904
            designer: Mead
            cost: $ 16,503

*71.   Amory, Francis I.
        townhouse   (half of double house; see Olney, R., No. 628)
        413 Commonwealth Avenue
        Boston, Mass.
            condition: extant
            begun: October, 1890   built: 1890-1892
            designer: McKim
            cost: $ 48,775
                  + 9,000
                    57,775

*72.   Andover Free Christian Church
        Andover, Mass.
            condition: extant
            begun: January, 1907   built: 1907-1908
            designer: Richardson [K]
            cost: $ 54,535

*73.   Andrew, John Forrester
        house
        Commonwealth Avenue and Hereford Street
        Boston, Mass.
            condition: extant
            begun: July, 1883   built: 1884-1886
            designer: McKim [K], with interiors by White
            cost: $ 83,809
                    51,522
                   135,331
            contractor: Norcross Brothers

*74.   Andrews, William Loring
        house
        deForest Road
        Montauk Point, N.Y.
            condition: extant
            begun: May, 1882   built: 1883
            cost: $ 6,803

22

*75. Appleton, Julia and Marian Alice
       house, "Homestead"
       Lenox, Mass.
           condition: demolished
           begun: September, 1883   built: 1884-1885
           designer: McKim [K]
           cost: $ 20,643

*76. Arnold, Benjamin Walworth
       house
       465 State Street
       Albany, N.Y.
           begun: October, 1901   built: 1902-1905
           designer: White [LGW, B, K]
           cost: $ 121,592
                 + 33,557
                   155,149
           contractor: J. C. Vreeland

 77. Astor, John Jacob, IV
       additions to house, "Ferncliff"
       Rhinebeck, N.Y.
           begun: July, 1897   built: 1898
           cost: $ 24,410

*78. Astor, John Jacob, IV
       tennis court, addition to "Ferncliff"
       Rhinebeck, N.Y.
           begun: March, 1902   built: 1902-1904
           designer: White [LGW, B, K]
           cost: $ 238,126

 79. Astor, William (estate of)
       house
       374 Fifth Avenue
       New York, N.Y.
           condition: demolished
           begun: December, 1879   built: 1880-1881
           designer: White (?)
           cost: $ 82,686

 80. Astor, Mrs. William
       additions to house
       Newport, R.I.
           begun: September, 1901   built: 1902
           cost: $ 47,010

ᵏ81. Atterbury, Charles L.
       house (later remodeled for William Merritt Chase, see No.192)
       Shinnecock, N.Y.
           begun: January, 1888   built: 1888
           designer: White [B]
           cost: unrecorded, unsupervised

82. Auchincloss, Henry B.
house
Glen Avenue
Llewellyn Park
Orange, N.J.
condition: extant
begun: October, 1882   built: 1883-1884
designer: White [B]
cost: $ 50,035

83. Ayers, Mrs. Henrietta
two houses
New Rochelle, N.Y.
begun: December, 1886   built: 1887
cost: $ 17,578

B

84. Babbott, Frank L.
monument
Greenwood Cemetery
Brooklyn, N.Y.
begun: 1909   built: 1909
cost: $ 2,060

85. Babylon Casino (for the Long Island Improvement Company)
Babylon, N.Y.
condition: demolished
begun: February, 1888   built: 1888
cost: $ 10,000

86. Baldwin, Charles A.
house
Colorado Spring, Colo.
begun: May, 1905   built: uncertain, project (?)
cost: $ 75,000 est.

87. Ballantine, Mrs. Isabella
additions and alterations to existing house
Morristown, N.J.
begun: December, 1911   built: 1912
cost: $ 49,303

88. Bancroft
monument
Worcester, Mass.
begun: 1892   built: 1892
designer: White [B]
cost: unrecorded

89.   Bank of Buffalo
       Main and Division Streets
       Buffalo, N.Y.
       condition: extant
       begun: February, 1916   built: 1916-1918
       cost: $ 321,030

*90.   Bank of Montreal
       First Phase, new building
       Craig Street
       Montreal, Quebec, Canada
       condition: extant
       begun: June, 1900   built: 1901-1904
       designer: McKim [K]; assoc. arch. A. T. Taylor
       cost: $ 769,765
             + 135,926
                905,691
       contractor: Norcross Brothers
       extant drawings: New-York Historical Society

*91.   Bank of Montreal
       Second Phase, renovation of original building
       St. James Street
       Montreal, Quebec, Canada
       condition: extant
       begun: June, 1900   built: 1903-1905
       designer: McKim [K]; assoc. arch., A. T. Taylor
       cost: $ 477,793
             +   64,391
                 542,184
       contractor: Norcross Brothers
       extant drawings: New-York Historical Society

*92.   Bank of Montreal
       Portage and Main Streets
       Winnipeg, Manitoba, Canada
       condition: extant
       begun: January, 1909   built: 1910-1912
       designer: Richardson [K]
       cost: $ 1,175,411
       contractor: Norcross Brothers
       extant drawings: New-York Historical Society

93.   Bank of Montreal
       alterations to existing building
       64-66 Wall Street
       New York, N.Y.
       condition: extant
       begun: July, 1909   built: 1909-1910
       cost: $ 49,990
             +133,539
              183,529
       contractor: Norcross Brothers
       extant drawings: New-York Historical Society

25

*94.   Bank of Montreal
        Darling and Market Streets
        Brandtford, Ontario, Canada
            condition: extant
            begun: May, 1913   built: 1913-1914
            cost: $ 61,847

95.   Bank of New Amsterdam
        alterations to existing building
        Broadway and 39th Street
        New York, N.Y.
            condition: demolished
            begun: July, 1891   built: 1891-1892
            cost: $ 10,074

96.   Barclay, Sackett M.
        house
        Cazenovia, N.Y.
            condition: extant
            begun: February, 1888   built: 1888-1889
            cost: $ 29,274
                 +   4,876
                    34,150
            contractor: Taylor & Elmslie

*97.   Barney, Charles Tracy
        townhouse
        10 E. 55th Street
        New York, N.Y.
            condition: demolished
            begun: July, 1880   built: 1881-1882
            cost: $ 150,408

98.   Barney, Charles Tracy
        townhouse
        67 Park Avenue
        New York, N.Y.
            condition: demolished
            begun: April, 1895   built: 1895
            designer: White [B]
            cost: $ 33,843

*99.   Barney, Charles Tracy
        townhouse, interiors
        67 Park Avenue
        New York, N.Y.
            condition: demolished
            begun: January, 1901   built: 1901-1902
            designer: White
            cost: c. $ 225,000

100. Barney, Charles Tracy
      interiors
      yacht, *Invincible*
          begun: 1900   built: 1900
          designer: White [B]

* 101. Battell, Joseph, Memorial Fountain (for Mary Eldridge)
      Norfolk, Conn.
          condition: extant
          begun: 1888 (?)   built: 1889
          designer: White [LGW, B]
          cost: unrecorded
          contractor: Norcross Brothers

102. Beaman, Charles Cotesworth
      "cottages" (number unspecified)
      Rockaway
      New York, N.Y.
          begun: July, 1881   built: 1881 (?)
          cost: $ 9,500

* 103. Beebe, J. Arthur
      townhouse
      199 Commonwealth Avenue
      Boston, Mass.
          condition: extant
          begun: August (?), 1888   built: 1888-(1889?)
          cost: $ 60,827

* 104. Beecher, Henry Ward, Memorial
      base for bronze figure
          (duplicate of bronze by J. Q. A. Ward, 1891)
      Amherst College
      Amherst, Mass.
          condition: extant
          begun: 1915   built: 1915
          cost: $ 1,145

* 105. Bell, Isaac, jr.
      house
      Bellevue Avenue and Perry Street
      Newport, R.I.
          condition: extant
          begun: September, 1881   built: 1881-1883
          cost: $ 36,009
                + 4,928
                  40,937

*106. Bellevue Hospital
        comprehensive plan
        26th to 29th Street at First Avenue
        New York, N.Y.
            plan begun: 1903 (through 1905)
            built: 1906 through 1920 (sections listed below)
                Later sections by successor firm:
                Administration Building, Pavilions C, D, F,
                and G, 1920 through 1940.
            condition: extant, remodeled
            designer and planner: McKim with Van der Bent [K]
            extant drawings: New-York Historical Society
                            Avery Library

107. Bellevue Hospital
        Boiler House and Coaling Station
        New York, N.Y.
            built: 1908-1911
            cost: $ 395,100
            contractor: P. J. Carlin

108. Bellevue Hospital
        Governeur Dispensary
        New York, N.Y.
            built: 1914-1916
            cost: $ 184,440
            extant drawings: New-York Historical Society
            contractor: John H. Parker

109. Bellevue Hospital
        landscaping (planting of trees)
        New York, N.Y.
            work done: 1911

110. Bellevue Hospital
        Laundry Building
        New York, N.Y.
            built: 1909-1911
            cost: $ 656,419
            extant drawings: New-York Historical Society

111. Bellevue Hospital
        Neponsit Beach Hospital, "Sea Breeze"
        New York, N.Y.
            built: 1916
            cost: $ 22,458
            contractor: Architectural Contracting Company

112. Bellevue Hospital
        Nurses' Training School, project
        New York, N.Y.
            begun: 1919
            cost: est. $ 350,000
            extant drawings: New-York Historical Society

*113. Bellevue Hospital
        Pathological Wing
        New York, N.Y.
            built: 1907-1911
            cost: $ 832,609
            contractor: T. Cockerill
            extant drawings: New-York Historical Society

114. Bellevue Hospital
        Pavilions A and B
        New York, N.Y.
            built: 1906-1910
            cost: $ 806,429
            extant drawings: New-York Historical Society

115. Bellevue Hospital
        Pavilions I and K
        New York, N.Y.
            built: 1912-1914
            cost: $ 1,701,392
            contractor: John H. Parker
            extant drawings: New-York Historical Society

*116. Bellevue Hospital
        Pavilions L and M
        New York, N.Y.
            built: 1911-1913
            cost: $ 902,721
            contractor: John T. Brady
            extant drawings: New-York Historical Society

117. Bend, George H.
        house (project ?)
        Riverdale-on-Hudson, N.Y.
            begun: September, 1882   built: 1883 (?)
            cost: c. $ 45,000

118. Bennett, Mrs. Thomas G.   (Hannah J.)
        house
        423 Prospect Street
        New Haven, Conn.
            condition: demolished
            begun: July, 1899   built: 1901-1903
            cost: $ 108,831
                 +   16,898
                    125,729
            contractor: G. M. Grant

119. Bennett, James Gordon, jr.
        cottages ("sketches of cottages at Newport, R.I.")
        Newport, R.I.
            not built, project
            begun: January, 1883
            cost: unrecorded

29

120. Bennett, James Gordon, jr.
    additions and alterations to New York *Herald* building
        (see also the new *New York Herald* building, No. 572)
    28 Ann Street
    New York, N.Y.
        condition: demolished
        begun: June, 1884   built: 1884
        cost: $ 21,519

121. Bennett, James Gordon, jr.
    house
    28 W. 21st Street
    New York, N.Y.
        condition: demolished
        cost: $ 23,749
             + 14,794
                38,543

122. Bennett, James Gordon, jr.
    alterations to house
    Fifth Avenue and 23rd Street
    New York, N.Y.
        condition: demolished
        begun: August, 1885   built: 1885
        cost: $ 4,611
        contractor: J. Cabus

123. Bennett, James Gordon, jr.
    interiors
    yacht, *Polyana*
        begun: February, 1882
        cost: flat fee, $ 500

*124. Bennett, James Gordon, jr.
    interiors
    yacht, *Namouna*
        begun: March, 1885   built: 1885
        designer: White [B]
        cost: $ 20,837

*125. Benson, A. W.
    house
    deForest Road
    Montauk Point, N.Y.
        condition: extant
        begun: July, 1882   built: 1882
        cost: unrecorded

126. Benson, Frank Sherman
     alterations to existing house, interiors
     127 E. 39th Street
     New York, N.Y.
        condition: demolished
        begun: August, 1888   built: 1888
        cost: $ 6,932
        contractor: J. Cabus

127. Benson, Frank Sherman
     alterations to existing house
     214 Columbia Heights
     Brooklyn, N.Y.
        begun: June, 1892   built: 1892-1893
        cost: $ 10,134

*128. Blair, Edward Tyler
      house
      1576 Lake Shore Drive
      Chicago, Ill.
         condition: extant
         begun: February, 1912   built: 1912-1914
         designer: Kendall [K]
         cost: $ 135,816
              +   20,408
                 156,224
         extant drawings: New-York Historical Society
                          Burnham Library, Art Institute of Chicago

129. Bloomingdale, Lyman
     mausoleum
     Salem Fields Cemetery
     Brooklyn, N.Y.
        condition: extant
        begun: July, 1905   built: 1905-1907
        cost: $ 20,000

*130. Booth, Edwin, Memorial
      monument
      Mount Auburn Cemetery
      Cambridge, Mass.
         condition: extant
         begun: 1895   built: 1895
         designer: White [LGW, B]
         cost: unrecorded

131. Boreel Mining Company
     alterations to office building
     115 Broadway
     New York, N.Y.
        condition: demolished
        begun: March, 1896   built: 1896-1897
        cost: $ 42,409

31

132.   Boston Gas Light Company
       offices
       24 West Street
       Boston, Mass.
          condition: demolished
          begun: June, 1890   built: 1890-1892
          cost: $ 60,728
                +   4,685
                   65,413

*133. Boston Public Library
       Copley Square
       Boston, Mass.
          condition: extant, enlarged
          begun: March, 1887   built: 1888-1895
          designer: McKim [K]
          cost: $ 2,203,178 (excluding art work and furniture)
          contractor: Woodbury & Leighton; Norcross Brothers
             Note: for the extensive art work see Addenda, p. 172

*134. Boston Symphony Hall
       Huntington and Massachusetts Avenues
       Boston, Mass.
          condition: extant
          begun: October, 1892   (design studied through 1893-1894)
          built: 1899-1901
          designer: McKim [K]
          cost: $ 487,460
          contractor: Norcross Brothers

*135. Bowditch, Ernest William
       house
       Milton, Mass.
          begun: January, 1898   built: 1898
          cost: $ 50,689

 136. Bowdoin, George Sullivan
       alterations to existing townhouse
       39 Park Avenue
       New York, N.Y.
          condition: demolished
          begun: December, 1898   built: 1898
          cost: $ 11,080

*137. Bowdoin College
       Walker Art Gallery   (for Mary and Sophia Walker)
       Brunswick, Maine
          condition: extant
          begun: July, 1891   built: 1892-1894
          designer: McKim [K]
          cost: $ 109,843
          contractor: Norcross Brothers
             murals: Athens by John LaFarge; Florence by Abbott H.
                     Thayer; Venice by Kenyon Cox; Rome (or The
                     Art-Idea) by Elihu Vedder

32

138. Bowdoin College
     Walker Memorial Gates
     Brunswick, Maine
         condition: extant
         begun: June, 1902   built: 1902
         designer: Kendall [K]
         cost: $ 3,574

*139. Bowery Savings Bank
     Bowery and Grant Street
     New York, N.Y.
         condition: extant
         begun: February, 1893   built: 1893-1895
         designer: White [LGW, B, K]
         cost: $ 519,664
             pediment sculpture: Frederick MacMonnies, 1894-1895

140. *Boy and Duck*, fountain
     "Vale of Cashmere"
     Prospect Park
     Brooklyn, N.Y.
         condition: extant
         begun: 1895 (?)   built: 1896
         designer: White and MacMonnies [LGW, B]

*141. Bradley, Arthur C.
     house
     Newport, Vt.
         condition: extant
         begun: September, 1891   built: 1892-1893
         cost: $ 31,646

142. Brattleboro school
     drawings for school house
     Brattleboro, Vt.
         begun: January, 1893
         cost: fee for draftsmen's time

143. Brearly School
     Park Avenue and 61st Street
     New York, N.Y.
         condition: demolished
         begun: August, 1911   built: 1912-1913
         designer: Richardson [K]
         cost: $ 205,725

*144. Breese, James L.
     house, "The Orchard"
     Southampton, N.Y.
         condition: extant
         begun: July, 1898   built: 1900 (?) -1907
         designer: White [LGW, B]
         cost: c. $ 48,830
             garden fountain: Janet Scudder

33

bridge (see Shore Road Commission, bridge project, No. 787).

*145. Bridgeport City Hall
        competition entry
        Bridgeport, Conn.
          not built
          begun: September, 1900
          cost: $ 400,000 est.

146.   Brigham, William H.
        house
        Greenwich, Conn.
          begun: August, 1887   built: 1887-1888
          cost: $ 13,198
          contractor: Taylor & Elmslie

147.   Brokaw, Isaac Vail
        house
        Elberon, N.J.
          condition: demolished
          begun: March, 1880   built: 1880
          cost: $ 7,069

148.   Bronson, Mrs. Frederick
        monument
        Fairfield Cemetery
        Fairfield, Conn.
          condition: extant
          begun: February, 1912   built: 1912
          cost: $ 760

149.   Bronson & King Bank
        interiors
        El Paso, Texas
          begun: June, 1886   built: 1886
          cost: c. $ 5,000

*150. The Brook Club
        interior alterations
        7 E. 40th Street
        New York, N.Y.
          condition: demolished
          begun: December, 1904   built: 1904-1905
          designer: White [B]
          cost: unrecorded

*151. Brooklyn Botanic Garden
        Administration Building, with laboratory and school
        1000 Washington Avenue
        Brooklyn, N.Y.
          condition: extant
          begun: December, 1913   built: 1914-1916
          designer: Kendall [K]
          extant drawings: New-York Historical Society

34

*152.   Brooklyn Institute of Arts and Sciences (Brooklyn Museum)
        comprehensive plan
        Eastern Parkway and Washington Avenue
        Brooklyn, N.Y.
            plan begun: May, 1893 (competition winner)
            built: 1895 through 1915
            condition: extant
            designer: McKim [K]
                sculpture: (Daniel Chester French, Director) Daniel
                Chester French, Herbert Adams, Karl Bitter, George T.
                Brewster, Kenyon Cox, John Gelert, Charles H. Heber,
                Charles Keck, Henry Augustus Lukeman, Attilio Pic-
                cirilli, Edward Clark Potter, John T. Quinn, and
                Janet Scudder. Pediment sculpture by D. C. French.

 153.   Brooklyn Institute of Arts and Sciences
        comprehensive plan for proposed additions
        Brooklyn, N.Y.
            plan begun: March, 1909 (continued through 1909)
            cost: flat fee, $ 50,000

*154.   Brooklyn Institute of Arts and Sciences
        approach and steps, center pavilion
        Brooklyn, N.Y.
            begun: January, 1906   built: 1906
            cost: unspecified
            contractor: P. J. Carlin
            extant drawings: New-York Historical Society

*155.   Brooklyn Institute of Arts and Sciences
        Center Wing
        Brooklyn, N.Y.
            begun: c. 1902   built: 1902-1903
            cost: $ 407,315
            contractor: P. J. Carlin

*156.   Brooklyn Institute of Arts and Sciences
        Pavilions A and B (West Wing)
        Brooklyn, N.Y.
            begun: September, 1895   built: 1895-1897
            cost: $ 297,087
            contractor: P. J. Carlin
            extant drawings: New-York Historical Society

*157.   Brooklyn Institute of Arts and Sciences
        Pavilion C (Center Pavilion)
        Brooklyn, N.Y.
            begun: August, 1900   built: 1900-1905
            cost: $ 347,485
            contractor: P. J. Carlin
            extant drawings: New-York Historical Society

*158.   Brooklyn Institute of Arts and Sciences
        Pavilions D and E (East Wing)
        Brooklyn, N.Y.
            begun: August, 1904   built: 1904-1906
            cost: $ 416,764
            extant drawings: New-York Historical Society

*159.   Brooklyn Institute of Arts and Sciences
        Pavilions F and G
        Brooklyn, N.Y.
            begun: July, 1913   built: 1913-1915
            cost: $ 405,409
            extant drawings: New-York Historical Society

 160.   Brooklyn Institute of Arts and Sciences
        power house
        Brooklyn, N.Y.
            begun: December, 1902   built: 1902-1904
            cost: $ 79,884
            contractor: P. J. Carlin
            extant drawings: New-York Historical Society

*161.   Brooklyn Municipal Building
        competition entry
        Brooklyn, N.Y.
            not built
            begun: 1904 (?) or 1909 (?)

 162.   Brooklyn Riding and Driving Club
        Brooklyn, N.Y.
            begun: February, 1890   built: 1890-1891
            designer: in collaboration with Stratton & Ellingwood
            cost: $ 160,000
                  +   25,000
                    185,000

*163.   Brooks, Phillips, Memorial
            setting for bronze figures (by Augustus Saint-Gaudens)
        Trinity Church
        Boston, Mass.
            condition: extant
            begun: 1904-1906 (figure started, 1893)   built: 1907-1910
            designer: White with Augustus Saint-Gaudens [LGW, B]
            cost: $ 21,292

*164.   Brown, Mrs. George Bruce (later Mrs. W. B. Cutting)
            townhouse
        Madison Avenue and 72nd Street
        New York, N.Y.
            condition: demolished
            begun: May, 1893   built: 1893-1894
            cost: $ 76,306
                  + 20,914
                    97,220

165. Brown, Henry W.
     house
     4807 Wayne Avenue
     Philadelphia (Germantown), Penna.
       condition: demolished
       begun: June, 1886   built: 1886-1887
       cost: $ 17,000

166. Brown, William R.
     stable
     White Plains, N.Y.
       begun: 1882   built: 1882
       cost: $ 5,000

*167. Brown University
      Rockefeller Hall (Faunce Hall), student union
      Providence, R.I.
        condition: extant
        begun: July, 1902   built: 1903-1904
        designer: McKim [K]
        cost: $ 84,125
        contractor: Norcross Brothers

*168. Browne, T. O., and J. M. Meredith
      apartment building
      66 Beacon Street
      Boston, Mass.
        condition: extant
        begun: May, 1890   built: 1890-1891
        designer: McKim
        cost: $ 133,482

*169. "The Buckingham" (for John Howard Whittemore)
      office building and auditorium
      Grand and Bank Streets
      Waterbury, Conn.
        condition: demolished
        begun: December, 1903   built: 1905-1906
        designer: Kendall and Van der Bent [K]
        cost: $ 179,884
        contractor: Tidewater Construction Company
        extant drawings: New-York Historical Society

170. Bull, Charles M.
     house
     Newport, R.I.
       begun: July, 1882   built: 1882-1883
       cost: $ 12,866

*171.   Burke, Winnifred Masterson, Foundation Hospital for Convales-
        cents (for Winnifred Masterson Burke Relief Foundation)
        Mamaroneck Avenue
        White Plains. N.Y.
            begun: April, 1912   built: 1912-1915
            cost: $ 1,237,018
            extant drawings: New-York Historical Society

 172.   Bush, John S.
        house
        Tremont, N.Y.
            begun: November, 1887   built: 1888-1890
            cost: unspecified

*173.   Butler, Joseph G., jr.
        art gallery (Butler Institute of American Art)
        524 Wick Avenue
        Youngstown, Ohio
            condition: extant
            begun: February, 1917   built: 1917-1920
            designer: Kendall
            cost: $ 165,736
            extant drawings: New-York Historical Society

*174.   Butler, Prescott Hall
        additions and alterations to house, "Bytharbor" (See No. 29)
        Moriches Road
        St. James, N.Y.
            condition: extant, remodeled
            begun: August, 1884   built, 1884
            cost: unspecified

*175.   Butler, Prescott Hall
        additions and alterations to house, "Bytharbor"
        Moriches Road
        St. James, N.Y.
            condition: extant, remodeled
            begun: February, 1894   built: 1894
            cost: unspecified

*176.   Butler, Prescott Hall
        townhouse
        22 Park Avenue
        New York, N.Y.
            condition: demolished
            begun: June, 1895   built: 1895-1897
            designer: White [LGW, B]
            cost: $ 121,221
                +   8,415
                  ─────────
                    129,636

C

*177. Cable Building
   office building (for the Broadway and Seventh Avenue Rail-
    road Company)
   Broadway and Houston Street
   New York, N.Y.
    condition: extant
    begun: April, 1892 built: 1892-1894
    designer: White [B]
    cost: $ 871,355

 178. Calumet Club
   alterations in the former Henry B. Hollins house, No. 399
   12 W. 56th Street
   New York, N.Y.
    condition: extant
    begun: June, 1914 built: 1914
    cost: $ 21,418

*179. Canfield, A. Cass
   house, stable, and cottage
   Westbury, N.Y.
    condition: demolished
    begun: March, 1902 built: 1902-1903
    designer: McKim [K]
    cost: $ 96,794
      + 22,416
      ‾‾‾‾‾‾‾
      119,210

 180. Canfield, Mrs. Cass
   additions and alterations to house
   Westbury, N.Y.
    condition: demolished
    begun: July, 1905 built: 1905
    cost: $ 2,810

 181. Cannon, LeGrand B.
   house ("cottage")
   Burlington, Vt.
    begun: September, 1882 built: 1883 (?)
    cost: unspecified

*182. Cataract Construction Company (Niagara Falls Power Company)
   "Echota," workers' housing complex
   Buffalo and Hyde Park Avenues
   Niagara Falls, N.Y.
    condition: extant (partially)
    begun: February, 1893 built: 1893-1894
    designer: White
    cost: $ 84,730 (for first 25 buildings)

*183. Cataract Construction Company
        flagstaff, in front of powerhouse
        Niagara Falls, N.Y.
            begun: 1895   built: 1895
            designer: White with MacMonnies
              see the *American Architect and Building News* 49
              (September 28, 1895), 138, pl. 1031.

*184. Cataract Construction Company
        Powerhouse
        Buffalo Avenue
        Niagara Falls, N.Y.
            condition: demolished (center arch now on Goat Island)
            begun: June, 1892   built: 1893
            designer: White with engineer, Coleman Sellers
            cost: unspecified

*185. Cataract Construction Company
        Transformer Building
        Buffalo Avenue
        Niagara Falls, N.Y.
            condition: extant
            begun: c. 1893   built: 1894
            designer: White with engineer, Coleman Sellers
            cost: $ 15,825

*186. Century Club (for the Century Association)
        7-11 W. 43rd Street
        New York, N.Y.
            condition: extant
            begun: September, 1889   built: 1890-1891
            designer: White with McKim, details by Wells [LGW, B, K]
            cost: $ 212,909

*187. Chanler, the Misses
        alterations and additions to existing house, "Rokeby"
        Barrytown, N.Y.
            begun: July, 1894   built: 1894-1896
            cost: $ 24,765
                 +   9,806
                    ‾‾‾‾‾‾
                    34,571

*188. Chanler, John Armstrong
        commercial building
        198 Broadway
        New York, N.Y.
            condition: demolished
            begun: March, 1899   built: 1899
            cost: $ 112,864
            contractor: Michael Reid

189. Chapin, Alfred Clark
      alterations to house
      24 E. 56th Street
      New York, N.Y.
         condition: demolished
         begun: June, 1900   built: 1901-1905
         designer: White
         cost: $ 12,674
            conservatory fountain by Janet Scudder

*190. Chapin, Chester William, Memorial
       base and setting for bronze figure, *The Puritan*,
          by Augustus Saint-Gaudens
       Merrick Park (now)
       Springfield, Mass.
          condition: extant but moved from original location
          begun: November, 1884   built: 1887
          designer: White with Saint-Gaudens [LGW, B]
          cost: $ 2,107 (for base alone)
          contractor: R. C. Fisher

191. Chapin, William C.
      house
      621 High Street
      Providence, R.I.
         begun: July, 1881   built: 1882-1883
         cost: $ 11,000

*192. Chase, William Merritt
       house and studio (alterations in C. L. Atterbury house, No. 81)
       Shinnecock, N.Y.
          no entry in Bill Books; c. 1895 (?)

*193. Cheever, John H.
       house, "Wave Crest"
       Far Rockaway
       New York, N.Y.
          begun: April, 1885   built: 1885-1886
          cost: $ 16,994

*194. Cheney, Anne W.
       house
       South Manchester, Conn.
          begun: September, 1887   built: 1888
          designer: White [LGW, B, K]
             mural, *The Days*, by Thomas W. Dewing

195. Cheney, Anne W.
      additions and alterations to house
      South Manchester, Conn.
         begun: 1902   built: 1902-1903
         designer: White
         contractor: J. Cabus

196. Cheney, Anne W.
further additions and alterations to house
South Manchester, Conn.
begun: 1912   built: 1912-1916 et seq.

197. Cheney, Robert
house
South Manchester, Conn.
begun: July, 1901   built: 1902-1906
designer: White (?)
cost: $ 74,608

*198. Cheney, Rush
house (completed by Henry G. Cheney)
South Manchester, Conn.
begun: September, 1881   built: 1883-1886
cost: c. $ 35,000

*199. Choate, Joseph Hodges
house, "Naumkeag"
Stockbridge, Mass.
condition: extant
begun: December, 1884 ~ built: 1886-1887
designer: White [LGW, B, K]
cost: $ 41,300
    4,789
   46,089
contractor: J. Clifford
garden fountain, *Young Faun with Heron*, by Frederick
MacMonnies (see No. 942)

200. Chubb, Mrs. Victoria
house
East Orange, N.J.
begun: February, 1891   built: 1891
cost: $ 13,206

Church of Saint Paul the Apostle; see No. 751

*201. Church of Christ at Dartmouth   (built 1794-1795)
"College Church"
alterations in chancel
Hanover, N.H.
condition: demolished
begun: July, 1889   built: 1889
designer: White [LGW, B]
cost: unrecorded, no fee charged

*202. Church of the Ascension
alterations in chancel
Fifth Avenue and 10th Street
New York, N.Y.
condition: extant
begun: September, 1885   built: 1885-1888
designer: White [LGW, B, K]
cost: $ 9,636 (for White's work alone); $ 25,896 total
[art work listed on facing page]

Church of the Ascension, art work:
mural, *The Ascension of Our Lord*, by John La Farge
angels in relief by Louis Saint-Gaudens
mosaic angels and rinceaux by David Maitland Armstrong
window, *Christ and Nicodemus*, by John La Farge
window, *The Annunciation*, by David Maitland Armstrong
pulpit designed by C. F. McKim, executed by J. Cabus

203. Church of the Ascension
alterations in church (provision for new organ)
New York, N.Y.
   condition: extant
   begun: 1894   built: 1894-1897
   cost: $ 12,161

*204. Church of the Ascension
Parish House
12 W. 11th Street
New York, N.Y.
   condition: extant
   begun: June, 1888   built: 1888-1889
   cost: $ 25,896
   extant drawings: New-York Historical Society

*205. Cincinnati, University of
comprehensive plan for new campus
Burnet Woods Campus
Cincinnati, Ohio
   not executed
   begun: February, 1902
   designer and planner: White (?) with W. S. Richardson
   cost: flat fee, $ 310
   extant drawings: New-York Historical Society

*206. Clarke, Thomas Benedict
townhouse
22 E. 35th Street
New York, N.Y.
   condition: extant
   begun: April, 1902   built: 1902
   designer: White
   cost: unsupervised, no fee

*207. Cochrane, Alexander
townhouse
257 Commonwealth Avenue
Boston, Mass.
   condition: extant
   begun: January, 1886   built: 1887-1888
   designer: McKim [K]
   cost: $ 60,810
        + 20,454
          81,264

208. Colgate, Robert, jr.
        alterations to existing house
        Quogue, N.Y.
            begun: February, 1885   built: 1885
            cost: $ 9,188
            contractor: Mead & Taft

209. College of the City of New York
        competition entry
        North Campus, Morningside Heights
        New York, N.Y.
            not built
            begun: July, 1897
            cost: flat fee, $ 350

*210. Colman, Samuel
        house
        7 Red Cross Avenue
        Newport, R.I.
            condition: extant
            begun: April, 1882   built: 1882-1883
            cost: $ 24,669

*211. Colony Club
        120-124 Madison Avenue
        New York, N.Y.
            condition: extant
            begun: April, 1904   built: 1905-1908
            designer: White [LGW, B, K]
                    Interiors by Elsie de Wolfe
            cost: $ 289,175
            contractor: Jacob & Young
            extant drawings: New-York Historical Society

*212. Columbia University
        comprehensive plan
        Morningside Heights Campus
        Broadway and 116th Street
        New York, N.Y.
            plan begun: May, 1892 (studied through 1894)
            built: 1895 through 1919
            condition: extant
            designer and planner: McKim [K]
            cost: flat fee for plan, $ 1,500
            extant drawings: Avery Library and Columbiana Collection,
                        Columbia University

*213. Columbia University
          comprehensive plan for expanded site
          Broadway, 114th Street to 120th Street
          New York, N.Y.
              plan begun: July, 1903
              built: 1904 through 1916
              condition: extant
              designer and planner: McKim and Kendall
              cost: flat fee for plan, $ 3,500
              extant drawings: Avery Library, Columbia University

          Later buildings by successor firm: Chemistry Building,
          Faculty Club, John Jay Hall, Natural Science Building,
          Physics Building, Women's Dormitory, 1920 through 1930.

    [Note: Because of the number of Columbia University commissions,
    the buildings are listed alphabetically by name.]

*214. Columbia University
          Avery Library and School of Architecture
          New York, N.Y.
              begun: April, 1911   built: 1911-1912
              designer: Kendall [K]
              cost: $ 315,423
              extant drawings: New-York Historical Society
                               Avery Library

*215. Columbia University
          Earl Hall
          New York, N.Y.
              begun: January, 1901   built: 1901-1902
              designer: McKim
              cost: $ 155,869
              contractor: Norcross Brothers
              extant drawings: New-York Historical Society
                               Avery Library

216. Columbia University
          Engineering Building
          New York, N.Y.
              begun: April, 1896   built: 1896-1898
              designer: McKim
              cost: $ 257,278
              contractor: James B. Smith
              extant drawings: New-York Historical Society
                               Avery Library

45

*217. Columbia University
       Fayerweather Hall
       New York, N.Y.
           begun: February, 1896   built: 1896-1898
           designer: McKim
           cost: $ 257,102
           contractor: Norcross Brothers
           extant drawings: New-York Historical Society
                            Avery Library

 218. Columbia University
       Furnald Hall
       New York, N.Y.
           begun: August, 1912   built: 1912-1914
           designer: Kendall
           cost: $ 315,511
           extant drawings: New-York Historical Society
                            Avery Library

*219. Columbia University
       Hamilton Hall
       New York, N.Y.
           begun: July, 1905   built: 1905-1907
           designer: Kendall [K]
           cost: $ 435,376
           extant drawings: New-York Historical Society
                            Avery Library

*220. Columbia University
       Hartley Hall
       New York, N.Y.
           begun: May, 1904   built: 1904-1907
           designer: McKim
           cost: $ 310,806
           contractor: Michael Reid
           extant drawings: New-York Historical Society
                            Avery Library

*221. Columbia University
       Havemeyer Hall
       New York, N.Y.
           begun: April, 1896   built: 1896-1898
           designer: McKim
           cost: $ 475,326
           contractor: J. B. Smith
           extant drawings: New-York Historical Society
                            Avery Library

*222. Columbia University
          Kent Hall
          New York, N.Y.
             begun: November, 1907   built: 1909-1911
             designer: Kendall [K]
             cost: $ 427,332
             contractor: J. H. Parker
             extant drawings: New-York Historical Society
                              Avery Library

*223. Columbia University
          Livingston Hall
          New York, N.Y.
             begun: May, 1904   built: 1904-1907
             designer: McKim
             cost: $ 304,792
             contractor: Michael Reid
             extant drawings: New-York Historical Society
                              Avery Library

*224. Columbia University
          Low Library (gift of Seth Low in memory of Abiel Low)
          New York, N.Y.
             begun: June, 1895   built: 1895-1898
             designer: McKim [K]
             cost: $ 1,106,729
             contractor: Norcross Brothers
             extant drawings: New-York Historical Society
                              Avery Library

 225. Columbia University
          Philosophy Building
          New York, N.Y.
             begun: July, 1910   built: 1910-1911
             designer: Kendall [K]
             cost: $ 307,578
             extant drawings: New-York Historical Society
                              Avery Library

*226. Columbia University
          President's House
          New York, N.Y.
             begun: August, 1911   built: 1911-1912
             designer: Kendall [K]
             cost: $ 165,656
             extant drawings: New-York Historical Society
                              Avery Library

*227. Columbia University
         Schermerhorn Hall
         New York, N.Y.
            begun: February, 1896   built: 1896-1898
            designer: McKim [K]
            cost: $ 432,324
            contractor: Norcross Brothers
            extant drawings: New-York Historical Society
                             Avery Library

228. Columbia University
         School of Journalism
         New York, N.Y.
            begun: June, 1912   built: 1912-1913
            designer: Kendall [K]
            cost: $ 450,582
            extant drawings: New-York Historical Society
                             Avery Library

229. Columbia University
         620 Fifth Avenue
         New York, N.Y.
            begun: 1917   built: 1917
            cost: $ 42,761
            extant drawings: New-York Historical Society

230. Columbia University
         University Hall
         New York, N.Y.
            condition: demolished
            begun: December, 1896   built: 1896-1901, incomplete
            designer: McKim
            cost: $ 100,963
            contractor: Norcross Brothers
            extant drawings: New-York Historical Society
                             Avery Library

[Note: Miscellaneous Columbia University commissions, not buildings,
follow in alphabetical order.]

231. Columbia University
         Alma Mater
         base for bronze figure by Daniel Chester French
         New York, N.Y.
            begun: 1900   built: 1903
            designer: McKim with Daniel Chester French

232. Columbia University
         entrance gateway
         116th Street
            begun: 1918 (?)   built: 1918-1919
            designer: Kendall (?)
            cost: $ 22,605
            extant drawings: New-York Historical Society

48

*233. Columbia University
  Exedra, setting for *Pan*, bronze figure by George Gray
    Barnard (for Clark Estate)
  New York, N.Y.
    begun: November, 1907   built: 1908
    designer: Kendall [K]
    cost: $ 11,740, for setting alone
    extant drawings: New-York Historical Society

234. Columbia University
  fountains
  Low Library forecourt
  New York, N.Y.
    built: 1907
    cost: $ 3,607
    extant drawings: New-York Historical Society

235. Columbia University
  Jefferson, Thomas
  base for bronze figure by William Ordway Partridge
  New York, N.Y.
    built: 1914

236. Columbia University
  Memorial, clock, Class of 1906
  New York, N.Y.
    built: 1916
    designer: Kendall (?)
    cost: $ 150

237. Columbia University
  Memorial, gate and fence, Class of 1891
  New York, N.Y.
    built: 1917
    designer: Kendall (?)
    cost: $ 6,801
    extant drawings: New-York Historical Society

*238. Columbia University
  Memorial, sundial, Class of 1885
  New York, N.Y.
    condition: partially extant
    built: 1914
    designer: Kendall
    cost: $ 6,675

239. Columbia University
  terraces
  Low Library forecourt
  New York, N.Y.
    begun: June, 1895   built: 1895-1898
    designer: McKim
    cost: $ 357,284
    extant drawings: New-York Historical Society

240. Columbia University
        Vam Amringe Memorial
        New York, N.Y.
            built: 1918
            designer: Kendall (?)
            cost: $ 17,183
            extant drawings: New-York Historical Society

241. Columbus Arch
        temporary arch
        Columbus Circle
        New York, N.Y.
            condition: demolished
            begun: 1892   built: 1892
            designer: White [B]

*242. Confederate Memorial
        competition entry
        Richmond, Va.
            not built
            begun: 1911

*243. Congregational Church (Congregational Society of Naugatuck)
        Division Street
        Naugatuck, Conn.
            condition: extant
            begun: April, 1901   built: 1901-1903
            designer: interior, Mead [K]
            cost: $ 98,320
            contractor: H. Wales Lines

*244. Cook, Charles T.
        house
        Lincoln Avenue
        Elberon, N.J.
            condition: partially extant
            begun: April, 1884   built: 1885
            designer: McKim (?)
            cost: $ 30,088

245. Coolidge, Thomas Jefferson
        library, alterations in existing house
        93 Beacon Street
        Boston, Mass.
            condition: partially extant
            begun: 1887   built: 1887
            cost: $ 3,481

*246. Coolidge, Thomas Jefferson
          house
          Manchester-by-the-Sea, Mass.
             condition: demolished
             begun: December, 1902   built: 1903-1904
             designer: McKim [K]
             cost: $ 151,289
                   + 32,234
                     183,523
             contractor: Norcross Brothers

*247. Cooper, Peter, Memorial
          base and setting for bronze figure by
             Augustus Saint-Gaudens
          Cooper Square
          Bowery and 7th Street
          New York, N.Y.
             condition: extant
             begun: 1891 (?)   built: 1896-1897
             designer: White with Saint-Gaudens [LGW, B]
             cost: $ 25,000 total, figure and base

*248. Corbin, P. and F., Company
          offices, addition to existing factory
          Park and Orchard Streets
          New Britain, Conn.
             condition: extant
             begun: October, 1891   built: 1892-1893
             designer: White (?)
             cost: $ 14,000

 249. Corn Exchange Bank
          unspecified work
          Seventh Avenue and 33rd Street
          New York, N.Y.
             begun: 1910   built: 1911
             cost: $ 17,177

*250. Cornell Medical School (for Oliver H. Payne)
          First Avenue and 28th Street
          New York, N.Y.
             condition: demolished
             begun: December, 1898   built: 1899-1901
             designer: White [LGW, B, K]
             cost: $ 671,952
                   + 64,246
                     736,198
             contractor: Michael Reid
             extant drawings: New-York Historical Society

251. Cornell Medical School
     additions and alterations to building
     First Avenue and 28th Street
     New York, N.Y.
          condition: demolished
          begun: June, 1909   built: 1910
          cost: $ 21,687
          contractor: Michael Reid
          extant drawings: New-York Historical Society

252. *Cosmopolitan Magazine*
     offices
     Irvington-on-Hudson, N.Y.
          begun: June, 1894   built: 1895
          designer: White [B, K]
          cost: flat fee, $413

253. Crawford, George
     hotel, project
     Park Avenue and 41st Street
     New York, N.Y.
          not built
          begun: 1892
          cost: est. $ 500,000

*254. Cresson, George V.
     house
     Narragansett Pier, R.I.
          begun: March, 1883   built: 1884
          cost: $ 20,568
               +   5,500
                  26,068

255. Cromwell, Frederick
     tower
     Bernardsville, N.J.
          begun: July, 1894   built: 1894
          cost: $ 1,976
          contractor: Sturgis Brothers

256. Cromwell, Frederick
     monument
     Greenwood Cemetery
     Brooklyn, N.Y.
          condition: extant
          begun: February, 1911   built: 1911
          cost: $ 1,784

     Cullum Memorial Hall
     see United States Military Academy at West Point, No. 855

*257. Cumming, Robert W.
         house
         368 Mt. Prospect Street
         Newark, N.J.
           begun: 1894 (?)   built: 1895-1896
           cost: $ 58,789
                 + 12,000
                   70,789
           contractor: Norcross Brothers

 258. Curtiss Securities Company
         unspecified work at 998 Fifth Avenue (see No. 615)
         New York, N.Y.
           begun: 1915   built: 1915
           cost: $ 29,247

 259. Cutting, Mrs. William Bayard
         monument
         Greenwood Cemetery
         Brooklyn, N.Y.
           condition: extant
           begun: 1914   built: 1914
           cost: $ 100

D

*260. Davis, Theodore R.
         house
         43 McDonough Street
         Brooklyn, N.Y.
           begun: July, 1881   built: 1885
           cost: c. $ 6,500, unsupervised

*261. deForest, Henry G.
         house
         deForest Road
         Montauk Point, N.Y.
           condition: extant
           begun: July, 1882   built: 1882
           cost: $ 6,449

*262. Detroit Bicentennial Memorial
         project for memorial column
         Belle Isle
         Detroit, Mich.
           not built
           begun: 1899
           designer: White
           cost: est. $ 1,000,000

*263. Deutscher Verein
       club
       101 W. 59th Street
       New York, N.Y.
          condition: demolished
          begun: November, 1889   built: 1890-1891
          cost: $ 228,658

 264. Dillon, Sidney
       townhouse
       23 W. 57th Street
       New York, N.Y.
          condition: demolished
          begun: March, 1886   built: 1886-1887
          cost: $ 41,028

 265. Dimock, Henry F.
       townhouse
       25 E. 60th Street
       New York, N.Y.
          condition: demolished
          begun: July, 1898   built: 1898-1899
          cost: $ 77,005

*266. "Downtown Building" (later the Columbia Trust Company)
          downtown branch of the Knickerbocker Trust, first 8 stories
       60 Broadway
       New York, N.Y.
          condition: demolished
          begun: April (?), 1906   built: May, 1907
                                           to October, 1909
          designer: White: [LGW, B, K]
          cost: $ 1,135,774
          contractor: George A. Fuller
          extant drawings: New-York Historical Society

*267. "Downtown Building"
       upper 14 stories
       New York, N.Y.
          condition: demolished
          built: 1909-1911
          cost: $ 815,229
          contractor: George A. Fuller

*268. Drayton, J. Coleman
       townhouse
       374-380 Fifth Avenue
       New York, N.Y.
          condition: demolished
          begun: October, 1882   built: 1882-1883

269. Duveen Brothers
        showrooms, art galleries
        302 Fifth Avenue
        New York, N.Y.
        condition: demolished
        begun: June, 1902   built: 1903-1907
        cost: $ 70,081

E

270. Eastman, George
        alterations to existing house
        Rochester, N.Y.
        begun: December, 1902   built: 1904-1905
        cost: $ 30,539
        contractor: P. Hiss

*271. Eastman Kodak Company
        office building
        235-239 W. 23rd Street
        New York, N.Y.
        condition: extant
        begun: March, 1906   built: 1906-1907
        designer: Kendall (?)
        cost: $ 182,998
        contractor: Michael Reid

272. Eastman Kodak Company
        offices, alterations
        Rochester, N.Y.
        begun: November, 1912   built: 1913-1914
        cost: $ 37,705

*273. Edgar, Commodore William
        house
        29 Old Beach Road
        Newport, R.I.
        condition: extant
        begun: August, 1884   built: 1884-1886
        designer: McKim [K]
        cost: $ 32,973
                9,896
              ‾‾‾‾‾‾
              42,869

274. Elizabeth General Hospital
        nurses' home
        Elizabeth, N.J.
        begun: June, 1914   built: 1914-1915
        cost: $ 22,830

275. Elwell, Mrs. Frank Edwin
     alterations to existing house
     131 W. 11th Street
     New York, N.Y.
        condition: partially extant
        begun: October, 1893   built: 1893
        cost: $ 5,801

276. Emmet, C. Temple
     house, "Challoner"
     Portchester, N.Y.
        begun: May, 1897   built: 1899
        cost: $ 21,374
        designer: White

*277. Emmett, Devereaux
     alterations to existing house and gardens
     St. James, N.Y.
        condition: extant
        begun: 1895   built: 1895
        designer: White
        cost: unsupervised

278. Emmons, Nathaniel H.
     monument
     location unspecified
        built: 1890
        designer: White [B]

279. Erie County Savings Bank
     competition entry
     location unspecified
        not built
        begun: February, 1890
        cost: flat fee, $ 500

*280. Estey, Julius J.
     monument
     Prospect Hill Cemetery
     Brattleboro, Vt.
        condition: extant
        begun: 1892   built: 1892
        cost: $ 4,300

281. Eyerman, John
     house
     Easton, Penna.
        condition: extant
        begun: March, 1888   built: 1888-1891
        cost: $ 20,953
              + 6,100
                27,053

F

*282. Fahnestock, Gibson   (for Harris Charles Fahnestock)
        townhouse
        30 W. 51st Street
        New York, N.Y.
            condition: extant
            begun: October, 1886   built: 1886-1889
            cost: unrecorded
            extant drawings: New-York Historical Society

283. Fahnestock, Harris Charles
        house
        Ocean Avenue
        Elberon, N.J.
            condition: demolished
            begun: December, 1879   built: 1880
            cost: $ 10,173

*284. Fahnestock, Harris Charles
        townhouse   (part of the Villard house group)
        457 Madison Avenue
        New York, N.Y.
            condition: extant
            begun: December, 1885   built: 1886-1888
            cost: $ 57,149
                 + 42,953
                  ‾‾‾‾‾‾‾
                  100,102
            extant drawings: New-York Historical Society

285. Fahnestock, Harris Charles
        townhouse   (part of the Villard house group)
        22 E. 51st Street
        New York, N.Y.
            condition: extant
            begun: 1886   built: 1887-1888
            cost: $ 45,576

286. Fahnestock, Harris Charles
        townhouse   (part of the Villard house group)
        24 E. 51st Street
        New York, N.Y.
            condition: extant
            begun: 1886   built: 1887-1888
            cost: $ 40,121

287. Fahnestock, Harris Charles
        townhouse
        47 W. 52nd Street
        New York, N.Y.
            condition: demolished
            begun: October, 1899   built: 1899-1900
            cost: $ 39,456

*288.   Fanwood School   (for Augustus D. Shepard)
          Park Avenue
          Scotch Plains, N.J.
             condition: extant
             begun: November, 1889   built: 1889-1890
             cost: $ 14,642

*289.   Fayette National Bank
          bank with offices above
          Lexington, Ky.
             begun: July, 1912   built: 1913-1914
             designer: Kendall (?)
             cost: $ 377,846

 290.   Federal Reserve Bank of New York
          competition entry
          Liberty and Nassau Streets
          New York, N.Y.
             not built
             begun: 1919
             cost: flat fee, $ 2,500

        Field, Dudley, Memorial Window
          see St. Paul's Church, No. 751

*291.   First Methodist Episcopal Church
          (now Lovely Lane United Methodist Church)
          church and Parish House
          St. Paul and 22nd Streets
          Baltimore, Md.
             condition: extant
             begun: August, 1883   built: 1884-1887
             designer: White [B]; Charles L. Carson, assoc. arch.
             cost: approx. $ 250,000
             contractor: Benjamin F. Bennett
             extant drawings: New-York Historical Society

*292.   First Presbyterian Church
          Parish House
          Fifth Avenue and 12th Street
          New York, N.Y.
             condition: remodeled
             begun: March, 1893   built: 1893-1894
             designer: Mead (?)
             cost: $ 54,951

*293.   First Presbyterian Church
          Douglas Street and McGallie Avenue
          Chattanooga, Tenn.
             begun: April, 1909   built: 1909-1911
             designer: Kendall [K], Bearden & Foreman, assoc. arch.
             cost: $ 99,081
             contractor: J. T. Wilson
             extant drawings: New-York Historical Society

294. First Unitarian Church
          church, project
          Cambridge, Mass.
          not built
          begun: April, 1900
          designer: McKim

295. Fish, Mrs. Clemence S. B.
          alterations to existing house
          53 Irving Place
          New York, N.Y.
          begun: June, 1887   built: 1887-1888
          designer: associated with Sidney V. Stratton
          cost: $ 34,135
                + 6,510
                  40,645

*296. Fish, Hamilton
          monument
          St. Phillips-in-the-Highlands Cemetery
          Garrison-on-Hudson, N.Y.
          condition: extant
          begun: 1892
          designer: White and Augustus Saint-Gaudens
          cost: unrecorded

*297. Fish, Stuyvesant
          townhouse
          25 E. 78th Street
          New York, N.Y.
          condition: extant
          begun: September, 1897   built: 1897-1900
          designer: White [LGW, B, K]
          cost: $ 90,030
                + 22,160
                 112,190

298. FitzGerald, W. J.
          monument
          Litchfield, Conn.
          condition: extant
          begun: May, 1885   built: 1885
          cost: $ 50

299. Flagler, John H.
          monument
          Mt. Auburn Cemetery
          Cambridge, Mass.
          condition: extant
          begun: January, 1888   built: 1888
          cost: $ 250

300. Fort Green Park Shelter
     Fort Green Park
     Brooklyn, N.Y.
         condition: extant
         begun: September, 1905   built: 1905-1906
         cost: $ 30,100
         contractor: P. J. Carlin

301. Francklyn, Charles G.
     alterations to existing townhouse
     15 Washington Square
     New York, N.Y.
         condition: demolished
         begun: March, 1881   built: 1881-1882
         cost: $ 3,942

*302. Franklin National Bank
      Chestnut Street
      Philadelphia, Penna.
          condition: demolished
          begun: August, 1915   built: 1915-1917
          designer: Richardson
          cost: $ 768,442
          extant drawings: New-York Historical Society

303. Freeman, Mrs. Alden
     monument
     Newark, N.J.
         condition: extant
         begun: December, 1915   built: 1915
         cost: $ 2,017

304. Freer, Charles Lang
     house, project
     Detroit, Mich.
         not built
         begun: January, 1900
         designer: White

*305. Frelinghuysen, Peter Hood Ballantine
      house and garage
      Normandie Heights
      Morristown, N.J.
          condition: extant
          begun: October, 1909   built: 1910-1913
          designer: Richardson [K]
          cost: $ 108,461 house
                  10,585 garage
                 119,046
          contractor: J. V. Schafer
          extant drawings: New-York Historical Society

60

*306. Freundschaft Society
       club
       Park Avenue and 72nd Street
       New York, N.Y.
          condition: demolished
          begun: November, 1885   built: 1887-1889
          designer: White [B, K]
          cost: $ 295,337

307.   Freundschaft Society
       alterations to club
       New York, N.Y.
          condition: demolished
          begun: July, 1893   built: 1893-1894
          cost: $ 32,717

G

*308. Garden City Hotel
       Park Avenue and 7th Street
       Garden City, N.Y.
          condition: demolished
          begun: February, 1894   built: 1895-1896
          designer: White [LGW, B, K]
          cost: $ 182,473

*309. Garden City Hotel
       reconstruction of burned sections; extensions; tower
       Garden City, N.Y.
          condition: demolished
          begun: September, 1899   built: 1900-1901
          designer: White
          cost: $ 231,405

310.   Garden City houses
       plans for "seven types of detached houses"
          begun: December, 1906   built: ?
          cost: flat fee, $ 1,214

311.   Garfield Memorial
       base for bronze figure by Augustus Saint-Gaudens
       Fairmount Park
       Philadelphia, Penna.
          condition: extant
          begun: 1894   built: 1895
          designer: White [LGW, B]
          extant drawings: New-York Historical Society

312.   Garfield Safe Deposit Company
       alterations to banking facilities
       71 W. 23rd Street
       New York, N.Y.
          condition: demolished
          begun: June, 1888   built: 1888
          cost: $ 22,382

313.   Garland, James A.
       house
       Ocean Avenue
       Elberon, N.J.
          condition: demolished
          begun: March, 1880   built: 1880
          cost: $ 9,544

*314. Garrett, John Work (Mary E.)
       renovation of townhouse
       77 W. Monument Street
       Baltimore, Md.
          condition: extant
          begun: June, 1882   built: 1884-1886
          designer: White
          cost: $ 100,524
               +   49,832
                  150,356

315.   Garrett, Robert
       townhouse
       11 W. Mount Vernon Place
       Baltimore, Md.
          condition: demolished
          begun: July, 1883   built: 1884-1887
          cost: $ 226,992
               + 110,889
                 337,881

316.   Garrett, Robert
       alterations to townhouse
       11 W. Mount Vernon Place
       Baltimore, Md.
          condition: demolished
          begun: July, 1892   built: 1892-1893
          cost: $ 27,900

*317. Germantown Cricket Club
       Manheim and Morris Streets
       Philadelphia (Germantown), Penna.
          condition: extant
          begun: September, 1889   built: 1890-1891
          designer: McKim [K]
          cost: $ 78,500

*318. Gibson, Charles Dana
          townhouse
          127 E. 73rd Street
          New York, N.Y.
              condition: extant
              begun: January, 1902   built: 1902-1903
              designer: White [LGW, B, K]
              cost: $ 44,726
                   + 5,008
                     ‾‾‾‾‾‾
                     49,734
              contractor: J. C. Vreeland

 319. Gilder, Richard Watson
          renovation of stable for townhouse; new facade
          103 E. 15th Street
          New York, N.Y.
              built: c. 1882
              designer: White
              cost: unrecorded

 320. Gilder, Richard Watson
          renovation of building for summer house
          Marion, Mass.
              built: c. 1885
              designer: White
              cost: unrecorded

*321. Girard Trust Company
          bank
          Broad and Chestnut Streets
          Philadelphia, Penna.
              condition: extant
              begun: March, 1905 (work started in Philadelphia in
                     June, 1904)
              built: 1905-1909
              designers: McKim and Richardson [K] with Allen Evans
                         of Furness, Evans and Company
              cost: $ 1,428,101
              extant drawings: New-York Historical Society

 322. Glover, John H.
          house
          Newport, R.I.
              begun: January, 1886   built: 1886 (?)
              cost: flat fee, $ 500, unsupervised

*323.   Goelet, Robert
         house, "Southside"
         Narragansett and Ochre Point Avenues
         Newport, R.I.
            condition: extant
            begun: February, 1882   built: 1883-1884
            designer: White [LGW, B]
            cost: $ 66,251
                  + 17,237
                     83,488

 324.   Goelet, Robert and Ogden
         commercial building
         402 Fifth Avenue and 2 W. 37th Street
         New York, N.Y.
            condition: demolished
            begun: July, 1889   built: 1890
            cost: $ 78,000

 325.   Goelet, Robert and Ogden
         additions and alterations to commercial building
         402 Fifth Avenue and 2 W. 37th Street
         New York, N.Y.
            condition: demolished
            begun: June, 1891   built: 1891-1892
            cost: $ 104,898

 326.   Goelet, Robert and Ogden
         commercial building
         Eighth Avenue and 135th Street
         New York, N.Y.
            begun: 1896   built: 1897
            cost: $ 45,280

*327.   Goelet, Robert and Ogden
         "Goelet Building" (office building)
         Broadway and 20th Street
         New York, N.Y.
            condition: extant
            begun: April, 1886   built: 1886-1887
            cost: $ 258,294

*328.   Goelet, Robert and Ogden
         Goelet offices
         9 W. 17th Street
         New York, N.Y.
            condition: demolished
            begun: June, 1885   built: 1886
            designer: White (?)
            cost: $ 55,319

*329. Goelet, Robert and Ogden
        "The Judge Building" (office building)
        Fifth Avenue and 16th Street
        New York, N.Y.
            condition: extant, remodeled and enlarged
            begun: June, 1888   built: 1888-1889
            cost: c. $ 500,000, unsupervised

*330. Goelet, Robert and Ogden
        mausoleum
        Woodlawn Cemetery
        New York, N.Y.
            condition: extant
            begun: August, 1899   built: 1899
            cost: $ 52,000
            extant drawings: New-York Historical Society

*331. Goodwin, James Junius
        double townhouse
        15-17 W. 54th Street
        New York, N.Y.
            condition: extant
            begun: August (?), 1896   built: 1896-1898
            designer: McKim and Mead [K]
            cost: $ 118,759
                 +   34,011
                    152,770

*332. Gorham Company
        386 Fifth Avenue
        New York, N.Y.
            condition: extant
            begun: May, 1903   built: 1904-1906
            designer: White [LGW, B, K]
            cost: $ 933,147
            extant drawings: New-York Historical Society

 333. Gorham Company
        addition, 384 Fifth Avenue
        New York, N.Y.
            condition: extant
            begun: May, 1905   built: 1905-1906
            cost: $ 99,832
            extant drawings: New-York Historical Society

 334. Gorham Company
        addition, 386 Fifth Avenue
        New York, N.Y.
            condition: extant
            begun: 1915   built: 1915
            cost: $ 16,232

*335. Goucher, The Reverend John Franklin
       house
       2313 St. Paul Street
       Baltimore, Md.
          condition: extant
          begun: January, 1890   built: 1890-1892
          cost: unrecorded, unsupervised

 336. Goucher College (Women's College of Baltimore)
       Conservatory of Music, project (for Rev. J. F. Goucher)
       St. Paul and 24th Streets
       Baltimore, Md.
          not built (?)
          begun: April, 1890
          designer: White

 337. Goucher College
       Fine Arts Building, project (for Rev. J. F. Goucher)
       St. Paul and 24th Streets
       Baltimore, Md.
          not built (?)
          begun: April, 1894
          designer: White

*338. Goucher College
       Girls' Latin School (for Rev. J. F. Goucher)
       St. Paul and 23rd Streets
       Baltimore, Md.
          condition: extant
          begun: January, 1891   built: 1891
          designer: White
          cost: unrecorded, unsupervised

*339. Goucher College
       Gymnasium, "Physical Culture Building" (for B. F. Bennett)
       St. Paul and 23rd Streets
       Baltimore, Md.
          condition: extant
          begun: November, 1887   built: 1887-1888
          designer: White
          cost: unrecorded, unsupervised, flat fee, $ 500
          contractor: Benjamin F. Bennett

 340. Governor's Island
       store house and comprehensive plan for the entire island
          and 90 acres of land under reclamation, project
       New York Harbor
       New York, N.Y.
          not built (at this time)
          begun: April, 1902
          designer and planner: McKim

66

341. Gracie, James K.
     house
     Oyster Bay, N.Y.
       begun: March, 1884   built: 1884
       designer: in collaboration with Sidney V. Stratton
       cost: $ 14,666

342. Guggenheim, Simon R.
     alterations to existing house
     743 Fifth Avenue
     New York, N.Y.
       condition: demolished
       begun: March, 1900   built: 1900
       cost: $ 1,352

343. Guggenheim, Simon R.
     townhouse, project
     Fifth Avenue and 75th Street
     New York, N.Y.
       not built
       begun: February, 1902

344. Guinand, H.
     hotel project
     Baltimore, Md.
       not built
       begun: April, 1886

*345. Guthrie, William Dameron
     townhouse
     28 Park Avenue
     New York, N.Y.
       condition: demolished
       begun: November, 1895   built: 1896-1897
       cost: $ 63,472
            + 20,401
            ‾‾‾‾‾‾‾‾
              83,873

H

*346. Hagin, Louis L.
     house, project
     Lexington, Ky.
       not built (?)
       begun: 1917
       cost: flat fee, $ 3,100

*347. *Hale, Nathan*
        base for bronze figure by Frederick MacMonnies
        City Hall Park
        New York, N.Y.
            condition: extant
            begun: 1889   built: 1889
            designer: White [LGW, B], with MacMonnies
            extant drawings: New-York Historical Society

 348. *Hale, Nathan*
        duplicate of original in City Hall Park
        Huntington, N.Y.
            built: 1894

 349. Halstead, Bryan D., Memorial (for Mrs. Rudolph Riege)
        Rutgers College
        New Brunswick, N.J.
            condition: extant
            begun: 1919   built: 1919
            cost: $ 280

 350. Hamilton, George
        alterations to existing townhouse
        27 W. 49th Street
        New York, N.Y.
            condition: demolished
            begun: July, 1882   built: 1882-1883
            cost: $ 5,823
                  + 6,318
                   12,141

*351. Hanna, Howard Melville
        house
        11505 Lake Shore Boulevard
        Bratenahl (Cleveland), Ohio
            condition: extant
            begun: October, 1908   built: 1909-1912
            designer: Richardson
            cost: $ 203,620
            contractor: Norcross Brothers
            extant drawings: New-York Historical Society

*352. Hanna, Leonard Colton
        house
        2717 Euclid Avenue
        Cleveland, Ohio
            condition: demolished
            begun: January, 1902   built: 1902-1905
            designer: White [B, K]
            cost: $ 145,977
                  + 37,445
                   183,422
            extant drawings: New-York Historical Society

353. Harkness, Mrs. S. V.
     monument
     Cleveland, Ohio
     begun: c. 1891   built: 1907
     cost: $ 1,375

*354. Harmonie Club
      4-8 E. 60th Street
      New York, N.Y.
         condition: extant
         begun: January, 1904   built: 1904-1907
         designer: White [LGW, B, K]
         cost: $ 463,717
         contractor: Tidewater Construction Company
         extant drawings: New-York Historical Society

355. Harper, James Thomas
     alterations to existing townhouse
     4 Gramercy Square
     New York, N.Y.
        begun: December, 1879   built: 1879
        designer: White
        cost: flat fee, $ 350

*356. Harrison, O. F.
      apartment building
      "The Percival"
      228-232 W. 42nd Street
      New York, N.Y.
         condition: demolished
         begun: March, 1882   built: 1882-1883
         cost: c. $ 55,000, unsupervised

*357. Harvard Club of New York
      27-29 W. 44th Street
      New York, N.Y.
         condition: extant
         begun: June, 1893   built: 1893-1894
         designer: McKim
         cost: unrecorded
         extant drawings: New-York Historical Society

*358. Harvard Club of New York
      addition to the rear, through to 45th Street
      New York, N.Y.
         condition: extant
         begun: December, 1900   built: 1902-1905
         designer: McKim [K]
         cost: $ 362,524
         extant drawings: New-York Historical Society

*359. Harvard Club of New York
      additions to the west side and behind, through to 45th Street
      New York, N.Y.
           condition: extant
           begun: May, 1913   built: 1913-1916
           designer: Kendall
           cost: $ 496,984
           extant drawings: New-York Historical Society

[Note: The numerous Harvard University commissions are listed buildings first, followed by named memorials, followed by class memorial
gates.]

*360. Harvard University
      Robinson Hall, School of Architecture
      Cambridge, Mass.
           condition: extant
           begun: July, 1899   built: 1900-1902
           designer: McKim [K]
           cost: $ 128,129
                 +   4,394
                   ‾‾‾‾‾‾‾
                    132,523
           contractor: L. D. Willcutt & Son

*361. Harvard University
      Stadium
      N. Harvard Street
      Allston, Mass.
           condition: extant
           begun: c. 1899   built: 1903 et seq.
           designer: McKim [K] for external shell and colonnade
           cost: unrecorded
           extant drawings: New-York Historical Society

*362. Harvard University
      Union (for Henry Lee Higginson)
      Cambridge, Mass.
           condition: extant
           begun: September, 1899   built: 1900-1901
           designer: McKim [K]
           cost: $ 196,921
                 +   42,050
                   ‾‾‾‾‾‾‾
                    238,971
           contractor: Norcross Brothers
           extant drawings: New-York Historical Society

*363. Harvard University
      Bradley, Robert S., Memorial
      Cambridge, Mass.
           condition: extant
           built: 1910
           designer: Kendall (?)
           cost: $ 4,026
           extant drawings: New-York Historical Society

364. Harvard University
         Lowell, James Russell, Memorial
         Cambridge, Mass.
            condition: extant
            built: 1907
            designer: Kendall (?)
            cost: $ 3,580

[Note: The numerous memorial gates for Harvard University follow,
first the named gates and then those donated by classes by the
year of the class.]

*365. Harvard University
         Johnston, Samuel, Memorial Gate
         Cambridge, Mass.
            condition: extant
            begun: 1889   built: 1889-1890
            designer: McKim [K]
            cost: $ 9,972
            extant drawings: New-York Historical Society

*366. Harvard University
         Meyer Gate (Class of 1879)
         Cambridge, Mass.
            condition: extant
            begun: 1890   built: 1890-1891
            designer: McKim
            cost: unrecorded
            extant drawings: New-York Historical Society

*367. Harvard University
         Porcellian (McKean) Gate
         Cambridge, Mass.
            condition: extant
            begun: c. 1890-1891   built: 1900-1901
            designer: McKim
            cost: $ 6,726
            extant drawings: New-York Historical Society

*368. Harvard University
         Class of 1857, Memorial Gate
         Cambridge, Mass.
            condition: extant
            begun: 1901   built: 1902
            designer: McKim
            cost: $ 5,524
            extant drawings: New-York Historical Society

*369. Harvard University
   Class of 1870, Memorial Gate
   Cambridge, Mass.
    condition: extant
    begun: 1899 built: 1900-1901
    designer: McKim
    cost: $ 3,905
    extant drawings: New-York Historical Society

*370. Harvard University
   Class of 1873, Memorial Gate
   Cambridge, Mass.
    condition: extant
    begun: 1899 built: 1900-1901
    designer: McKim
    cost: $ 4,030
    extant drawings: New-York Historical Society

 371. Harvard University
   Class of 1874, Memorial Gate
   Cambridge, Mass.
    condition: extant
    begun: 1899 built: 1900-1901
    designer: McKim
    cost: $ 2,780
    extant drawings: New-York Historical Society

*372. Harvard University
   Class of 1875, Memorial Gate
   Cambridge, Mass.
    condition: extant
    begun: 1899 built: 1900-1901
    designer: McKim
    cost: $ 4,162
    extant drawings: New-York Historical Society

*373. Harvard University
   Class of 1876, Memorial Gate
   Cambridge, Mass.
    condition: extant
    begun: 1899 built: 1900-1901
    designer: McKim
    cost: $ 5,108
    extant drawings: New-York Historical Society

*374. Harvard University
   Class of 1877, Memorial Gate
   Cambridge, Mass.
    condition: extant
    begun: 1899 built: 1900-1901
    designer: McKim
    cost: $ 12,916
    extant drawings: New-York Historical Society

*375. Harvard University
        Class of 1880, Memorial Gate
        Cambridge, Mass.
            condition: extant
            begun: 1901   built: 1902
            designer: McKim (?)
            cost: $ 16,173
            extant drawings: New-York Historical Society

*376. Harvard University
        Class of 1885, Memorial Gate
        Cambridge, Mass.
            condition: extant
            begun: 1901   built: 1903-1904
            designer: McKim (?)
            cost: $ 7,501
            extant drawings: New-York Historical Society

*377. Harvard University
        Class of 1886, Memorial Gate
        Cambridge, Mass.
            condition: extant
            begun: 1899   built: 1900-1901
            designer: McKim
            cost: $ 3,035
            extant drawings: New-York Historical Society

*378. Harvard University
        Classes of 1887-1888, Memorial Gate
        Cambridge, Mass.
            condition: extant
            begun: 1905   built: 1905-1906
            designer: McKim (?) with Kendall (?)
            cost: $ 13,049
            extant drawings: New-York Historical Society

*379. Harvard University
        Class of 1889, Memorial Gate
        Cambridge, Mass.
            condition: extant
            begun: 1899   built: 1900-1901
            designer: McKim
            cost: $ 4,613
            extant drawings: New-York Historical Society

*380. Harvard University
        Class of 1890, Memorial Gate
        Cambridge, Mass.
            condition: extant
            begun: 1899   built: 1900-1901
            designer: McKim
            cost: $ 4,194
            extant drawings: New-York Historical Society

381. Haskell, Llewellyn, Memorial
     Llewellyn Park
     Orange, N.J.
          condition: extant
          built: 1880
          designer: White [B]
          cost: unrecorded

     Havana Tobacco Company Store
     see American Tobacco Company, No. 65

382. Havemeyer, James
     townhouse, project
     50 W. 37th Street
     New York, N.Y.
          not built
          begun: November (?), 1885
          cost: flat fee, $ 75

383. Havemeyer, Theodore
     house, project
     Newport, R.I.
          not built (?)
          begun: October (?), 1881
          cost: c. $ 35,000

384. Havemeyer Sugar Company
     offices, project
     Greenpoint, N.Y.
          not built
          begun: October (?), 1885
          cost: flat fee, $ 250

385. Hayden Furniture Company
     alterations to showrooms
     1 E. 34th Street
     New York, N.Y.
          condition: demolished
          begun: December, 1891   built: 1892
          cost: $ 18,670

386. Haydock, Mrs. Hannah W.
     house
     Morristown, N.J.
          condition: demolished
          begun: December, 1890   built: 1891-1892
          cost: $ 15,233

387. Hazard, Rowland Gibson
     house, project
     Peace Dale, R.I.
          not built (?)
          begun: November, 1886
          cost: flat fee, $ 200

74

388. Hazard, Roland Gibson
      additions and alterations to existing house, "The Acorns"
      Peace Dale, R.I.
         begun: October, 1891   built: 1892-1893
         designer: McKim
         cost: $ 50,947

389. Hearst School for Girls
      competition entry
      Washington, D.C.
         not built
         begun: January, 1897
         cost: c. $ 182,028

390. Hecker, Frank J.
      mausoleum
      Woodward Lawn Cemetery
      Detroit, Mich.
         condition: extant
         begun: February, 1897   built: 1897?
         designer: White

391. Henderson, Charles R.
      house, alterations
      Southampton, N.Y.
         begun: October, 1886   built: 1887
         cost: $ 6,856
         contractor: Mead & Taft

392. Henderson Estate Company
      house
      Livingston Avenue
      Staten Island, N.Y.
         begun: June, 1891   built: 1892
         cost: $ 8,098

393. Henderson Estate Company
      two houses, "no's 18 & 19"
      Livingston Avenue
      Staten Island, N.Y.
         begun: December, 1892   built: 1893
         cost: $ 5,150 each; total, $ 10,300

*394. Henry, Charles Wolcott
      house
      Tulpehocken Street and Wayne Avenue
      Wissahickon Heights
      Philadelphia (Germantown), Penna.
         condition: demolished
         begun: May, 1887   built: 1887-1889
         designer: McKim (?)
         cost: $ 35,837
              +   8,993
                 44,830

75

Herald Building
see *New York Herald*, No. 572

395. Hewitt, Abram Stevens
      alterations to existing townhouse
      9 Lexington Avenue
      New York, N.Y.
          condition: demolished
          begun: February, 1885   built: 1886-1888
          cost: $ 47,979
                + 19,633
                  67,612

396. Higginson, James J.
      alterations to existing townhouse
      16 E. 41st Street
      New York, N.Y.
          condition: demolished
          begun: October, 1879   built: 1879
          designer: White
          cost: c. $ 6,500

397. Higginson, James J.
      further alterations to existing townhouse
      16 E. 41st Street
      New York, N.Y.
          condition: demolished
          begun: December, 1890   built: 1890
          cost: $ 7,449
                + 3,900
                  11,349

398. Hitchcock, Dr. Charles
      alterations to existing townhouse
      61 W. 36th Street
      New York, N.Y.
          condition: demolished
          begun: 1883   built: 1883
          designer: McKim
          cost: flat fee, $ 250

*399. Hollins, Henry B.
       townhouse
       12 W. 56th Street
       New York, N.Y.
           condition: extant
           begun: September, 1899   built: 1899-1901
           designer: White [B]
           cost: $ 129,587
                   29,505
                  159,092
           contractor: Michael Reid

400. Hollins, Henry B.
     alterations to townhouse
     12 W. 56th Street
     New York, N.Y.
        condition: extant
        begun: June, 1903   built: 1903
        cost: $ 8,183

401. Holmes, Artemas H.
     interiors of townhouse   (part of the Villard house group)
     453 Madison Avenue
     New York, N.Y.
        condition: partially extant
        begun: November, 1884   built: 1884
        cost: $ 12,039

402. Holt, Henry
     house
     Premium Point
     New Rochelle (Larchmont), N.Y.
        condition: demolished
        begun: February, 1883   built: 1883-1885
        designer: McKim [B]
        cost: c. $ 10,000

403. Homans, Edward C.
     unspecified work
     Gould's Island, N.Y.
        begun: August (?), 1881
        cost: c. $ 8,000

404. Home Life Insurance Company
     unspecified work
     no location given in New York, N.Y.
        begun: April, 1886
        cost: flat fee, $ 50, "on sketches furnished"

*405. Home Life Insurance Company
     competition entry
     237 Broadway
     New York, N.Y.
        not built
        begun: March, 1892
        cost: flat fee, $ 250

*406. Honore, A. C.
     mausoleum
     Graceland Cemetery
     Chicago, Ill.
        condition: extant
        begun: January, 1905   built: 1905
        cost: $ 18,100
        contractor: C. G. Blake

*407. Hooker, Mrs. Blanche Ferry
    alterations and additions to existing house
    Greenwich, Conn.
        begun: May, 1907   built: 1907-1908
        designer: Fenner [K]
        cost: $ 23,292
        contractor: G. Mertz
        extant drawings: New-York Historical Society

408. Hooker, Mrs. Blanche Ferry
    additions (lodge and garage)
    Greenwich, Conn.
        begun: December, 1909   built: 1909-1911
        designer: Fenner [K]
        cost: $ 38,857

409. Hooker, Mrs. Blanche Ferry
    further additions and alterations
    Greenwich, Conn.
        begun: January, 1911   built: 1911-1912
        designer: Fenner (?)
        cost: $ 90,056

*410. Hopkins, Mrs. Mark
    house
    Great Barrington, Mass.
        begun: May, 1885   built: 1885-1886
        designer: White (?); McKim [K]
        cost: c. $ 200,000
        contractor: Norcross Brothers

*411. Hotel Imperial   (for Robert and Ogden Goelet)
    Broadway and 32nd Street
    New York, N.Y.
        condition: demolished
        begun: March, 1889   built: 1889-1891
        designer: White [B, K]
        cost: $ 800,644
            murals in lobby and dining room by Thomas W. Dewing
            and Edwin Austin Abbey

*412. Hotel Imperial
    extension, 32nd Street
    New York, N.Y.
        condition: demolished
        begun: May, 1891   built: 1891-1894
        designer: White [B, K]
        cost: $ 265,970

413. Hotel Imperial
         second extension, 31st Street
         New York, N.Y.
            condition: demolished
            begun: June, 1895   built: 1895-1896
            designer: White
            cost: $ 106,784

*414. Hotel Pennsylvania
         (for the Pennsylvania Terminal Real Estate Company)
         Seventh Avenue and 32nd Street
         New York, N.Y.
            condition: extant
            begun: October, 1915   built: 1916-1920
            cost: $ 12,116,099
            extant drawings: New-York Historical Society

415. Hotel Windsor
         alterations to hotel
         Saratoga, N.Y.
            begun: March, 1880   built: 1880
            designer: White
            cost: $ 24,000

*416. Howe, Dr. Robert T.
         house
         Mount Vernon, N.Y.
            condition: extant
            begun: December, 1886   built: 1886-1887
            cost: $ 5,887

*417. Hoyt, Alfred M.
         house
         deForest Road
         Montauk Point, N.Y.
            condition: extant
            begun: March, 1882   built: 1882-1883
            cost: $ 14,083

*418. Hoyt, Alfred M.
         townhouse
         934 Fifth Avenue
         New York, N.Y.
            condition: demolished
            begun: April, 1883   built: 1884-1885
            cost: $ 127,643
                 + 18,968
                   146,611

419. Hoyt, Alfred M.
    alterations to townhouse
    934 Fifth Avenue
    New York, N.Y.
        condition: demolished
        begun: April, 1891   built: 1891
        cost: $ 3,269

420. Hoyt, Henry R.
    stable
    109 E. 76th Street
    New York, N.Y.
        condition: demolished
        begun: July, 1893   built: 1893
        cost: $ 21,747

*421. Hunt Memorial Building
    student union
    Hartford Medical College
    Hartford, Conn.
        begun: March, 1897   built: 1897-1898
        cost: $ 19,337
        extant drawings: New-York Historical Society

422. Husted, Miss M. E.
    house
    Broadalbin, N.Y.
        begun: July, 1889   built: 1889 (?)
        cost: c. $ 16,000

I

*423. Illinois, University of
    Women's Building
    Wright Street
    Champaign-Urbana, Ill.
        condition: extant, remodeled
        begun: November, 1903   built: 1904-1905
        designer: McKim and Fenner [K]
        cost: $ 70,738

*424. Interborough Rapid Transit Company   (IRT)
    powerhouse
    Eleventh Avenue and 59th Street
    New York, N.Y.
        condition: extant
        begun: November, 1901   built: 1903-1904
        designer: White [LGW, B, K]
        cost: flat fee, $ 3,500; unsupervised

425. Iselin, Mrs. Adrian
     monument
     Fairfield, Conn.
        condition: extant
        begun: September, 1915   built: 1915
        cost: $ 762
        extant drawings: New-York Historical Society

426. Iselin, Charles Oliver
     house
     Hunter's Island
     New York, N.Y.
        begun: October, 1882   built: 1882-1883
        designer: in collaboration with Sidney V. Stratton
        cost: $ 6,522

427. Ives, Brayton
     house
     Lowmoor
     Seabright, N.J.
        begun: November, 1886   built: 1887
        cost: $ 10,973

428. Ives, Brayton
     stable addition
     Lowmoor
     Seabright, N.J.
        begun: June, 1888   built: 1888
        cost: $ 3,322
        contractor: A. P. Cubberly

J

429. Jackson, Dr. F. W.
     townhouse
     68 W. 55th Street
     New York, N.Y.
        condition: demolished
        begun: November, 1904   built: 1904
        cost: $ 12,000

430. Johnston, John Taylor
     gate lodge
     Plainfield, N.J.
        begun: 1885   built: 1885-1887
        cost: $ 4,052

431. Jones, Dwight Arven
    house
    Englewood, N.J.
        begun: October, 1886   built: 1886-1887
        cost: $ 12,620

432. Jones, J. H.
    library addition to existing house
    Bartow-on-the-Sound, N.Y.
        begun: November, 1880   built: 1880-1881
        cost: c. $ 4,000

433. Jones, Mrs. Mary
    alterations to existing townhouse
    743 Fifth Avenue
    New York, N.Y.
        condition: demolished
        begun: August, 1899   built: 1899-1900
        cost: $ 28,611

    "The Judge Building"
    see Robert and Ogden Goelet, No. 329

*434. Judson Memorial Church (Berean Baptist Church)
    Washington Square South and Thompson Street
    New York, N.Y.
        condition: extant
        begun: December, 1888   built: 1890-1893
        designer: White [LGW, B, K]
        cost: $ 240,578
        extant drawings: New-York Historical Society
            windows by John La Farge
            baptistry by Herbert Adams (from a design by
                Augustus Saint-Gaudens)

*435. Judson Memorial Church
    Judson Hall and Tower
    54 Washington Square South
    New York, N.Y.
        condition: extant
        begun: August, 1895   built: 1895-1896.
        designer: White [B]
        cost: $ 41,200
        extant drawings: New-York Historical Society

K

*436. Kane, John Innes
   townhouse
   610 Fifth Avenue
   New York, N.Y.
      condition: demolished
      begun: March, 1904   built: 1904-1908
      designer: McKim and Richardson [K]
      cost: $ 511,472
      contractor: Michael Reid
      extant drawings: New-York Historical Society

437. Kane, John Innes
   mausoleum
   Greenwood Cemetery
   Brooklyn, N.Y.
      condition: extant
      begun: September, 1914   built: 1914
      cost: $ 4,842
      extant drawings: New-York Historical Society

438. Kansas City Casino
   Kansas City, Mo.
      begun: October, 1887   built: 1887-1888
      cost: unsupervised

439. Keene brothers
   "houses and shops"
   Lynn, Mass. (?)
      begun: January, 1886   built: 1886 (?)
      cost: fees, $400

440. Kelly, Eugene, jr.
   alterations to existing townhouse
   19 Washington Square North
   New York, N.Y.
      condition: extant
      begun: August, 1886   built: 1886
      cost: $ 21,995
            + 4,798
            ─────────
              26,793

*441. Kimball, William W.
   monument
   Graceland Cemetery
   Chicago, Ill.
      condition: extant
      begun: April, 1907   built: 1907-1908
      cost: $ 33,444
      contractor: C. G. Blake
      extant drawings: New-York Historical Society

*442.　King, David H., jr.
　　　addition, dining room, to "Kingscote"
　　　Bellevue Avenue and Bowery Street
　　　Newport, R.I.
　　　　condition: extant
　　　　begun: January, 1880　　built: 1881
　　　　designer: White
　　　　cost: $ 9,018
　　　　　　 + 3,409
　　　　　　　 12,427

443.　King, David H., jr.
　　　house, project
　　　Washington, D.C.
　　　　not built
　　　　begun: March, 1882
　　　　cost: c. $ 15,000

444.　King, David H., jr.
　　　house, first phase
　　　Premium Point
　　　New Rochelle (Larchmont), N.Y.
　　　　begun: April, 1883　　built: 1883
　　　　cost: $ 7,700

445.　King, David H., jr.
　　　house, second phase
　　　Premium Point
　　　New Rochelle, N.Y.
　　　　begun: September, 1887　　built: 1887-1888 (?)
　　　　cost: c. $ 20,000, unsupervised

446.　King, David H., jr.
　　　house, additions to "Kingscote" (?)
　　　Newport, R.I.
　　　　begun: February, 1897　　built: 1897 (?)
　　　　cost: $ 30,530

*447.　King, David H., jr.
　　　townhouse complex (5 units)
　　　West End Avenue and 83rd Street
　　　New York, N.Y.
　　　　condition: demolished
　　　　begun: December, 1885　　built: 1886 (?)
　　　　cost: est. $ 75,000, unsupervised
　　　　contractor: David H. King, jr.

*448. King, David H., jr.
       "King Model Houses" ("Striver's Row")
       Seventh to Eighth Avenue, 139th Street, north side only
       New York, N.Y.
          condition: extant
          begun: September, 1891   built: 1891-c. 1892
          designer: White [B]
          cost: c. $ 500,000, unsupervised
          contractor: David H. King, jr.

 449. King, David H., jr.
       unspecified work
       9 W. 42nd Street
       New York, N.Y.
          condition: demolished
          begun: February, 1897   built: 1897
          cost: $ 21,850

*450. King, George Gordon
       house, "Edgehill"
       Harrison Avenue
       Newport, R.I.
          condition: extant
          begun: October, 1887   built: 1888
          cost: c. $ 25,000

*451. King, George Gordon
       additions to house, "Edgehill"
       Newport, R.I.
          condition: extant
          begun: August, 1902   built: 1902-1904
          cost: $ 48,594
                + 3,066
                  51,660

*452. King, George Gordon
       further additions to house, "Edgehill"
       Newport, R.I.
          condition: extant
          begun: 1906 built: 1907
          cost: $ 12,057

 453. King, George Gordon
       alterations to existing townhouse
       16 E. 84th Street
       New York, N.Y.
          condition: partially extant
          begun: 1903   built: 1903-1904
          cost: $ 1,607

*454. King, LeRoy
       house
       Newport, R.I.
          condition: extant
          begun: April, 1884   built: 1884-1886
          cost: c. $ 20,000

455. King, Mrs. Edward (Mary)
     townhouse
     431 Fifth Avenue
     New York, N.Y.
         condition: demolished
         begun: May, 1882   built: 1882-1883
         cost: $ 44,199

456. King, Mrs. Edward (Mary)
     townhouse
     724 Fifth Avenue
     New York, N.Y.
         condition: demolished
         begun: February, 1883   built: 1883-1884
         cost: $ 62,495
             + 12,291
               74,786

*457. King's Mountain Battlefield Memorial
      planning
      York County, N.C.
          begun: 1910   built: 1910
          cost: $ 23,940
          extant drawings: New-York Historical Society

*458. Kip, George G.
      Baptismal Font
      St. Peter's Church (see Nos. 752, 753)
      Morristown, N.J.
          condition: extant
          begun: May, 1893   built: 1893
          designer: White (?)
          cost: $ 3,842

459. Knickerbocker Club
     alterations to existing club
     Fifth Avenue and 32nd Street
     New York, N.Y.
         condition: extant
         begun: September, 1891   built: 1891
         cost: $ 8,065

*460. Knickerbocker Trust and Knickerbocker Safe Deposit Company
      358 Fifth Avenue
      New York, N.Y.
          condition: demolished
          begun: March, 1901   built: 1902-1904
          designer: White [LGW, B, K]
          cost: $ 618,256 (bank)
              +   42,269 (safe deposit vaults)
                 660,525
          contractor: Charles T. Wills
          extant drawings: New-York Historical Society

Knickerbocker Trust Company
see "Downtown Building," Nos. 266, 267

L

*461. The Lambs Club
        128 W. 44th Street
        New York, N.Y.
          condition: demolished
          begun: June, 1903   built: 1904-1905
          designer: White [LGW, B, K]
          cost: $ 169,097

*462. Langdon, Woodbury
        addition, dining room wing, to
          the Governor John Langdon Mansion (1783-1784)
        Pleasant Street
        Portsmouth, N.H.
          condition: extant
          begun: August, 1905   built: 1906
          cost: $ 19,927

*463. Lathrop, Bryan
        townhouse
        120 E. Bellevue
        Chicago, Ill.
          condition: extant
          begun: April, 1891   built: 1891-1893
          designer: McKim
                    Holabird & Roche, supervisory architects
          cost: $ 39,528
                + 6,000
                  45,528
          extant drawings: New-York Historical Society
                           Burnham Library, Art Institute of
                             Chicago

464.   Lawrence, William V.
        hospital project, Lawrence Hospital
        Bronxville
        New York, N.Y.
          not built
          begun: 1917
          cost: c. $ 137,500

465.   Leland, Mrs. Francis L.
        alterations to existing townhouse
        1 W. 37th Street
        New York, N.Y.
          condition: demolished
          begun: March, 1886   built: 1886
          cost: $ 495

466. Leland, Mrs. Francis L.
     further alterations to townhouse
     1 W. 37th Street
     New York, N.Y.
        condition: demolished
        begun: August, 1888   built: 1888-1890
        cost: $ 1,104

467. Lenox Episcopal Church
     competition entry
     Lenox, Mass.
        not built, but travel to Lenox continued through mid-1885
        begun: December, 1883
        cost: flat fee, $ 500

468. Leverich, James H.
        "on plan for portable house"
        not built (?)
        begun: c. July, 1882
        cost: single bill, August, 1882, for $ 30

469. Library of Congress
        "for examining plans and drawings of J. L. Smithmeyer and
        P. Peltz for the building for the Library of Congress,
        and opinion on the same in the case of Smithmeyer and
        Peltz vs. the United States: as per letter to the Attorney
        General dated March 22, 1889, by William Rutherford Mead."
        begun: March, 1889
        cost: consultant's fee, $ 200

*470. *Lincoln* (Seated)
        base and setting for bronze figure by Augustus Saint-Gaudens
        Grant Park
        Chicago, Ill.
           condition: extant
           begun: c. 1902-1904 (figure begun, 1897)   built: 1907-192
           designer: White [LGW, B] with Saint-Gaudens
           cost: $ 41,420, base and setting only
           extant drawings: New-York Historical Society

*471. *Lincoln* (Standing)
        base and setting for bronze figure by Augustus Saint-Gaudens
        Lincoln Park
        Chicago, Ill.
           condition: extant
           begun: c. 1884-1885 (figure begun 1884)   built: 1887
           designer: White [LGW, B, K] with Saint-Gaudens
           cost: $ 30,000 total, setting and figure
           extant drawings: New-York Historical Society

472. *Logan, General John A.*
     base and setting for bronze equestrian figure
         by Augustus Saint-Gaudens
     Grant Park
     Chicago, Ill.
         condition: extant
         begun: c. 1894 (figure begun 1890)   built: 1897
         designer: White (?)
         cost: $ 50,000 total, setting and figure

473. Lorillard, Pierre, jr.
     house
     Tuxedo Park, N.Y.
         begun: March, 1887   built: 1888-1891
         designer: White [B, K]
         cost: $ 59,954
               + 15,378
                 75,332

     Lovely Lane United Methodist Church
     see First Methodist Episcopal Church, No. 291

*474. Low, William Gilman
     house
     Bristol, R.I.
         condition: demolished
         begun: November, 1886   built: 1886-1887
         cost: $ 13,432
         contractor: Taylor & Elmslie

*475. Lydig, Philip M.
     interiors, alterations in existing townhouse
     32 W. 52nd Street
     New York, N.Y.
         condition: demolished
         begun: September, 1903, through 1905
         designer: White [B, K]

476. Lyons, J. C., Building and Operating Company
     double townhouse, north half
         (see Whitney, Payne, No. 910)
     973 Fifth Avenue
     New York, N.Y.
         condition: extant
         begun: December, 1902   built: 1903-1905
         designer: White [B]
         cost: $ 133,467

M

*477. McCormick, Cyrus Hall
        house, "Clayton Lodge"
        Richfield Springs, N.Y.
            condition: demolished, stables extant
            begun: November, 1880   built: 1881-1882
            cost: $ 15,000
                  + 6,533
                    ‾‾‾‾‾‾
                    21,533

 478. MacCurdy, Dr. J. J.
        house and barn
        Pleasantville, N.Y.
            begun: June, 1916   built: 1916-1918
            cost: $ 71,705

*479. Mackay, Clarence Hungerford
        house, "Harbor Hill"
        Roslyn Road
        Roslyn, N.Y.
            condition: demolished, gate lodge extant
            begun: August, 1899   built: 1900-1902
            designer: White [LGW, B, K]
            cost: $ 525,613 house
                   174,272 interiors
                    21,955 lodge
                     1,729 lodge interiors
                    41,251 terraces
                    10,092 tower
                  + 16,770 walls, miscellaneous
                   ‾‾‾‾‾‾‾
                   791,482
            extant drawings: New-York Historical Society

 480. Mackay, Clarence Hungerford
        addition, library, to "Harbor Hill"
        Roslyn, N.Y.
            condition: demolished
            begun: November, 1906   built: 1906
            cost: $ 30,442

*481. Mackay, Clarence Hungerford
        hunting lodge
        Jamestown, N.C.
            begun: September, 1903   built: c. 1905
            cost: unsupervised

*482. McKinley Birthplace National Memorial
        museum
        Niles, Ohio
            condition: extant
            begun: February, 1915   built: 1915-1918
            cost: $ 278,840
            extant drawings: New-York Historical Society

483. McLane, Allan
     house
     Narragansett Pier, R.I.
          begun: August, 1885   built: 1885-1886
          cost: $ 12,626
          contractor: J. Thompson

484. Maconochie (?)
     hotel, project
     Narragansett Pier, R.I.
          not built
          begun: January, 1896
          cost: est. $ 90,000

*485. Madison Square Garden
      amphitheater, theaters, restaurants
      Madison Avenue, Fourth Avenue, 26th and 27th Streets
      New York, N.Y.
           condition: demolished
           begun: July, 1887   built: 1889-1891
           designer: White [LGW, B, K]
           cost: $ 1,380,536
           contractor: David H. King, jr.
           extant drawings: New-York Historical Society
                Diana atop tower by Augustus Saint-Gaudens

*486. Madison Square Presbyterian Church
      church and parish house
      Madison Avenue and 24th Street
      New York, N.Y.
           condition: demolished
           begun: April, 1903   built: 1904-1906
           designer: White [LGW, B, K]
           cost: $ 306,022
           contractor: Charles T. Wills
           extant drawings: New-York Historical Society

*487. Madison Square Presbyterian Church
      pediment relief sculpture, installation
      New York, N.Y.
           condition: reinstalled in library wing, Metropolitan
                     Museum of Art, see No. 509
           installed: June, 1910
                The Church Pastoral and the Church Militant, designed
                by H. Siddons Mowbray and modeled by Adolph A. Weinman

*488. Manchester Public Library (for T. J. Coolidge)
      Summer Street
      Manchester-by-the-Sea, Mass.
           condition: extant
           begun: May, 1886   built: 1886-1887
           designer: McKim (?)
           cost: $ 18,020
           contractor (interiors): J. Cabus
                memorial window by David Maitland Armstrong and
                Louis C. Tiffany

489. Manhattan Company and Merchants Bank
     competition entry
     40 Wall Street
     New York, N.Y.
         not built
         begun: March, 1883
         cost: flat fee, $ 250

490. Marlborough, Consuelo Vanderbilt Spencer-Churchill, Duchess of
     monument
     Woodlawn Cemetery
     New York, N.Y.
         begun: 1906
         designer: White [B]

     "The Marlborough" apartment building
     see New York Life Insurance Company, No. 575

*491. Maryland Society Battle Monument
     memorial
     Prospect Park
     Brooklyn, N.Y.
         condition: extant
         begun: c. 1892   built: 1892
         designer: White [B]

492. Massachusetts Mutual Life Insurance Company
     competition entry
     Springfield, Mass.
         not built
         begun: August, 1894
         cost: flat fee, $ 500

*493. Massapequa Land Company
     Massapequa railroad station and park, project (?)
     Massapequa, N.Y.
         begun: July, 1908   built: 1908 (?)
         cost: c. $ 10,000

494. Mastin, Thomas H.
     house, first design
     Commonwealth Avenue
     Kansas City, Mo.
         begun: November, 1887   not built
         cost: c. $ 125,000

*495. Mastin, Thomas H.
     house, second design
     Commonwealth Avenue
     Kansas City, Mo.
         begun: April, 1888   built: 1888-1889 (?)
         cost: $ 50,000, unsupervised

496. May, Mrs. Isabella T.
        building (unspecified)
        Mercer and 3rd Streets
        New York, N.Y.
           condition: demolished
           begun: 1888   built: 1889
           cost: c. $ 150,000

497. Merchants Bank
        alterations to banking facilities
        40 Wall Street
        New York, N.Y.
           condition: demolished
           begun: May, 1880   built: 1880
           cost: flat fee, $ 75

498. Merchants Club (in New York Life Insurance Company building)
        346-348 Broadway
        New York, N.Y.
           condition: dismantled
           begun: December, 1896   built: 1896
           designer: White (?)
           cost: $ 6,626

*499. Metcalf, Edwin D.
        house
        126 W. North Street
        Buffalo, N.Y.
           condition: extant
           begun: July, 1882   built: 1882-1884
           cost: $ 17,757
                  +   5,707
                     23,464

*500. Metropolitan Club
        Fifth Avenue and 60th Street
        New York, N.Y.
           condition: extant
           begun: November, 1891   built: 1892-1894
           designer: White [LGW, B, K]
           cost: $ 1,200,000
           extant drawings: New-York Historical Society

501. Metropolitan Hotel
        alterations to facade
        Broadway and Prince Street
        New York, N.Y.
           condition: demolished
           begun: December, 1891   built: 1891
           cost: $ 3,850

93

*502. Metropolitan Museum of Art
       comprehensive plan
       Fifth Avenue and 82nd Street
       New York, N.Y.
          condition: extant
          plan begun: 1904 (through 1906)
          designer and planner: McKim with Kendall and Richardson
                                  [K]

 503. Metropolitan Museum of Art
       boiler house
       New York, N.Y.
          condition: extant
          begun: 1912   built: 1912-1914
          cost: $ 408,291

 504. Metropolitan Museum of Art
       carpentry shop
       New York, N.Y.
          condition: extant
          begun: 1913   built: 1913-1914
          cost: $ 59,503

 505. Metropolitan Museum of Art
       carriage entrance
       New York, N.Y.
          condition: remodeled
          begun: 1912   built: 1913-1914
          cost: $ 14,662

 506. Metropolitan Museum of Art
       pediment from Madison Square Presbyterian Church,
          installation in library wing
       New York, N.Y.
          condition: extant
          begun: 1920   built: 1920
          cost: $ 7,644

*507. Metropolitan Museum of Art
       Section E, North Extension
       New York, N.Y.
          condition: extant
          begun: 1907   built: 1907-1909
          cost: $ 416,324
                + 71,050
                  ‾‾‾‾‾‾‾
                   487,374

 508. Metropolitan Museum of Art
       Section F, the Morgan Wing
       New York, N.Y.
          condition: extant
          begun: 1907   built: 1907-1909
          cost: $ 514,255

509. Metropolitan Museum of Art
        Section G, Library Wing
        New York, N.Y.
            condition: extant
            begun: 1908   built: 1908-1910
            cost: $ 83,589
            contractor: J. F. Walsh

*510. Metropolitan Museum of Art
        Section H, North Extension
        New York, N.Y.
            condition: extant
            begun: 1910   built: 1910-1913
            cost: $ 819,873

*511. Metropolitan Museum of Art
        Sections J and K, South Extension
        New York, N.Y.
            condition: extant
            begun: 1914   built: 1914-1916
            cost: $ 740,918

512. Miller, Dr. George N.
        townhouse
        811 Madison Avenue
        New York, N.Y.
            condition: demolished
            begun: November, 1891   built: 1892-1893
            designer: White [B]
            cost: $ 38,322
                 + 14,017
                 ───────
                   52,339

513. Miller, Dr. George N.
        stable, addition to existing house
        Rhinebeck, N.Y.
            begun: December, 1891   built: 1892 (?)
            cost: flat fee, $ 150

514. Miller, J. C.
        house (project ?)
        47 W. 119th Street
        New York, N.Y.
            begun: June, 1886   built: 1886 (?)
            cost: flat fee, $ 250

*515. Miller, James C.
        apartment building
        359 W. 47th Street
        New York, N.Y.
            condition: extant
            begun: September, 1886   built: 1886-1887
            cost: $ 20,000

95

516. Miller, William Starr
       house
       Newport, R.I.
          begun: April, 1882   built: 1883
          cost: $ 22,187
                + 7,471
                  29,658

517. Miller, William Starr
       house
       Rhinebeck, N.Y.
          begun: May, 1892   built: 1892
          cost: fees only, $ 463.45 total, based on
                est. $ 50,000

*518. Mills, Ogden
       house
       Staatsberg, N.Y.
          begun: April, 1894   built: 1895-1897
          designer: White [B, K]
          cost: c. $ 100,000

*519. Minneapolis Museum of Fine Arts (Minneapolis Institute of Arts)
       Third Avenue and 24th Street
       Minneapolis, Minn.
          condition: extant
          begun: December, 1911   built: 1913-1914
          designer: Richardson [K]
          cost: $ 459,782
          contractor: J. and W. A. Elliott
          extant drawings: New-York Historical Society

520. Mitchell, Roland G.
       house
       Wading River, N.Y.
          begun: August, 1905   built: 1905-1907
          cost: $ 76,688

*521. Modjeska, Helena
       house
       Santiago Canyon
       Santa Ana, Calif.
          begun: 1888   built: 1888 et seq.
          cost: unsupervised, unrecorded

522. Montauk Point Association (Henry G. deForest, treasurer)
       club house, casino, stable, and laundry
       deForest Road
       Montauk Point, N.Y.
          condition: demolished
          begun: October, 1881   built: 1881-1882
          cost: $ 19,430

523. Montauk Point Association
     additions and alterations to club house
     deForest Road
     Montauk Point, N.Y.
         condition: demolished
         begun: April, 1883   built: 1883
         cost: $ 4,517

*524. Montclair High School
      school, project
      Montclair, N.J.
          not built
          begun: December, 1905
          cost: est. $ 187,375

525. Montclair Presbyterian Church
     chapel
     Church Street and Claremont Avenue
     Montclair, N.J.
         condition: demolished
         begun: September, 1883   built: 1883-1885
         cost: $ 11,414

*526. Moore, William H.
      townhouse
      4 E. 54th Street
      New York, N.Y.
          condition: extant
          begun: March, 1900   built: 1900
          cost: $ 88,417

*527. Morgan, Edwin Dennison, jr.
      house, "Beacon Rock"
      Harrison Avenue
      Newport, R.I.
          condition: extant
          begun: October, 1888   built: 1889-1891
          designer: White and McKim [B, K]
          cost: $ 204,496
                +   23,841
                   238,337
          extant drawings: New-York Historical Society

*528. Morgan, Edwin Dennison, jr.
      house, "Wheatley Hills," central section
      Wheatley, N.Y.
          condition: demolished
          begun: December, 1890   built: 1890-1891
          designer: McKim (?)
          cost: $ 86,495

97

* 529. Morgan, Edwin Dennison, jr.
        additions to house, "Wheatley Hills," west wing and gardens
        Wheatley, N.Y.
            condition: demolished
            begun: January, 1898   built: 1898-1900
            designer: McKim [K]
            cost: $ 40,591

* 530. Morgan, John Pierpont
        library
        33 E. 36th Street
        New York, N.Y.
            condition: extant
            begun: March, 1902   built: 1903-1907
            designer: McKim [K]
            cost: $ 922,532
                 + 232,137
                 1,154,669
            contractor: Charles T. Wills
            extant drawings: New-York Historical Society
                             Morgan Library
              lunettes and ceiling murals by H. Siddons Mowbray
              recumbent lionesses by Edward Clark Potter
              relief sculpture by Andrew O'Connor

  531. Morris County Savings Bank
        bank, project
        Morristown, N.J.
            not built
            begun: June, 1890
            cost: est. $ 30,000

  532. Morton, Levi Parsons
        additions and alterations to existing house
        Newport, R.I.
            begun: February, 1881   built: 1881
            cost: $ 7,700

* 533. Morton, Levi Parsons
        townhouse
        681 Fifth Avenue
        New York, N.Y.
            condition: demolished
            begun: September, 1896   built: 1897-1898
            designer: White [B, K]
            cost: $ 76,746
                 + 28,383
                 105,129

534. Morton, Levi Parsons
additions to townhouse
681 Fifth Avenue
New York, N.Y.
condition: demolished
begun: March, 1912   built: 1912-1913
cost: $ 340,532

535. Mott, John L. B.
house
Bellport, N.Y.
begun: October, 1890   built: 1891-1893
cost: $ 13,950

536. Moulton, Gilman S.
townhouse, project
Fifth Avenue and 76th Street
New York, N.Y.
not built
begun: January, 1896
cost: est. $ 80,000

537. Mount Morris Bank and Safe Deposit Company
competition entry
Mount Morris, N.Y.
not built
begun: c. December, 1881
cost: flat fee, $ 200

538. Mount Royal Club
Sherbrooke Street
Montreal, Quebec, Canada
condition: demolished
begun: May, 1904   built: 1904-1907
designer: Richardson [K]
cost: $ 130,380
contractor: Lessard and Harris
extant drawings: New-York Historical Society

*539. Municipal Building, City of New York
Park Row and Chambers Street
New York, N.Y.
condition: extant
begun: November, 1907   built: 1909-1916
designer: Kendall and Van der Bent [K]
cost: $ 1,351,422 foundations
          5,924,433 structure
          3,311,635 interiors, painting
            467,342 elevators
            225,320 tower
         11,280,152
contractor: Thompson-Starrett
extant drawings: New-York Historical Society
sculpture by Adolph A. Weinman

99

540. Munsey, Frank Andrew
        house
        Lewiston, Maine
            begun: February, 1910   built: 1910 (?)
            cost: est. $ 17,000

*541. Munsey Building ("Times Building") (first building)
        office building
        1329 E Street, NW
        Washington, D. C.
            condition: extant, remodeled
            begun: February, 1905   built: 1905-1907
            cost: $ 751,510
            contractor: George A. Fuller
            extant drawings: New-York Historical Society

*542. Munsey Building ("Times Building")
        alterations to first building
        Washington, D. C.
            condition: extant
            begun: 1912   built: 1913
            cost: $ 207,923

*543. Munsey Building (second building)
        office building, next to first building
        1327 E Street, NW
        Washington, D. C.
            condition: extant
            begun: February, 1912   built: 1914-1918
            cost: $ 1,305,412
            contractor: George A. Fuller
            extant drawings: New-York Historical Society

*544. Munsey Building
        office building
        Fayette and Calvert Streets
        Baltimore, Md.
            condition: extant
            begun: May, 1908   built: 1910-1913
            cost: $ 1,275,593
            contractor: George A. Fuller

545. Munsey Building
        alterations
        Baltimore, Md.
            condition: extant
            begun: c. 1913   built: 1914
            cost: $ 74,988

546. Munsey Building
      office building
      8 W. 40th Street
      New York, N.Y.
        condition: demolished
        begun: April, 1915   built: 1915-1916
        cost: $ 164,929

N

*547. Narragansett Pier Casino
      Ocean Road
      Narragansett Pier, R.I.
        condition: partially extant
        begun: October, 1883   built: 1884-1886
        designer: White (?); McKim [K]
        cost: $ 66,480

      Narragansett Pier Life-Saving Station
      see U. S. Coast Guard, No. 850

*548. National Cash Register Company
      auditorium and garage
      Dayton, Ohio
        condition: extant, remodeled
        begun: July, 1911   built: 1911-1914
        designer: Richardson [K]
        cost: $ 304,180

*549. National City Bank (for James Stillman)
      bank (alterations and additions to Merchants' Exchange,
          Isaiah Rogers, 1836-1842)
      55 Wall Street
      New York, N.Y.
        condition: extant
        begun: 1904 through 1906   built: 1907-1910
        designer: McKim and Richardson [K]
        cost: $ 2,232,272
        contractor: George A. Fuller
        extant drawings: New-York Historical Society

550. National City Bank
      alterations
      New York, N.Y.
        condition: extant
        begun: 1914   built: 1914
        cost: $ 13,951

551. National City Bank
        further alterations
        55 Wall Street
        New York, N.Y.
            condition: extant
            begun: 1916   built: 1916
            cost: $ 27,130

*552. Naugatuck, Conn.
        fountain and landscaping of town green
        (for J. H. Whittemore)
        Naugatuck, Conn.
            condition: extant
            begun: 1894   built: 1894-1895
            cost: $ 7,000, for fountain only
            contractor: New England Granite Works
            extant drawings: New-York Historical Society

*553. "Naugatuck Bank"
        bank, project
        Church Street
        Naugatuck, Conn.
            not built
            begun: 1906

*554. Naugatuck City Hall
        project
        Church Street
        Naugatuck, Conn.
            not built
            begun: 1906

*555. Naugatuck National Bank
        Church and Division Streets
        Naugatuck, Conn.
            condition: demolished
            begun: May, 1892   built: 1892-1893
            designer: Mead [K]
            cost: $ 14,293
            contractor: H. S. Hotchkiss

*556. Naugatuck Public Grammar School
        Salem School
        Meadow Street
        Naugatuck, Conn.
            condition: extant
            begun: September, 1892   built: 1892-1894
            designer: Mead (?)
            cost: $ 71,290
            contractor: H. Wales Lines Company

*557. Naugatuck Public High School
       Hillside High School
       Hillside Avenue
       Naugatuck, Conn.
          condition: extant, renovated
          begun: January, 1901   built: 1902-1905
          designer: White [B]; Mead, Kendall, and Van der Bent [K]
          cost: $ 247,874
          contractor: Tidewater Construction Company

 558. Nebraska State Capitol
       competition entry
       Lincoln, Neb.
          not built
          cost: flat fee, $ 2,000

*559. Nevada, University of
       Mackay School of Mines and replanning of campus
       Reno, Nevada
          condition: extant
          begun: June, 1906   built: 1906-1908
          designer: Richardson [K]
          cost: $ 72,323
          contractor: Northwestern Construction Company
          extant drawings: New-York Historical Society

 560. New Britain City Hall
       remodeling of the Russell and Erwin building (see No. 741)
       35 W. Main Street
       New Britain, Conn.
          condition: extant
          begun: July, 1907   built: 1908-1909
          cost: $ 31,377

*561. New England Trust Company
       Devonshire and Milk Streets
       Boston, Mass.
          condition: extant
          begun: April, 1904   built: 1905-1907
          designer: McKim [K]
          cost: $ 443,832
          contractor: Norcross Brothers

 562. New Haven Public Library
       competition entry
       New Haven, Conn.
          not built
          begun: April, 1907

 563. New Jersey Central Railroad
       competition entry
          begun: August, 1889
          cost: flat fee, $ 500

564. New Jersey State House
        project
        Trenton, N.J.
            not built
            cost: flat fee, $ 1,000

565. New York Association for Improving the Condition of the Blind
        hospital, project
        Rockaway (?)
        New York, N.Y. (?)
            not built
            cost: flat fee, $ 930

566. New York Association for Improving the Condition of the Blind
        hospital, Pavilions A and B
        Rockaway Point
        New York, N.Y.
            begun: May, 1914   built: 1914-1915
            cost: $ 230,359

*567. New York Central and Hudson River Railroad Company
        Grand Central Station
        competition entry
        Park Avenue and 42nd Street
        New York, N.Y.
            not built
            begun: February, 1903
            designer: White [B]
            cost: flat fee, $ 2,000
            extant drawings: New-York Historical Society

568. New York City Aquarium
        project for remodeling of Castle Garden
        Battery Park
        New York, N.Y.
            not built
            begun: 1902
            cost: unrecorded

*569. New York City Board of Education Building
        competition entry
        Park Avenue and 58th Street
        New York, N.Y.
            not built
            begun: March, 1892
            designer: White (?)

*570. New York City Hospital
        hospital, project
        Eleventh Avenue, 54th to 55th Streets
        New York, N.Y.
            not built
            begun: 1911
            cost: est. $ 3,000,000

*571. New York Clearing House Association
          competition entry
          77-81 Cedar Street
          New York, N.Y.
              not built
              begun: January, 1894
              designer: White (?)
              cost: flat fee, $ 500

*572. *New York Herald* Building   (for James Gordon Bennett, jr.)
          Broadway and 34th Street
          New York, N.Y.
              condition: demolished
              begun: June, 1890   built: 1892-1895
              designer: White [LGW, B]
              cost: c. $ 400,000
              contractor: David H. King, jr.
              bronze bell ringers by Antonin Jean Carles (now in
              Herald Square)

573. New York Institute for the Education of the Blind
          hospital, project
          New York, N.Y.
              not built
              begun: January, 1918
              cost: est. $ 673,553

574. New York Life Insurance Company
          apartment building
          E. 107th Street
          New York, N.Y.
              begun: May, 1890   built: 1890
              cost: $ 15,199

575. New York Life Insurance Company
          alterations in "The Marlborough" apartment building
          356-358 W. 58th Street
          New York, N.Y.
              condition: demolished
              cost: $ 2,332

*576. New York Life Insurance Company
          New York Life Insurance Company Building
          20 W. Ninth Street
          Kansas City, Mo.
              condition: extant
              begun: January, 1887   built: 1887-1890
              designer: White and Mead [B, K]
              cost: $ 1,134,875
              contractor: Norcross Brothers

*577. New York Life Insurance Company
       New York Life Insurance Company Building
       Farnum and 17th Streets
       Omaha, Neb.
            condition: extant
            begun: January, 1887   built: 1887-1890
            designers: White and Mead [B, K]
                       (this is a duplicate of the Kansas City
                       building)
            cost: $ 955,874
            contractor: Norcross Brothers

*578. New York Life Insurance Company
       New York Life Insurance Company Building, Main Offices
            rear section
       Elm and Leonard Streets
       New York, N.Y.
            condition: extant
            begun: c. 1893   built: 1894-1898
            designer: White [B, K]
            cost: $ 2,270,402
            extant drawings: New-York Historical Society

*579. New York Life Insurance Company
       New York Life Insurance Company Building, Main Offices
            front section
       346-348 Broadway
       New York, N.Y.
            condition: extant
            begun: c. 1893   built: 1896-1899
            designer: White [B, K]
            cost: $ 1,775,454
            extant drawings: New-York Historical Society

*580. New York Life Insurance Company
       New York Life Insurance Company Building, Main Offices
            Directors' Room
       346-348 Broadway
       New York, N.Y.
            condition: extant, moved to new building by Cass Gil-
                       bert, 1926-1928
            begun: August, 1896   built: c. 1899
            designer: White [B, K]

       New York Life Insurance Company
       see Plaza Hotel, Nos. 665 and 666

*581. New York Life Insurance Company
       "The Yosemite" apartment building
       1054 Fourth Avenue (Park Avenue)
       New York, N.Y.
            condition: demolished
            begun: November, 1887   built: 1888-1890
            cost: $ 400,697

*582. New York, New Haven, and Hartford Railroad Company
       Waterbury Passenger Station
       Meadows Street
       Waterbury, Conn.
          condition: extant
          begun: 1906-1907   built: 1908-1909
          designer: Richardson [K]
          cost: $ 254,131
                + 14,728
                  268,859
          contractor: Horton & Hemenway
          extant drawings: New-York Historical Society

*583. New York Post-Graduate Hospital and Medical School
       Second Avenue and 20th Street
       New York, N.Y.
          condition: demolished
          begun: March, 1910   built: 1910-1912
          designer: Kendall and Van der Bent [K]
          cost: $ 878,184

 584. New York Post-Graduate Hospital and Medical School
       alterations to building
       New York, N.Y.
          condition: demolished
          begun: 1919   built: 1919
          cost: $ 13,850

*585. New York Public Library
       competition entry
       New York, N.Y.
          not built (won third place)
          begun: May, 1897
          designer: McKim

*586. New York Public Library, Branch
       Carnegie Library No. 2, Chatham Square
       31 E. Broadway
       New York, N.Y.
          condition: extant
          begun: 1902   built: 1902-1903
          designer: McKim and Kendall [K]
          cost: $ 72,314
          contractor: Michael Reid

*587. New York Public Library, Branch
       Carnegie Library No. 6, 125th Street
       224 E. 125th Street
       New York, N.Y.
          condition: extant
          begun: 1902   built: 1903-1904
          designer: McKim and Kendall [K]
          cost: $ 68,097
          contractor: Michael Reid

*588. New York Public Library, Branch
      Carnegie Library No. 10
      103 W. 135th Street
      New York, N.Y.
          condition: extant
          begun: 1903   built: 1903-1905
          designer: McKim and Kendall [K]
          cost: $ 68,373
          contractor: Michael Reid

*589. New York Public Library, Branch
      Carnegie Library No. 11, Rivington Street
      61 Rivington Street
      New York, N.Y.
          condition: extant
          begun: 1904   built: 1904-1905
          designer: McKim and Kendall [K]
          cost: $ 66,401
          contractor: Michael Reid

*590. New York Public Library, Branch
      Carnegie Library No. 14, Thompkins Square
      331 E. 10th Street
      New York, N.Y.
          condition: extant
          begun: 1903   built: 1903-1905
          designer: McKim and Kendall [K]
          cost: $ 75,141
          contractor: Michael Reid

*591. New York Public Library, Branch
      Carnegie Library No. 23, Kingsbridge
      New York, N.Y.
          begun: 1904   built: 1904-1905
          designer: McKim and Kendall [K]
          cost: $ 19,283
          contractor: Michael Reid

*592. New York Public Library, Branch
      Carnegie Library No. 29, St. Gabriel's
      303 E. 36th Street
      New York, N.Y.
          condition: demolished
          begun: 1906   built: 1906-1908
          designer: McKim and Kendall [K]
          cost: $ 81,540
          contractor: Michael Reid

*593. New York Public Library, Branch
      Carnegie Library No. 32, 115th Street
      203 W. 115th Street
      New York, N.Y.
          condition: extant
          begun: 1907   built: 1907-1909
          designer: McKim and Kendall [K]
          cost: $ 79,218
          contractor: I. A. Hopper

*594. New York Public Library, Branch
      Carnegie Library No. 35, Hamilton Grange
      Amsterdam Avenue and W. 145th Street
      New York, N.Y.
          condition: extant
          begun: 1905   built: 1905-1906
          designer: McKim and Kendall [K]
          cost: $ 99,459

*595. New York Public Library, Branch
      Carnegie Library No. 37, Mt. Morris
      9 W. 124th Street
      New York, N.Y.
          condition: extant
          begun: 1907   built: 1907-1909
          designer: McKim and Kendall [K]
          cost: $ 84,581
          contractor: Michael Reid

*596. New York Public Library, Branch
      Carnegie Library No. 42, Woodstock
      759 E. 160th Street
      New York, N.Y.
          begun: 1912   built: 1912-1914
          designer: Kendall
          cost: $ 104,822

*597. New York State Building
      World's Columbian Exposition
      Chicago, Ill.
          condition: demolished
          begun: April, 1892   built: 1892-1893
          designer: McKim [K]
          cost: $ 150,559
          contractor: George A. Fuller
              sculpture by Olin L. Warner

*598. New York University
          comprehensive plan
          University Heights Campus
          University Avenue and W. 180th Street
          New York, N.Y.
              plan begun: 1892-1893
              built: 1894 through 1901
              condition: extant
              designer and planner: White [LGW, B, K]

*599. New York University
          Ambulatory, "Hall of Fame"
          New York, N.Y.
              built: 1900-1901
              cost: $ 108,862
              contractor: J. J. Tucker

*600. New York University
          Dormitory
          New York, N.Y.
              built: 1896-1897
              cost: $ 164,314
              contractor: Michael Reid

*601. New York University
          Gould Library and Administration Offices
          New York, N.Y.
              built: 1896-1903
              cost: $ 692,368

*602. New York University
          Hall of Languages
          New York, N.Y.
              built: 1894
              cost: $ 68,628
              contractor: Norcross Brothers

*603. New York University
          museum
          New York, N.Y.
              built: 1896-1898
              cost: $ 67,030
              contractor: J. J. Tucker

 604. New York University
          retaining walls, terraces
          New York, N.Y.
              built: 1895
              cost: $ 89,037

605. Newark Memorial Building
        competition entry
        Newark, N.J.
            not built
            begun: 1916
            cost: est. $ 1,741,000

*606. Newbold, Thomas
        townhouse
        15 E. 79th Street
        New York, N.Y.
            condition: extant
            begun: July, 1916   built: 1916-1918
            designer: Kendall (?)
            cost: $ 147,819
            extant drawings: New-York Historical Society

*607. Newcomb, H. Victor
        house
        1265 Ocean Avenue
        Elberon, N.J.
            condition: partially extant, extensively remodeled
            begun: March, 1880   built: 1880
            cost: $ 32,976

608. Newcomb, H. Victor
        townhouse
        683 Fifth Avenue
        New York, N.Y.
            condition: demolished
            begun: October, 1881   built: 1881-1882
            cost: $ 33,981
                 +   8,339
                    42,320

609. Newcomb, H. Victor
        stable
        108 W. 54th Street
        New York, N.Y.
            condition: demolished
            begun: September, 1893   built: 1893
            cost: $ 4,516

*610. Newhall, Daniel S.
        house
        151 Old Eagle School Road
        Strafford (Eagle Station), Penna.
            condition: extant
            begun: June, 1886   built: 1886
            designer: McKim (?)
            cost: flat fee, $ 500

111

611. Newhall, George M.
        house (interiors or alterations ?)
        Manheim and Pulaski Streets
        Philadelphia (Germantown), Penna.
        condition: demolished
        begun: October, 1879
        designer: White (?)
        cost: flat fee, $ 50

*612. Newport Casino (for James Gordon Bennett, jr.)
        194 Bellevue Avenue
        Newport, R.I.
        condition: extant (partially damaged by fire, 1953)
        begun: August (?), 1879   built: 1880
        designer: White [B]; McKim [K]
        cost: $ 64,100

613. Newport Casino
        additions
        Newport, R.I.
        condition: extant
        begun: July, 1881   built: 1881
        designer: White (?)
        cost: $ 21,931

*614. Nickerson, George A.
        townhouse
        303 Commonwealth Avenue
        Boston, Mass.
        condition: extant
        begun: March, 1895   built: 1895-1897
        designer: McKim [K]
        cost: $ 77,160
             + 18,050
               95,210

*615. 998 Fifth Avenue (for Century Holding Company)
        apartment building
        998 Fifth Avenue at 81st Street
        New York, N.Y.
        condition: extant
        begun: August, 1910   built: 1910-1914
        designer: Richardson [K]
        cost: $ 806,909
        extant drawings: New-York Historical Society

616. Northern Pacific Railroad Company
        hospital
        Main and W. Ward Streets
        Brainerd, Minn.
        begun: August, 1883   built: 1883
        designer: in collaboration with Cass Gilbert
        cost: c. $ 25,000

*617. Northern Pacific Railroad Company
        Mandan Station ("for account of Mandan and other stations")
        Mandan, N.D.
            begun: April, 1884   built: 1884
            cost: expenses, $ 59

 618. Northern Pacific Railroad Company
        offices, alterations
        Fourth Street
        St. Paul, Minn.
            begun: August, 1883   built: 1883
            designer: in collaboration with Cass Gilbert
            cost: $ 4,636

*619. Northern Pacific Railroad Company
        "Portland House," hotel
        Sixth, Seventh, Yamhill, and Morrison Streets
        Portland, Ore.
            condition: demolished
            begun: c. January, 1882   built: 1883-1885, basement
                and ground floors only. Building completed, 1888,
                by Whidden & Lewis.
            designer: McKim (?)
            cost: est. $ 142,442

*620. Northern Pacific Railroad Company
        Portland Terminal Station (for Portland Union Depot Company)
        Seventh, Eighth, Hoyt, and Marshall Streets
        Portland, Ore.
            not built (Another design by Van Brunt & Howe built later)
            begun: c. January, 1882
            designer: McKim (?)
            cost: flat fee, $ 10,000

 621. Northern Pacific Railroad Company
        steam packet interiors (for Oregon Railway and Navigation
        Company, a subsidiary: "on designs furnished for
        interior woodwork on steamers")
            designs prepared: c. October, 1883
            cost: flat fee, $ 300

*622. Northern Pacific Railroad Company
        Tacoma Terminal Station and Hotel
        Tacoma, Wash.
            condition: demolished
            begun: 1884   built: 1884 (hotel only)
            designer: McKim (?)
            cost: $ 39,450

O

*623. Oakland City Hall
          competition entry
          Oakland, Calif.
             not built
             begun: July, 1910
             cost: flat fee, $ 1,000

  624. Odell, Edward V.
          house
          New Rochelle, N.Y.
             begun: March, 1887   built: 1887
             cost: $ 9,051

  625. Oelrichs, Herman
          additions and alterations to existing townhouse
          1 E. 57th Street
          New York, N.Y.
             condition: demolished
             begun: June, 1896   built: 1896-1897
             cost: $ 129,670

*626. Oelrichs, Herman
          house, "Rosecliff"
          Bellevue and Marine Avenues
          Newport, R.I.
             condition: extant
             begun: August, 1897   built: 1899-1902
             designer: White [LGW, B, K]
             cost: $ 248,799
                    + 49,244
                      ───────
                      298,043
             extant drawings: New-York Historical Society

*627. Olmsted, A. H.
          house
          91 Elm Street
          Hartford, Conn.
             condition: demolished
             begun: September, 1884   built: 1885-1887
             cost: $ 25,000
                    + 5,000
                      ──────
                      30,000

*628. Olney, Richard
          townhouse (half of double house; see Amory, F. I., No. 71)
          415 Commonwealth Avenue
          Boston, Mass.
             condition: extant
             begun: October, 1890   built: 1890-1892
             designer: McKim (?)
             cost: $ 39,606

*629. Orange Free Library
        Main Street and Essex Avenue
        Orange, N.J.
            condition: extant
            begun: March, 1900   built: 1900-1901
            designer: McKim (?)
            cost: $ 96,452
                stained glass window by D. Maitland and
                Helen Armstrong

*630. Orr, Alexander Ector
        house
        deForest Road
        Montauk Point, N.Y.
            condition: demolished
            begun: July, 1882   built: 1882
            cost: $ 5,000

*631. Osborn, Charles J.
        house
        South Barry Avenue
        Mamaroneck, N.Y.
            condition: partially demolished
            begun: August, 1883   built: 1884-1885
            designer: White [LGW, B, K]
            cost: $ 126,008
                 +   55,302
                    181,310
                mural paintings by Thomas W. Dewing and
                Francis Lathrop

*632. Osborn, Charles J.
        mausoleum
        Woodlawn Cemetery
        New York, N.Y.
            condition: extant
            begun: April, 1909   built: 1909
            cost: $ 3,900

P

633. Pack, Charles L.
        mausoleum
        Cleveland, Ohio
            condition: extant
            begun: July, 1908   built: 1908
            cost: $ 7,470

*634. Page, Thomas Nelson
        house
        1759 R Street, NW
        Washington, D.C.
            condition: extant
            begun: January, 1896   built: 1896-1897
            designer: White [LGW, B, K]
            cost: $ 72,890
            extant drawings: New-York Historical Society

635. Page, Thomas Nelson
        alterations to house
        Washington, D.C.
            condition: extant
            begun: June, 1903   built: 1903
            cost: flat fee, $ 400
            extant drawings: New-York Historical Society

636. Palmer, Potter
        art gallery, addition to house
        Lake Shore Drive and Schiller Street
        Chicago, Ill.
            condition: demolished
            begun: July, 1892   built: 1892-1893
            cost: flat fee, $ 500

*637. Palmer, Mrs. Potter
        mausoleum
        Graceland Cemetery
        Chicago, Ill.
            condition: extant
            begun: 1904   built: 1905-1906
            cost: $ 45,600
            contractor: C. B. Blake
            extant drawings: New-York Historical Society

638. *Pan of Rohallion*
        fountain, base and setting for bronze figure by
            Frederick MacMonnies
        "Rohallion," the E. D. Adams house (see No. 54)
        Seabright, N.J.
            built: 1889
            designer: White [B] with MacMonnies

*639. Panama-Pacific Exposition
        Court of the Universe
        San Francisco, Calif.
            condition: demolished
            begun: 1912-1914   built: 1914-1915
            designer: Richardson
            cost: flat fee, $ 10,000
            extant drawings: New-York Historical Society
                sculpture: *Nations of the East* (atop the Arch of the
                Rising Sun) by A. Stirling Calder, Leo Lentelli, and
                Frederick G. R. Roth; *Fountain of the Rising Sun* by
                Adolph A. Weinman; Column of Progress with reliefs
                by Isidore Konti, surmounted by *Adventurous Archer* by
                Hermon A. MacNeil; *Guardian Angel* (repeated atop arch
                columns) by Leo Lentelli; *Star* (repeated atop the
                colonnade) by A. Stirling Calder.

640.   Park, Hobart J.
        house
        Portchester, N.Y.
            begun: December, 1906   built: 1907-1908
            designer: Mead and Fenner [K]
            cost: $ 158,605

641.   Park, William Gray
        house
        Cazenovia, N.Y.
            condition: extant
            begun: October, 1892   built: 1893
            cost: $ 33,440
            contractor: V. J. Hedden

642.   Park, William Gray
        alterations to existing townhouse
        47 Fifth Avenue
        New York, N.Y.
            condition: partially extant
            begun: September, 1893   built: 1893
            cost: $ 8,656

643.   Park, William Gray
        house, project
        Westbury, N.Y.
            not built
            begun: August, 1902
            cost: est. $ 100,000

*644. Park & Tilford
        store and offices
        Columbus Avenue and 72nd Street
        New York, N.Y.
            condition: extant
            begun: May, 1892   built: 1892-1893
            cost: $ 189,625
            extant drawings: New-York Historical Society

645. Park & Tilford Company
          store and offices
          Broadway and 39th Street
          New York, N.Y.
             condition: demolished
             begun: August, 1895   built: 1895-1896
             cost: $ 70,840

646. Park Avenue Hotel
          alterations to existing hotel
          Park Avenue and 32nd Street
          New York, N.Y.
             condition: demolished
             begun: December, 1890   built: 1890-1891
             cost: c. $ 30,000

647. Park Avenue Hotel
          further alterations to hotel
          New York, N.Y.
             condition: demolished
             begun: January, 1902   built: 1902-1903
             cost: $ 78,395

*648. Parkman, Francis, Memorial
          base and setting for figure by Daniel Chester French
          Boston (Jamaica Plain), Mass.; initial studies only
             condition: extant , built after designs by H. Bacon
             begun: c. 1895
             designer: McKim with Daniel Chester French
             cost: unrecorded

649. Parrish, Samuel L.
          house
          Southampton, N.Y.
             begun: January, 1889   built: 1889
             cost: $ 10,000

650. Parsons, Herbert
          alterations to existing townhouse
          112 E. 35th Street
          New York, N.Y.
             condition: partially extant
             begun: January, 1901   built: 1901
             cost: $ 3,730

*651. Patterson, Robert Wilson
           house
           Astor Street and Burton Place
           Chicago, Ill.
              condition: extant
              begun: April, 1892   built: 1892-1895
              designer: White [B]
              cost: $ 68,117
                    + 21,657
                      89,774
              contractor: George A. Fuller
              extant drawings: New-York Historical Society

*652. Patterson, Robert Wilson
           house
           15 Dupont Circle
           Washington, D.C.
              condition: extant
              begun: May, 1900   built: 1901-1903
              designer: White [LGW, B, K]
              cost: $ 134,248
                    + 48,972
                      183,220
              contractor: George A. Fuller
              extant drawings: New-York Historical Society

       Paulist Fathers' Church
          see St. Paul the Apostle (Church of the Paulist Fathers),
          No. 749

653.   Pendleton, F. K.
           house, project
           Shinnecock, N.Y.
              not built
              begun: December, 1887
              designer: White [B]
              cost: flat fee, $ 25

654.   Penn, William, Memorial Tablet
           All Hallows Church
           Barking, By-the-Tower
           London, England
              condition: extant
              begun: 1911   built: 1911

655.   Pennsylvania Railroad Company
           "on parlor car, No. 1"
           parlor car interiors
              begun: June, 1886
              designer: White (?)
              cost: flat fee, $ 1,000

119

*656.   Pennsylvania Railroad Company
        New York Terminal Station
          "Penn Station"
        Seventh and Eighth Avenues, 31st to 33rd Streets
        New York, N.Y.
          condition: demolished
          begun: May, 1902 (through 1904)
          built: Hudson River tunnel, 1904-1906
                 East River tunnel, 1904-1908
                 excavations, 1904-1905
                 station house and power station, 1905-1911
          opened: station fully operational November, 1910
          designers: McKim and Richardson [K]
              with Samuel Rea, Third Vice-President, PRR Co.
              George Gibbs, Chief Engineer, PRR Co.
              Westinghouse, Church, Kerr & Company, engineers
          cost: $ 10,271,383 total
          contractors: George A. Fuller, general contractor
                       Norcross Brothers, granite masonry
                       American Bridge Company, steel fabrication
                       New York Contracting Company, substructure
              murals by Jules Guerin
              sculpture by Adolph A. Weinman

*657.   Pennsylvania Railroad Company
        Power Station
        New York Terminal Station, "Penn Station"
        242 W. 31st Street
        New York, N.Y.
          condition: extant
          begun: c. 1905   built: 1905-1908
          designer: McKim and Richardson [K] with Westinghouse,
              Church, Kerr & Company, engineers
          cost: not recorded separately
          contractor: George A. Fuller et al.

        "The Percival"
        see Harrison, O. F., No. 356

* 658. Phelps Association
          "Wolf's Head" Fraternity (Yale University)
          77 Prospect Street
          New Haven, Conn.
            condition: extant
            begun: August, 1884   built: 1884-1885
            designer: McKim (?)
            cost: $ 18,000
            extant drawings: New-York Historical Society

*659. Phoenix, Phillips and Lloyd
       townhouse
       21 E. 33rd Street
       New York, N.Y.
          condition: demolished
          begun: December, 1882   built: 1882-1884
          cost: $ 37,247
                + 13,690
                  50,937
          extant drawings: New-York Historical Society

660. *The Pilgrim*
       base for bronze figure by Augustus Saint-Gaudens
       (revised version of the Deacon Chapin Memorial,
       The Puritan, see No. 190)
       Fairmount Park
       Philadelphia, Penna.
          condition: extant
          begun: 1903   built: 1905
          designer: White [LGW, B] with Augustus Saint-Gaudens
          cost: unrecorded

661. Pinchot, James W.
       alterations to existing townhouse
       2 Gramercy Park
       New York, N.Y.
          condition: partially extant
          begun: September, 1887   built: 1887
          cost: c. $ 5,000

662. Pinchot, James W.
       "The Tecumseh" apartment building
       Broadway and 66th Street
       New York, N.Y.
          condition: demolished
          begun: July, 1891   built: 1891-1892
          cost: $ 62,872

*663. Players' Club
       alterations to the former Edwin Booth home
       16 Gramercy Park South
       New York, N.Y.
          condition: extant
          begun: August, 1888   built: 1888-1889
          designer: White [LGW, B]
          cost: $ 7,500
          extant drawings: New-York Historical Society

664. Players' Club
       further alterations
       New York, N.Y.
          condition: extant
          begun: July, 1893   built: 1893
          cost: $ 2,242

*665. Plaza Hotel (for the New York Life Insurance Company)
        alterations to existing hotel
        Fifth Avenue and 59th Street
        New York, N.Y.
            condition: demolished
            begun: December, 1888   built: 1888-1891
            cost: c. $ 1,723,626
            extant drawings: New-York Historical Society

666. Plaza Hotel (for the New York Life Insurance Company)
        further alterations
        New York, N.Y.
            condition: demolished
            begun: 1899   built: 1899
            cost: $ 53,647

667. Plimpton, George Arthur
        additions and alterations to existing townhouse
        70 Fifth Avenue
        New York, N.Y.
            condition: demolished
            begun: August, 1892   built: 1895-1896
            cost: $ 52,118

668. Plymouth Rock Portico (for the Pilgrim Society)
        Plymouth, Mass.
            condition: extant
            begun: December, 1917   built: 1917-1921
            cost: $ 51,800

669. Poidebard Silk Company
        offices (?)
        North Bergen, N.J.
            begun: October, 1882   built: 1882-1883
            cost: $ 25,556

*670. Polifeme, A. C.
        commercial building
        7 E. 48th Street
        New York, N.Y.
            condition: extant
            begun: April, 1911   built: 1911
            cost: $ 60,833
            extant drawings: New-York Historical Society

*671. Poor, Henry William
        interiors in existing townhouse
        1 Lexington Avenue
        New York, N.Y.
            condition: demolished
            begun: July, 1899   built: 1899-1901
            designer: White [LGW, B]
            cost: $ 137,844

672. Poor, Henry William
        stable and squash court
        134 E. 22nd Street
        New York, N.Y.
            condition: demolished
            begun: July, 1899   built: 1899-1901
            designer: White [LGW, B]
            cost: $ 22,344

*673. Pope, Alfred Artmore
        house, "Hill-Stead"
        671 Farmington Avenue
        Farmington, Conn.
            condition: extant
            begun: October, 1898   built: 1898-1901
            designer: White [K] with Theodate Pope
            cost: c. $ 50,000
            extant drawings: New-York Historical Society

674. Pope, Alfred Artmore
        additions and alterations to "Hill-Stead"
        Farmington, Conn.
            condition: extant
            begun: June, 1907   built: 1907
            cost: $ 12,000

675. Princeton Club
        club, project
        Park Avenue and 58th Street
        New York, N.Y.
            not built
            begun: April, 1917

*676. Princeton University
        Athletic Field fence and gate (for Ferris S. Thompson)
        Princeton, N.J.
            condition: extant
            begun: February, 1910   built: 1910-1911
            designer: Richardson [K]
            cost: $ 35,740

*677. Princeton University
        Cottage Club
        51 Prospect Avenue
        Princeton, N.J.
            condition: extant
            begun: January, 1904   built: 1904-1908
            designer: McKim [K]
            cost: $ 119,793
            extant drawings: New-York Historical Society

678. Princeton University
        Cottage Club, library and gallery (for S. S. Palmer)
        51 Prospect Avenue
        Princeton, N.J.
            condition: extant
            begun: June, 1905   built: 1906
            cost: $ 19,969
            extant drawings: New-York Historical Society

*679. Princeton University
        FitzRandolph Memorial Gates (for Nathaniel Van Wickle)
        Nassau and Witherspoon Streets
        Princeton, N.J.
            condition: extant
            begun: November, 1903   built: 1904-1905
            designer: McKim and Kendall [K]
            cost: $ 17,636
            extant drawings: New-York Historical Society

680. Princeton University
        Olden Street gates
        Olden Street
        Princeton, N.J.
            condition: extant
            begun: December, 1912   built: 1913
            cost: $ 6,244
            extant drawings: New-York Historical Society

*681. Prison Ship Martyrs' Monument
        Fort Greene Park
        Brooklyn, N.Y.
            condition: extant
            begun: c. 1906 (c. 1900 [B])   built: 1907-1909
            designer: White [LGW, B, K]
            cost: $ 173,224
            contractor: P. J. Carlin
            extant drawings: New-York Historical Society
                bronze tripod atop memorial column by Adolph
                A. Weinman

*682. Prospect Park
        plan for embellishments; Grand Army Plaza entrance
        Brooklyn, N.Y.
            condition: extant
            begun: February, 1889   built: 1889
            designer: White (?)
            cost: c. $ 134,021
            extant drawings: New-York Historical Society

[Note: Park furniture and embellishments for Prospect Park follow
in alphabetical order.]

683. Prospect Park
        children's garden house
        Brooklyn, N.Y.
            condition: extant
            begun: June, 1917   built: 1917
            cost: $ 6,493

*684. Prospect Park
        croquet shelter
        Brooklyn, N.Y.
            condition: extant
            begun: April, 1904   built: 1904
            cost: $ 22,390
            contractor: L. Wechsler
            extant drawings: New-York Historical Society

*685. Prospect Park
        entrance, Ninth Avenue and 15th Street
        Brooklyn, N.Y.
            condition: extant
            begun: April, 1907   built: 1907-1908
            cost: $ 18,325
            extant drawings: New-York Historical Society

*686. Prospect Park
        entrance, Parkside (Willink) and Ocean Avenue
        Brooklyn, N.Y.
            condition: extant
            begun: October, 1890   built: 1890
            cost: $ 101,667
            extant drawings: New-York Historical Society
                includes two pylon bases for Frederick MacMonnies'
                The Horse Tamers (*The Triumph of Mind over Brute
                Force*), installed 1899

687. Prospect Park
        McCarren shelter
        Brooklyn, N.Y.
            condition: extant
            begun: July, 1912   built: 1912-1914
            cost: $ 19,040
            extant drawings: New-York Historical Society

*688. Prospect Park
        miscellaneous, "pedestals, balustrades" and "fences,
            columns, shelters, houses, etc."
        Brooklyn, N.Y.
            condition: extant
            begun: March, 1895   built: 1895 et seq.
            cost: $ 30,770
            contractor: W. and T. Lamb
            extant drawings: New-York Historical Society

689. Prospect Park
      "outlook tower, rose garden, and martyrs monument"
      Brooklyn, N.Y.
         condition: extant
         begun: November, 1895   built: 1895 et seq.
         cost: $ 86,000
         extant drawings: New-York Historical Society

690. Prospect Park
      "pergola entrance"
      Brooklyn, N.Y.
         begun: April, 1904   built: 1904
         cost: $ 24,500
         contractor: J. Hynes
         extant drawings: New-York Historical Society

*691. Prospect Park
      Stranahan, James, Memorial
         base for bronze figure by Frederick MacMonnies
      Brooklyn, N.Y.
         condition: extant
         begun: 1890   built: 1891
         designer: White [LGW, B] with Frederick MacMonnies
         cost: c. $ 20,000 total, figure and base
         extant drawings: New-York Historical Society

692. Prudential Insurance Company
      competition entry
      Newark, N.J.
         not built
         begun: February, 1890
         cost: flat fee, $ 500

*693. Puck Building
      World's Columbian Exposition
      Chicago, Ill.
         condition: demolished
         begun: July, 1892   built: 1893
         cost: $ 29,391
         contractor: George A. Fuller

694. Pulitzer, Joseph
      alterations to townhouse (former C. T. Barney house, No. 97)
      10 E. 55th Street
      New York, N.Y.
         condition: demolished
         begun: July, 1891   built: 1891
         cost: $ 17,590

695. Pulitzer, Joseph
    further alterations to townhouse (former C. T. Barney house)
    10 E. 55th Street
    New York, N.Y.
        condition: demolished
        begun: December, 1894   built: 1894
        cost: $ 16,612

696. Pulitzer, Joseph
    tower, addition to "Chatwold"
    Bar Harbor, Maine
        condition: demolished
        begun: September, 1895   built: 1896-1897
        designer: White (?)
        cost: c. $ 31,000

*697. Pulitzer, Joseph
    townhouse
    7 E. 73rd Street
    New York, N.Y.
        condition: extant
        begun: September, 1900   built: 1901-1903
        designer: White [LGW, B, K]
        cost: $ 289,731
             +   79,579
               369,310
        contractor: Michael Reid

*698. Pulitzer Fountain
    competition entry
    Grand Army Plaza
    Fifth Avenue and 58th Street
    New York, N.Y.
        not built
        begun: 1913
        cost: flat fee, $ 1,000

    The Puritan
    see Chapin, Chester W., Memorial, No. 190

699. Pyle, James Tolman
    additions and alterations to existing townhouse
    673 Fifth Avenue
    New York, N.Y.
        condition: demolished
        begun: June, 1895   built: 1896
        cost: $ 67,698

700. Pyle, James Tolman
     house, "Glen Alpin"
     Morristown, N.J.
        condition: extant
        begun: August, 1901   built: 1902-1903
        designer: White [B, K]
        cost: $ 94,489
        extant drawings: New-York Historical Society

*701. Pyne, Percy Rivington
     townhouse
     680 Park Avenue
     New York, N.Y.
        condition: extant
        begun: January, 1906   built: 1910-1912
        designer: McKim and Kendall [K]
        cost: $ 348,899
        extant drawings: New-York Historical Society

Q

*702. Quogue Episcopal Church
     Quogue Street
     Quogue, N.Y.
        condition: extant
        begun: June, 1884   built: 1884
        designer: White (?) with Sidney V. Stratton
        cost: $ 3,175

R

*703. Racquet and Tennis Club
     370 Park Avenue
     New York, N.Y.
        condition: extant
        begun: July, 1916   built: 1916-1919
        designer: Kendall (?)
        cost: $ 1,105,547
        extant drawings: New-York Historical Society

*704. Radcliffe College
     comprehensive planning
     Garden Street
     Cambridge, Mass.
        not built
        plan begun: February, 1897
        designer: McKim

128

*705. Radcliffe College
Gymnasium
10 Garden Street
Cambridge, Mass.
condition: extant
begun: April, 1897   built: 1898-1899
designer: McKim [K]
cost: $ 58,438
contractor: Norcross Brothers

*706. Ramona Industrial School for Indian Girls
Santa Fé, N.M.
begun: October, 1887   built: c. 1888
designer: White [B]
cost: unrecorded
extant drawings: New-York Historical Society

707. Recess Club   (club rooms)
60 Broadway
New York, N.Y.
begun: 1911   built: 1912
cost: $ 41,240

*708. Redmond, Geraldyn
house
701 Park Avenue (half of double house, see Villars, No.874)
New York, N.Y.
condition: demolished
begun: November, 1912   built: 1913-1915
designer: Kendall [K]
cost: $ 206,503

709. Redmond, Geraldyn
mausoleum
Tivoli, N.Y.
begun: September, 1917   built: 1917
cost: $ 1,044
extant drawings: New-York Historical Society

710. Reid, Michael
unspecified work
Mercer Street
New York, N.Y.
condition: demolished
begun: February, 1896   built: 1896
cost: c. $ 65,000, unsupervised
contractor: Michael Reid

711. Reid, Michael
        unspecified work
        3 Worth Street
        New York, N.Y.
            condition: demolished
            begun: February, 1896   built: 1896
            cost: c. $ 33,750, unsupervised
            contractor: Michael Reid

712. Reid, Michael
        unspecified work
        29th Street
        New York, N.Y.
            condition: demolished
            begun: February, 1896   built: 1896
            cost: c. $ 26,700
            contractor: Michael Reid

713. Reid, Michael
        unspecified work
        Eighth Avenue and 135th Street
        New York, N.Y.
            condition: demolished
            begun: June, 1897   built: 1897
            cost: c. $ 45,280, unsupervised
            contractor: Michael Reid

714. Reid, Michael
        unspecified commercial building
        93 Bowery
        New York, N.Y.
            condition: extant, extensively remodeled
            begun: June, 1898   built: 1898
            cost: c. $ 14,000, unsupervised
            contractor: Michael Reid

715. Reid, Whitelaw
        house, project
        Adirondack, N.Y.
            not built
            begun: February, 1910
            cost: est. $ 15,000

716. Reid, Whitelaw
        alterations to Villard house (see Villard, Henry, No. 869)
        451 Madison Avenue
        New York, N.Y.
            condition: extant
            begun: June, 1887   built: 1887-1889
            designer: White (?)
            cost: $ 30,979
                library mural panels, *Music* and *Drama*, by John La Farge
                rondel panel, *Reflection*, by George W. Breck
                panel, *Pavanne*, by Edwin Austin Abbey, 1895

717. Reid, Whitelaw
      additions and further additions to the Villard house
      451 Madison Avenue
      New York, N.Y.
         condition: partially extant
         begun: September, 1890   built: 1890-1892
         designer: White (?)
         cost: $ 33,330
                + 10,015
                  43,345

*718. Reid, Whitelaw
      library, further additions and alterations to Villard house
      New York, N.Y.
         condition: partially extant
         begun: November, 1909   built: 1910-1913
         designer: Kendall (?)
         cost: $ 446,153
         extant drawings: New-York Historical Society

719. Reid, Whitelaw
      house, "Ophir Farm"
      Purchase, N.Y.
         begun: June, 1890   built: 1890-1893
         cost: $ 101,442

720. Reid, Whitelaw
      additions to house, "Ophir Farm"
      Purchase, N.Y.
         begun: February, 1911   built: 1911-1913
         cost: $ 408,781
                + 580,108
                  988,889

*721. Rhode Island State Capitol
      90 Smith Street
      Providence, R.I.
         condition: extant
         begun: c. September, 1891 through 1894   built: 1894-1903
         designer: McKim and Mead [K]
         cost: $ 2,368,773
         contractor: Norcross Brothers
         extant drawings: New-York Historical Society

722. Riverdale Country School
      dormitory and houses
      Riverdale, N.Y.
         begun: January, 1917   built: 1918-1921
         cost: $ 252,072

723. Rives, George L.
      stable
      Newport, R.I.
         begun: December, 1892   built: 1893
         cost: $ 9,380

724. Roanoke Rapids Power Company
     United Industrial Company spinning mill
     Roanoke Rapids, N.C.
         condition: partially extant
         begun: c. November, 1894   built: 1895
         designer: White
         cost: flat fee, $ 228.75

*725. Roanoke Rapids Power Company
      c. 50 houses, free-standing and duplexes
         ("on cottages, grounds, etc., at Weldon, North Carolina")
      Roanoke Rapids, N.C.
         condition: partially extant
         begun: c. January, 1895   built: 1895
         designer: White
         cost: flat fee, $ 270.15

726. Roanoke Rapids Power Company
     Baptist Church
     Roanoke Rapids, N.C.
         condition: demolished
         begun: 1895   built: 1895
         designer: White
         cost: unrecorded, unsupervised

*727. Robb, J. Hampden
      house
      23 Park Avenue
      New York, N.Y.
         condition: extant
         begun: May, 1889   built: 1889-1891
         designer: White [LGW, B, K]
         cost: $ 111,940
               +   52,289
                  164,229

728. Robb, J. Hampden
     house, project
     Southampton, N.Y.
         not built
         begun: February, 1885
         cost: est. $ 15,000

729. Robbins, Daniel Cock
     house, project
     Skaneateles, N.Y.
         not built
         begun: September, 1883
         cost: est. $ 7,500

*730. Roberts, Lewis
"The Pocantico" hotel and adjacent cottages
Pocantico Hills, N.Y.
condition: demolished
begun: August, 1882   built: 1882-1883
cost: $ 30,000 hotel
          12,000 cottages (number unspecified, c. 10?)
extant drawings: New-York Historical Society (hotel only)

731. Robinson, Jeremiah P., jr.
house
Wakefield, R.I.
begun: July, 1883   built: 1883-1885
cost: c. $ 20,000

732. Rogers, Archibald
alterations to existing townhouse
340 Madison Avenue
New York, N.Y.
condition: demolished
begun: March, 1883   built: 1883
cost: $ 4,190

733. Rogers, George W.
unspecified work (residential ?)
Eleventh Avenue and 83rd Street
New York, N.Y.
not built
begun: January, 1886
cost: flat fee, $ 250

*734. Rollins, Philip A.
townhouse
28 E. 78th Street
New York, N.Y.
condition: extant
begun: c. December, 1899   built: 1900-1902
designer: McKim and Mead [K]
cost: $ 85,967
        + 16,793
        102,760
contractor: Michael Reid
extant drawings: New-York Historical Society

735. Roosevelt, Elliott
alterations to existing townhouse
29 E. 38th Street
New York, N.Y.
condition: demolished
begun: September, 1884   built: 1884
designer: in collaboration with Sidney V. Stratton
cost: $ 2,640

736. Root, Elihu
       house
       Clinton, N.Y.
          begun: September, 1912   built: 1915-1916
          cost: $ 19,842
          extant drawings: New-York Historical Society

*737. Root, Robert K.
       house
       650 Delaware Avenue
       Buffalo, N.Y.
          condition: demolished
          begun: July, 1894   built: 1895-1896
          designer: White [B]
          cost: $ 52,614
                + 6,693
                  59,307
          extant drawings: New-York Historical Society

738. Rowland, George
       house
       Greenwich, Conn.
          begun: May, 1893   built: 1893-1894
          cost: $ 10,312

*739. Royal Trust Company
       105 St. James Street
       Montreal, Quebec, Canada
          condition: extant
          begun: December, 1911   built: 1912-1914
          designer: Richardson [K]
          cost: $ 901,605

740. Russell, Henry E.
       house, project
       Adirondack, N.Y.
          not built
          begun: December, 1885
          cost: flat fee, $ 100

741. Russell, Henry E.
       stable
       E. 76th Street
       New York, N.Y.
          begun: May, 1892   built: 1892-1893
          cost: $ 15,620

*742. Russell, Mrs. Henry E.
       mausoleum
       Woodlawn Cemetery
       New York, N.Y.
          condition: extant
          begun: August, 1893   built: 1894
          cost: $ 25,531
          extant drawings: New-York Historical Society

*743. Russell, H. E. and C. B. Erwin
       hotel   (RussWin Hotel)
       35 W. Main Street
       New Britain, Conn.
          condition: extant, interior remodeled for New Britain
                    City Hall, see No. 560
          begun: July, 1883   built: 1884-1885
          designer: Joseph Morrill Wells [K]
          cost: $ 105,533

 744. Rutherford, Lewis M.
       monument
       no location given
          begun: July, 1902   built: 1902
          cost: flat fee, $ 250

S

*745. Saint Bartholomew's Church
          Cornelius Vanderbilt II Memorial Doors, facade remodeling
       Park Avenue and 51st Street
       New York, N.Y.
          condition: extant, moved from original location at
                    Madison Avenue and 44th Street
          begun: 1900   built: 1901-1903
          designer: White [LGW, B, K]
          cost: $ 133,996
          contractor: Michael Reid
          extant drawings: New-York Historical Society
             Sculpture supervised by Daniel Chester French
             Central Portal by Daniel Chester French and Andrew
                O'Connor
             North Portal (present) by Herbert Adams
             South Portal (present) by Philip Martiny

 746. Saint James' Church
          three memorial windows
             (James and Ann T. Clinch Memorial Window, Charles Clinch
             Memorial Window, and John L. and Sarah N. Smith Memorial
             Window)
       Smithtown, N.Y.
          condition: extant
          begun: 1895   built: 1895
          designer: White [LGW, B]

 747. Saint John the Divine Cathedral Church
          competition entry
          not built
          begun: 1889
          cost: flat fee, $ 500

748. Saint John's Church
      alterations in chancel
      16th and H Streets, NW
      Washington, D.C.
          condition: extant
          begun: May, 1919   built: 1919
          cost: $ 44,254
          extant drawings: New-York Historical Society

749. Saint Luke's Hospital
      Duluth, Minn.
          begun: February, 1919 built: 1919-1921
          cost: flat fee, $ 4,700

*750. Saint Marys Falls Canal Memorial Obelisk
      Sault Sainte Marie, Mich.
          condition: extant
          begun: July, 1905   built: c. 1907
          designer: McKim
          cost: flat fee, $ 250

*751. Saint Paul the Apostle, Church of
      (Church of the Paulist Fathers)
      altar and ciborium, alterations in chancel, side altars
      Columbus Avenue and 59th Street
      New York, N.Y.
          condition: extant
          begun: October, 1887   built: 1888-1890
          designer: White [LGW, B]
          cost: $ 26,418
          contractor: Batterson, See & Eisele (main altar)
                      Robert C. Fisher (side altars)
          extant drawings: New-York Historical Society
          Angels by Frederick MacMonnies
          Lamp by Philip Martiny

*752. Saint Paul's Church (for Charles E. Butler)
      Main and Church Streets
      Stockbridge, Mass.
          condition: extant
          begun: c. April, 1883   built: 1883-1885
          designer: McKim [K], baptistry by White
          cost: unrecorded, services donated
          contractor: John T. Tucker
              Angels in relief in baptistry by Louis Saint-Gaudens

753. Saint Paul's Church
      Dudley Field Memorial Window
      Stockbridge, Mass.
          condition: extant
          begun: 1885   built: 1885
          designer: in collaboration with Louis Comfort Tiffany
          contractor: Louis Comfort Tiffany

136

*754. Saint Peter's Church
        comprehensive plan, construction of Section A, choir, chapel,
            and vestries
        Miller Road and South Street
        Morristown, N.J.
            condition: extant
            begun: August, 1886   built: 1887-1890
            designer: McKim [K]
            cost: $ 71,679
                 + 11,012
                   ‾‾‾‾‾‾
                    82,691
            contractor: J. H. Sturgis & Co.
            extant drawings: New-York Historical Society
                Chapel window by Edwin Austin Abbey and Louis Comfort
                Tiffany, installed 1893

*755. Saint Peter's Church
        Section B, nave
        Morristown, N.J.
            condition: extant
            built: 1890-1892
            designer: McKim [K]
            cost: $ 43,258
            extant drawings: New-York Historical Society

*756. Saint Peter's Church
        Section C, tower
        Morristown, N.J.
            condition: extant
            begun: 1905   built: 1907-1908
            designer: McKim [K]
            cost: c. $ 60,000
            extant drawings: New-York Historical Society

        Saint Peter's Church, Baptistry
        see Kip, George C., No. 457

*757. Saint Peter's Rectory
        Miller Road and Maple Avenue
        Morristown, N.J.
            condition: extant
            begun: December, 1897   built: 1898-1899
            designer: McKim
            cost: $ 29,683
            extant drawings: New-York Historical Society

[Note: In addition to designing the church and rectory, the firm
also served as quasi-official architects for Saint Peter's, designing the World War memorial tablets; the Hudson Struck Memorial tablet, 1920; the vestibule; the communion rail gates, 1936; and the
sacristy.]

758. Saloman, William
      unspecified work
      104 E. 37th Street and 108 E. 40th Street
      New York, N.Y.
         condition: demolished
         begun: 1891   built: 1891
         cost: $ 19,917

759. Sampson, Edward C.
      alterations to existing townhouse
      10 W. 48th Street
      New York, N.Y.
         condition: demolished
         begun: December, 1883   built: 1883
         cost: $ 4,580

760. Sampson, Edward C.
      further alterations to existing townhouse
      New York, N.Y.
         condition: demolished
         begun: November, 1886   built: 1886
         cost: $ 2,815

761. Sampson and Proctor   (A. Sampson; A. Phimister Proctor)
      unspecified work (studios ?)
      168 W. 51st Street
      New York, N.Y.
         condition: demolished
         begun: 1911   built: 1912
         cost: $ 22,211

*762. Sanger, Henry
      house
      deForest Road
      Montauk Point, N.Y.
         condition: extant
         begun: May, 1882   built: 1882-1883
         cost: $ 10,095

*763. Satterlee, Herbert L. (for J. P. Morgan)
      townhouse
      37 E. 36th Street
      New York, N.Y.
         condition: demolished
         begun: May, 1903 (or 1902 ?)   built: 1903-1904
         designer: McKim
         cost: $ 130,153

764. Saunders, Emmett A.
     house
     404 Whitney Avenue
     New Haven, Conn.
        condition: demolished
        begun: January, 1894   built: 1894-1895
        cost: $ 35,387
        extant drawings: New-York Historical Society

765. Sealy, George
     house
     Galveston, Texas
        condition: extant
        begun: September, 1885   built: 1887-1891
        designer: White
        cost: $ 77,980
              + 22,020
              100,000

766. Sealy, Mrs. George
     monument
     Galveston, Texas
        condition: extant
        begun: May, 1904   built: 1904
        cost: flat fee, $ 300

*767. Second National Bank
     250 Fifth Avenue
     New York, N.Y.
        condition: extant
        begun: October, 1907   built: 1908
        designer: Richardson [K]
        cost: $ 262,885
        contractor: George A. Fuller
        extant drawings: New-York Historical Society

768. Second National Bank
     additions and alterations to bank building
     New York, N.Y.
        condition: extant
        begun: 1913   built: 1914
        cost: $ 79,875

*769. Selfridge, Admiral Thomas O., jr.
     house
     1867 Kalorama Avenue, NW
     Washington, D.C.
        condition: demolished
        begun: December, 1897   built: 1898-1899
        designer: McKim
        cost: $ 25,126

139

*770. Senate Park Commission (for U.S. Senate. District Committee)
comprehensive plan for Mall and park system improvement
Washington, D.C.
    period of work: May, 1901, to March, 1902
    designer and planner: McKim
    cost: expenses, $ 10,390
    extant drawings: Fine Arts Commission, National Archives

*771. Shaw, Colonel Robert Gould, Memorial
setting for bronze relief by Augustus Saint-Gaudens
Boston Common
Boston, Mass.
    condition: extant
    begun: 1890-1891 (figure begun 1881-1882)
    built: 1897
    designer: McKim [K], with Augustus Saint-Gaudens
    cost: $ 23,113, for setting only
    extant drawings: New-York Historical Society
                     Houghton Library, Harvard University

772. Sheldon, Frederic
unspecified work (interior alterations ?)
no location given
    begun: October, 1879   built: 1879 (?)
    designer: White
    cost: flat fee, $ 100

773. Shepard, Augustus D.
house
Fanwood, N.J.
    begun: May, 1886   built: 1886-1887
    cost: $ 33,005

*774. Shepard, Elliott Fitch
house, "Woodlea"
Scarborough, N.Y.
    begun: September, 1890   built: 1892-1895
    designer: White [B]; Mead [K]
    cost: $ 808,764

775. Shepard, Elliott Fitch
stables for Fifth Avenue Stage Lines
Madison and Park Avenues, 88th to 89th Streets
New York, N.Y.
    condition: demolished
    begun: July, 1889   built: 1889-1890
    cost: $ 123,540

*776. Sherman, General William Tecumseh, Memorial
    base and setting for bronze equestrian figure
      by Augustus Saint-Gaudens
    Grand Army Plaza
    New York, N.Y.
      condition: extant, moved sixteen feet south of
           original position
      begun: 1902 (figure begun 1892 and redone in 1897)
      built: 1902-1903
      designer: McKim with Augustus Saint-Gaudens
      cost: c. $ 30,000 for base and setting ($ 45,000 total)
      extant drawings: New-York Historical Society

*777. Sherman, William Watts
    library, alterations to house by H. H. Richardson
    Shepard Avenue
    Newport, R.I.
      condition: extant
      begun: August, 1881   built: 1881
      designer: White
      cost: $ 18,000

*778. Sherry, Louis
    casino, project
    Narragansett Pier, R.I.
      not built
      begun: April, 1894
      cost: est. $ 21,000

779. Sherry, Louis
    casino
    Narragansett Pier, R.I.
      condition: demolished
      begun: October, 1904   built: 1905
      cost: $ 65,972
      contractor: J. Bristow

780. Sherry, Louis
    cottages, two
    Narragansett Pier, R.I.
      condition: demolished
      begun: November, 1891   built: 1891
      cost: $ 14,000

*781. Sherry, Louis
    hotel, project
    London, England
      not built
      begun: April, 1902
      cost: unrecorded

782. Sherry, Louis
        mausoleum
        Woodlawn Cemetery
        New York, N.Y.
            condition: extant
            begun: April, 1906   built: 1906-1907
            cost: $ 7,500

783. Sherry, Louis
        restaurant and cottages
        Narragansett Pier, R.I.
            condition: demolished
            begun: January, 1888   built: 1888-1889
            cost: flat fee, $ 500

784. Sherry, Louis
        "Sherry's" restaurant, alterations
        Fifth Avenue and 37th Street
        New York, N.Y.
            condition: demolished
            begun: January, 1890   built: 1890
            cost: c. $ 25,000

*785. Sherry, Louis
        "Sherry's" restaurant and hotel
        Fifth Avenue and 44th Street
        New York, N.Y.
            condition: demolished
            begun: May, 1896   built: 1897-1898
            designer: White [B, K]
            cost: $ 1,322,611

786. Sherry, Louis
        "Sherry's" restaurant and hotel, addition
        New York, N.Y.
            condition: demolished
            begun: April, 1907   built: 1907
            cost: $ 60,625

*787. Shinnecock Hills Golf Club
        clubhouse
        North Road
        Shinnecock Hills, N.Y.
            condition: extant
            begun: March, 1892   built: 1895
            designer: White [B, K]
            cost: $ 7,445
            extant drawings: New-York Historical Society

*788. Shore Road Commission
        bridge, project
        Third Avenue and 68th Street
        New York, N.Y.
            not built
            begun: April, 1898
            cost: est. $ 50,000

*789. Short Hills Music Hall (Casino)   (for Stewart Hartshorn)
        The Crescent
        Short Hills, N.J.
            condition: extant
            begun: November, 1879   built: 1880
            designer: White
            cost: c. $ 9,000

*790. Skinner, Mrs. Frances L.
        house
        6 Red Cross Avenue
        Newport, R.I.
            condition: extant
            begun: April, 1882   built: 1882
            cost: $ 7,553

*791. *Slocum, General Henry W.*
        base for equestrian figure by Frederick MacMonnies
        Eastern Parkway, east of the Grand Army Plaza
        Brooklyn, N.Y.
            condition: extant, moved from Bedford Avenue, 1928
            begun: February, 1903   built: 1905
            designer: White with Frederick MacMonnies [LGW]
            cost: $ 9,800
            extant drawings: New-York Historical Society

792. Smith, Ann Marie, Monument
        monument
        Newport Cemetery
        Newport, R.I.
            condition: extant
            begun: 1887
            designer: White with Augustus and Louis Saint-Gaudens
            cost: unrecorded

143

793. Smith, W. W.
"on houses at Washington" (unspecified number)
Washington, Penna.
begun: June, 1884   built: 1884 (?)
cost: flat fee, $ 100

794. Soldiers' Monument (For Joseph W. Stickler)
Athens, Penna.
begun: July, 1900   built: 1900
cost: $ 8,150
extant drawings: New-York Historical Society

*795. State Savings Bank
Fort and Shelby Streets
Detroit, Mich.
condition: extant, enlarged
begun: January, 1898   built: 1899-1900
designer: White [LGW, B, K]
Donaldson & Meier, associate architects
cost: $ 291,290
contractor: Norcross Brothers
extant drawings: New-York Historical Society
lunette mural by Thomas W. Dewing

*796. State Street Exchange
competition entry
Boston, Mass.
not built
begun: c. September, 1887
cost: unrecorded, no fee

797. Sterling, John W.
mausoleum
Woodlawn Cemetery
New York, N.Y.
condition: extant
begun: August, 1910   built: 1910-1911
cost: $ 24,900

798. Stevens, Frederick W.
house
Newport, R.I.
begun: September, 1882   built: 1882
cost: $ 16,591

799. Stewart, D.
monument
Greenwood Cemetery
Brooklyn, N.Y.
condition: extant
begun: c. 1885
designer: White [B]
cost: unrecorded

800. Stier, Joseph F.
     commercial building, project
     5-11 Broadway
     New York, N.Y.
        not built
        begun: May, 1894
        cost: flat fee, $ 5,000

801. Stillman, James
     house
     Cornwall-on-Hudson, N.Y.
        begun: July, 1882   built: 1884
        designer: McKim with Frederick Law Olmsted

802. Stillman, James
     townhouse
     9 E. 72nd Street
     New York, N.Y.
        condition: demolished
        begun: June, 1900   built: 1903-1904
        designer: White [B]
        cost: $ 55,353

803. Stillman, James Alexander
     alterations in house, "Mondanne"
     Pocantico Hills, N.Y.
        begun: July, 1905   built: 1905-1907
        cost: $ 10,100

*804. Stockbridge Casino
      Stockbridge, Mass.
         condition: extant, moved
         begun: April, 1887   built: 1887
         cost: unrecorded
         extant drawings: New-York Historical Society

*805. Stokes, William E. D.
      townhouse
      2 W. 54th Street
      New York, N.Y.
         condition: demolished
         begun: July, 1898   built: 1898-1900
         designer: White (?)
         cost: $ 71,701
               + 28,738
               100,439
         extant drawings: New-York Historical Society

806. Stone, Mrs. Caroline
     house
     Llewellyn Park
     Orange, N.J.
        begun: June, 1886   built: 1886-1887
        cost: $ 11,450

145

Stranahan, James, Memorial
see Prospect Park, Stranahan, James, Memorial, No. 690

807. Street, William A.
house
Seabright, N.J.
begun: October, 1882   built: 1883
cost: $ 34,924
+   1,245
36,169

808. Strong, Ashbel W., and Samuel Chandler
project, unspecified building
Cleveland, Ohio
not built
begun: December, 1896
cost: $ 1,920, expenses

809. Strong, Charles S.
alterations to existing building
no location given
begun: January, 1882
cost: $ 3,840

810. Stuyvesant, A. Van Horne
alterations to existing house
Elberon, N.J.
condition: demolished
begun: 1886   built: 1886
cost: $ 4,985

*811. Swift, Edwin F.
townhouse
Hereford and Beacon Streets
Boston, Mass.
condition: demolished
begun: July, 1898   built: 1898-1899
cost: $ 196,178
extant drawings: New-York Historical Society

T

812. Taylor, George C.
     house and cottage
     Moriches, N.Y.
          begun: June, 1884   built: 1884 (?)
          cost: c. $ 30,000, unsupervised

*813. Taylor, Henry Augustus Coit
     house
     Annandale Road
     Newport, R.I.
          condition: demolished
          begun: July, 1882 (through September, 1884)
          built: 1885-1886
          designer: McKim [K]
          cost: $ 57,734
               + 8,048
                 65,782
          extant drawings: New-York Historical Society

*814. Taylor, Henry Augustus Coit
     mausoleum
     Woodlawn Cemetery
     New York, N.Y.
          condition: extant
          begun: March, 1900   built: 1900-1901
          designer: White [B]; McKim [K]
          cost: $ 137,040
          extant drawings: New-York Historical Society

*815. Taylor, Henry Augustus Coit
     townhouse
     3 E. 71st Street
     New York, N.Y.
          condition: demolished
          begun: April, 1892   built: 1894-1896
          designer: McKim [K]
          cost: $ 193,704
               + 82,029
                275,733
          extant drawings: New-York Historical Society

816. Taylor, Henry Augustus Coit
     alterations to townhouse
     New York, N.Y.
          condition: demolished
          begun: December, 1907   built: 1907
          cost: $ 2,007

147

*817. Taylor, Henry Augustus Coit
      townhouses (double house)
      2-4 E. 72nd Street
      New York, N.Y.
         condition: demolished
         begun: April, 1892   built: 1894-1896
         designer: McKim
         cost: $ 65,832
               + 18,696
                 84,528
         extant drawings: New-York Historical Society

      "The Tecumseh"
      see Pinchot, James W., No. 662

*818. Tesla, Nicola
      Wardenclyffe electrical broadcasting station
      Shoreham, N.Y.
         condition: partially extant
         begun: April, 1902   built: 1902
         designer: White
         cost: $ 1,168, expenses

819. Thaw, A. Blair
      house
      Sparkill, N.Y.
         begun: January, 1890   built: 1891-1892
         cost: $ 121,212
               + 17,129
                 138,341
         extant drawings: New-York Historical Society

820. Thomas, Dr. T. Gaillard
      "on houses on St. Ann's Avenue" (number unspecified)
      Bronx
      New York, N.Y.
         begun: May, 1886   built: 1886 (?)
         cost: c. $ 50,000

821. Thompson, Charles G.
      townhouse
      17 W. 36th Street
      New York, N.Y.
         condition: demolished
         begun: July, 1893   built: 1893-1894
         cost: $ 26,952
               + 18,587
                 45,539

822. Thurston, William R.
      unspecified work
      no location given
         begun: November, 1879
         cost: unrecorded

823. Thurston, William R., jr.
      alterations to house
      Morristown, N.J.
         condition: demolished
         begun: May, 1885   built: 1885
         cost: $ 6,100

*824. Tiffany, Charles Lewis
      triple house
      19 E. 72nd Street
      New York, N.Y.
         condition: demolished
         begun: April, 1882   built: 1883-1885
         designer: White [LGW, B, K]
         cost: c. $ 100,000
         extant drawings: New-York Historical Society

825. Tiffany, Charles Lewis
      alteration to house, porch
      New York, N.Y.
         condition: demolished
         begun: September, 1887   built: 1887
         cost: $ 3,881

*826. Tiffany & Company
      mercantile building and offices
      401 Fifth Avenue
      New York, N.Y.
         condition: extant
         begun: June, 1903   built: 1903-1906
         designer: White [LGW, B, K]
         cost: $ 2,061,737
         contractor: Charles T. Wills
         extant drawings: New-York Historical Society

827. Tiffany & Company
      addition to building
      391 Fifth Avenue
      New York, N.Y.
         condition: extant
         begun: February, 1909   built: 1909
         cost: $ 161,917

*828. Tiffany & Company
      stable (later garage)
      140 E. 41st Street
      New York, N.Y.
         condition: demolished
         begun: August, 1904   built: 1905
         designer: McKim (?)
         cost: $ 60,349

*829. Tilton, Samuel
        house
        Sunnyside Place
        Newport, R.I.
            condition: extant
            begun: November, 1880   built: 1881-1882
            designer: White
            cost: $ 13,000
                 + 3,000
                   16,000

        "Times Building"
        see Munsey Building, No. 542

830. Towle, Stevenson
        house
        Rye Neck, Rye, N.Y.
            begun: June, 1890   built: 1890-1891
            cost: $ 15,551
                 + 3,925
                   19,476

831. Tracy, Francis H.
        monument
        Forest Lawn Cemetery
        Buffalo, N.Y.
            condition: extant
            begun: 1888   built: c. 1888
            designer: White with Augustus Saint-Gaudens

*832. Trinity Church and Parish House   (for Mrs. Clarence Mackay)
        Northern Boulevard
        Roslyn, N.Y.
            condition: extant
            begun: November, 1905   built: 1906-1907
            designer: White, finished by Richardson [LGW, B, K]
            cost: $ 43,238 church
                 + 14,958 parish house
                   58,196
            contractor: G. A. Varney
            extant drawings: New-York Historical Society

833. Trinity School
        alterations
        Washington, Penna.
            begun: July, 1881   built: 1881
            cost: $ 12,500

834. Truesdell, George
        hotel, project
        Eckington Place
        Washington, D.C.
            not built
            begun: January, 1893
            cost: flat fee, $ 2,000

150

835. Tuckerman, Lucius
        alterations to existing townhouse
        41 W. 4th Street
        New York, N.Y.
            condition: demolished
            begun: March, 1881   built: 1881-1882
            cost: $ 1,745

*836. Tuckerman, Walter C.
        house
        Oyster Bay, N.Y.
            begun: July, 1882   built: 1882
            cost: $ 18,700
                 + 3,500
                  22,200

837. Tulane University
        plan for new buildings
        New Orleans, La.
            not built
            begun: March, 1892
            cost: flat fee, $ 200

838. Turnbull, Robert I.
        alterations to existing house
        Morristown, N.J.
            condition: demolished
            begun: July, 1885   built: 1885
            cost: $ 9,306
                 + 2,825
                  12,131
            contractor: Mead & Taft

839. Twombly, Hamilton McKown
        "Florham Farms," first phase
        farm house, hay barn, carriage house, engine house,
        water tower, dairy farm, training stables, garden
        and gardener's cottage, piggery
        Madison Avenue at Convent and Danforth Avenues
        Madison, N.J.
            condition: partially extant
            begun: June, 1890   built: 1891-1894
            designer: McKim and Mead [K]
            cost: $ 185,191
            contractor: various contractors:
                        James Clark & Co.
                        Smith & Fanning
                        Thomas J. Allen
                        and others

151

840. Twombly, Hamilton McKown
        "Florham Farms," second phase
        main house
        Madison, N.J.
            condition: extant
            begun: March, 1894   built: 1894-1897
            designer: McKim and Mead [K]
            cost: $ 417,096
                 +   60,440
                    477,536
            contractor: Norcross Brothers
            extant drawings: New-York Historical Society

841. Twombly, Hamilton McKown
        "Florham Farms," third phase
        stables
        Madison, N.J.
            condition: partially extant
            begun: January, 1895   built: 1896-1897
            cost: $ 97,662
            contractor: Norcross Brothers

842. Twombly, Hamilton McKown
        "Florham Farms," fourth phase
        lodge and entrance gates
        Madison, N.J.
            condition: extant
            begun: March, 1899   built: 1899
            cost: $ 25,042
            contractor: Reeve & Burr

843. Twombly, Hamilton McKown
        mausoleum
        Woodlawn Cemetery
        New York, N.Y.
            condition: extant
            begun: c. 1896   built: 1896
            designer: White [B]
            cost: unrecorded

844. Tyson, Mrs. George (Emily D.)
        house
        Hale Street
        Beverly, Mass.
            condition: partially extant
            begun: June, 1883   built: 1883
            cost: $ 23,115
                 +   4,847
                    27,962

U

845. Union Club
     alterations in existing club facilities
     Fifth Avenue and 21st Street
     New York, N.Y.
        condition: demolished
        begun: July, 1891   built: 1891-1892
        cost: $ 11,185

846. United Society of New Haven   (The Reverend Artemas J. Haynes)
     memorial tablets in United Church
     New Haven Green
     New Haven, Conn.
        condition: extant
        begun: March, 1911   built: 1911-1913
        cost: $ 1,030

*847. U.S. Army War College
      comprehensive plan and construction of barracks, houses,
        mess, and main building
      Fort Lesley J. McNair
      Washington, D.C.
        condition: extant
        begun: August, 1902   built: 1903-1908
        designer: McKim and Richardson [K]
        cost: $ 1,361,463, unsupervised
        contractor: U.S. Army Corps of Engineers
        extant drawings: U.S. Army War College
                         New-York Historical Society

848. U.S. Army War College
     Engineers' School
     Fort McNair
     Washington, D.C.
        condition: extant
        begun: August, 1912   built: 1912-1914
        cost: $ 114,879

849. U.S. Army War College
     laboratory
     Fort McNair
     Washington, D.C.
        condition: extant
        begun: 1918   built: 1918
        cost: flat fee, $ 600

*850. U.S. Coast Guard
      life-saving station
      Narragansett Pier, R.I.
        condition: extant
        begun: April, 1889   built: 1889
        cost: $ 8,450

*851. U.S. Custom House, New York City
            competition entry
            New York, N.Y.
                not built
                begun: 1900
                designer: McKim
                extant drawings: New-York Historical Society

 852. U.S. Immigration Station, Ellis Island, New York City
            competition entry
            New York, N.Y.
                not built
                begun: September, 1897
                designer: White and Whitney Warren

*853. U.S. Military Academy at West Point
            competition entry for comprehensive plan
            West Point, N.Y.
                not implemented
                begun: October, 1902
                designer: White
                cost: flat fee, $ 2,000
                extant drawings: New-York Historical Society

*854. U.S. Military Academy at West Point
            Battle Monument
            West Point, N.Y.
                condition: extant
                begun: July, 1891   built: 1891-1896
                designer: White [LGW, B, K]
                cost: $ 56,752
                extant drawings: New-York Historical Society
                    Victory, atop the column, by Frederick MacMonnies

*855. U.S. Military Academy at West Point
            Cullum Memorial Hall
            West Point, N.Y.
                condition: extant
                begun: November, 1893   built: 1895-1898
                designer: White [LGW, B, K]
                cost: $ 217,273
                contractor: Probst Construction Company
                extant drawings: New-York Historical Society

 856. U.S. Military Academy at West Point
            Officers' Mess Hall
            West Point, N.Y.
                condition: extant
                begun: June, 1900   built: 1902-1903
                designer: White
                cost: $ 102,929
                contractor: J. H. Parker

154

*857. U.S. Post Office, New York City
Eighth Avenue and Ninth Avenue, 31st to 33rd Streets
New York, N.Y.
    condition: extant
    begun: c. April, 1908   built: 1908-1913
    designer: Kendall [K]
    cost: $ 4,308,829
    extant drawings: New-York Historical Society

U.S. Senate. District Committee
see Senate Park Commission, No. 768

858. University Club
alterations in existing facilities
Madison Avenue and 26th Street
New York, N.Y.
    condition: demolished
    begun: July, 1889   built: 1889-1893
    designer: McKim (?)
    cost: $ 3,451
          + 10,316
             13,767

*859. University Club
new building
1 W. 54th Street
New York, N.Y.
    condition: extant
    begun: June, 1896   built: 1897-1900
    designer: McKim [K]
    cost: $ 1,108,541
    contractor: Charles T. Wills
        university seals on exterior walls by Kenyon Cox and
            Daniel Chester French
        authors' portraits on keystones by Charles N. Niehaus
        library vaults and panels by H. Siddons Mowbray,
            1902-1904

860. University Club
addition to club building
8 W. 55th Street
New York, N.Y.
    condition: extant
    begun: March, 1916   built: 1918-1920
    designer: Kendall (?)
    cost: $ 1,033,969

V

861. Van Cortlandt, Robert B.
     alterations to existing house
     Mount Kisco, N.Y.
          begun: January, 1902   built: 1902
          cost: $ 16,063

*862. Vanderbilt, Cornelius and William Kissam
     office building
     15 Beekman Street
     New York, N.Y.
          condition: extant
          begun: February, 1892   built: 1892-1893
          designer: McKim (?)
          cost: $ 387,241

863. Vanderbilt, Cornelius and William Kissam
     addition and alterations to office building
     15 Beekman Street
     New York, N.Y.
          condition: extant
          begun: 1917   built: 1917
          cost: $ 10,502

*864. Vanderbilt, Frederick William
     house
     Hyde Park, N.Y.
          condition: extant
          begun: May, 1895   built: 1896-1899
          designer: McKim with Mead
          cost: $ 427,057 house
                  94,409 interiors
                  42,377 barn, cottages, miscellaneous outbuildings
                 563,843
          extant drawings: New-York Historical Society
             interiors by Georges A. Glaenser and Ogden Codman with
                McKim, Mead & White
             Gold Room ceiling mural by Edward E. Simmons, 1897
             drawing room ceiling mural by H. Siddons Mowbray, 1897

*865. Vanderbilt, Mrs. William Kissam (Virginia)
     townhouse
     666 Fifth Avenue
     New York, N.Y.
          condition: demolished
          begun: May, 1904   built: 1905-1907
          designer: White [LGW, B, K]
          cost: $ 399,054
          contractor: Jacob & Young
          extant drawings: New-York Historical Society

866. Vanderbilt, Mrs. William Kissam (Virginia)
     alterations to townhouse
     666 Fifth Avenue
     New York, N.Y.
         condition: demolished
         begun: 1912   built: 1912
         cost: $ 12,700

*867. Vanderpoel, The Reverend Wynant
      house
      South and James Streets
      Morristown, N.J.
          condition: demolished
          begun: June, 1884   built: 1884-1885
          cost: $ 13,577
                   3,464
                  17,041
          extant drawings: New-York Historical Society

*868. Vassar College
      auditorium ("Students' Building")
      Poughkeepsie, N.Y.
          condition: extant
          begun: April, 1912   built: 1912-1914
          designer: Mead and Kendall [K]
          cost: $ 168,222
          extant drawings: New-York Historical Society

*869. Villard, Henry (Heinrich Hilgard)
      houses, Villard House Group (the Villard residence and
          five adjoining residences; see below)
      451-457 Madison Avenue (Villard house, 451 Madison Avenue)
      New York, N.Y.
          condition: extant
          begun: January, 1882   built: 1883-1885
          designer: White, McKim, details by Joseph Morrill Wells
                    [LGW, B, K]
          cost: $ 326,289 no. 451 and general work
                  260,845 interiors of no. 451
                  150,000 adjoining houses, shell only
                  737,134
              interiors by White, relief sculpture of zodiac
              clock by Augustus Saint-Gaudens

      [Note: The Villard residence was sold, 1885, to Whitelaw
      Reid, see No. 717; no. 453 was sold, 1883, to Artemas H.
      Holmes, see No. 401; no. 455 was sold, 1883, to Edward D.
      Adams, see No. 53; no. 457 and nos. 22 and 24 E. 51st
      Street were sold, 1883, to Harris C. Fahnestock, see Nos.
      284, 285, and 286.]

*870. Villard, Henry
       additions and alterations to existing house, "Thorwood"
       Dobbs Ferry, N.Y.
          condition: demolished
          begun: February, 1880   built: 1880
          cost: $ 14,750

 871. Villard, Henry
       further additions, "Thorwood"
       Dobbs Ferry, N.Y.
          condition: demolished
          begun: June, 1891   built: 1891-1892
          designer: White
          cost: $ 76,206
                   9,121
                  85,327

 872. Villard, Henry
       "on works other than on Madison Ave."
       (unspecified work, further additions to "Thorwood" ?)
          begun: January, 1883   built: 1882 (?)
          cost: $ 503
                 + 5,544
                    6,047

 873. Villars, The Countess de Laugier
       garage and other work
       Tivoli, N.Y.
          begun: April, 1916   built: 1916
          designer: Kendall (?)
          cost: $ 19,260
          extant drawings: New-York Historical Society

*874. Villars, The Countess de Laugier
       townhouse
       703 Park Avenue (half of double house, see Redmond, No. 708)
       New York, N.Y.
          condition: demolished
          begun: November, 1912   built: 1913-1915
          designer: Kendall [K]
          cost: $ 119,212
                 + 24,324
                   143,536

*875. Virginia, University of
       comprehensive plan for restoration of Rotunda and new
          academic buildings
       Charlottesville, Va.
          plan begun: January, 1896 (through March, 1896)
          built: 1896 through 1907
          condition: extant, Rotunda restored to Jefferson's plan
          designer: White [LGW, B, K]

876. Virginia, University of
     boiler house
     Charlottesville, Va.
        condition: demolished
        begun: January, 1896   built: 1896-1898
        cost: $ 8,500
        extant drawings: University of Virginia
                         New-York Historical Society

*877. Virginia, University of
     Cabell Hall (liberal arts)
     Charlottesville, Va.
        condition: extant
        begun: January, 1896   built: 1896-1898
        cost: $ 78,484
        extant drawings: University of Virginia
                         New-York Historical Society
             mural, *The School of Athens*, by G. W. Breck

*878. Virginia, University of
     Cocke Hall (mechanical engineering)
     Charlottesville, Va.
        condition: extant
        begun: January, 1896   built: 1896-1898
        cost: $ 39,460
        extant drawings: University of Virginia
                         New-York Historical Society

*879. Virginia, University of
     Garrett Hall refectory
     Charlottesville, Va.
        condition: extant
        begun: May, 1906   built: 1906-1907
        designer: White
        cost: c. $ 10,900

880. Virginia, University of
     law library, project
     Charlottesville, Va.
        not built
        begun: c. 1910
        extant drawings: New-York Historical Society (undated)

*881. Virginia, University of
     President's House, "Carr's Hill"
     Charlottesville, Va.
        condition: extant
        begun: 1912   built: 1913
        cost: $ 32,226
        extant drawings: University of Virginia
                         New-York Historical Society

*882.   Virginia, University of
             Rotunda, library   (Thomas Jefferson, 1817, 1821-1826)
             restoration with new rear wall and wings
          Charlottesville, Va.
             condition: extant, remodeled
             begun: January, 1896   built: 1898-1899
             cost: $ 109,058
             extant drawings: University of Virginia
                             New-York Historical Society

*883.   Virginia, University of
             Rouss Hall (physics)
          Charlottesville, Va.
             condition: extant
             begun: January, 1896   built: 1896-1898
             cost: $ 33,968
             extant drawings: University of Virginia
                             New-York Historical Society

W

884.   Walcott, A. F.
             alterations to existing townhouse
             46 E. 26th Street
          New York, N.Y.
             condition: demolished
             begun: August, 1892   built: 1892-1893
             cost: $ 30,685
                   + 14,865
                     45,550

        Walker Art Gallery
        see Bowdoin College, Walker Art Gallery, No. 137

885.   Wanamaker, Thomas B.
             alterations to existing townhouse
             1900 Rittenhouse Square
          Philadelphia, Penna.
             condition: demolished
             begun: January, 1902   built: 1902-1905
             designer: White
             cost: c. $ 60,550

*886.   Warder, Benjamin Head
             monument
             Rock Creek Cemetery
          Washington, D.C.
             condition: extant
             begun: c. 1894   built: 1894
             designer: White (?)
             cost: unrecorded

160

*887. Warren, George Henry
        office building
        Broadway and 20th Street
        New York, N.Y.
            condition: demolished
            begun: March, 1890   built: 1891
            designer: White (?)
            cost: $ 322,117

888. Washburn, W. D.
        house, project
        Minneapolis, Minn.
        not built
            begun: November, 1881
            cost: est. $ 50,000

889. Washington Memorial Arch (temporary)
        Fifth Avenue at Washington Square
        New York, N.Y.
            condition: demolished
            begun: c. February, 1889   built: 1889
            designer: White [B]
            cost: unrecorded

*890. Washington Memorial Arch (permanent)
        Washington Square
        New York, N.Y.
            condition: extant
            begun: 1889-1890   built: 1890-1892
            designer: White [B, K]
            cost: c. $ 125,000
            contractor: David H. King, jr.
                spandrel reliefs by Frederick MacMonnies, 1894-1895
                Washington in Peace, pier group, by A. Stirling
                    Calder, 1918
                Washington in War, pier group, by Hermon A. MacNiel,
                    1916

891. *Washington, George*
        base for bronze equestrian figure by Daniel Chester French
            and Edward C. Potter
        Place d'Iena
        Paris, France
            condition: extant
            begun: September, 1899   built: 1900
            designer: McKim and Daniel Chester French
            cost: $ 7,665, base only
            extant drawings: New-York Historical Society

161

892. Waterbury, James M.
        alterations to existing townhouse
        43 Fifth Avenue
        New York, N.Y.
            condition: demolished
            begun: February, 1883   built: 1883
            cost: $ 3,884

893. Waterbury, James M.
        house
        Baychester, N.Y.
            begun: March, 1885   built: 1885-1886
            cost: $ 11,523

894. Waterbury, James M.
        project, "for House in the South"
        no location given
            not built (?)
            begun: September, 1886
            designer: in collaboration with Sidney V. Stratton

895. Wells, Dr. William L.
        house
        New Rochelle, N.Y.
            begun: August, 1886   built: 1886-1887
            cost: $ 8,965
            contractor: Taylor & Elmslie

896. Westcott, Robert F.
        house
        Orange, N.J.
            begun: July, 1882   built: 1883
            cost: $ 8,633
                 + 3,158
                  11,791

897. Westcott, Robert F.
        project, "on cottages at Orange"
        Orange, N.J. (?)
            begun: January, 1884   built: (?)
            cost: flat fee, $ 250

898. Wetherill, Mrs. K. A.
        alterations to existing house
        St. James, N.Y.
            begun: June, 1894   built: 1895
            designer: White [B]
            cost: flat fee, $ 1,129

899. White, Horace
     alterations to existing townhouse
     51 E. 55th Street
     New York, N.Y.
        condition: demolished
        begun: August, 1880   built: 1881-1883
        cost: $ 7,142
             + 39,737
               46,879

*900. White, Horace
     house
     Ocean Avenue
     Elberon, N.J.
        condition: demolished
        begun: November, 1880   built: 1881
        cost: $ 25,810

901. White, James F.
     alterations to commercial building
     54 Worth Street
     New York, N.Y.
        condition: demolished
        begun: December, 1893   built: 1894
        cost: $ 6,821

*902. White, Stanford
     alterations, interiors, in existing townhouse
     121 E. 21st Street
     New York, N.Y.
        condition: demolished
        begun: 1884 et seq.   built: 1884 et seq.
        designer: White

*903. White, Stanford
     alterations and additions to existing house, "Box Hill"
     Moriches Road
     St. James, N.Y.
        condition: extant
        begun: 1892 et seq.   built: 1892 et seq.
        designer: White

*904. The White House
     restoration of public areas and first floor
     1600 Pennsylvania Avenue, NW
     Washington, D.C.
        condition: extant
        begun: April, 1902   built: July, 1902 to December, 1902
        designer: McKim [K]
        cost: $ 477,037
        contractor: Norcross Brothers
        extant drawings: New-York Historical Society

905. The White House
     Executive Office Wing addition
     1600 Pennsylvania Avenue, NW
     Washington, D.C.
        condition: extant, greatly remodeled
        begun: April, 1902   built: 1902-1903
        designer: McKim
        cost: $ 46,712
              + 9,213
              55,925
        contractor: Norcross Brothers
        extant drawings: New-York Historical Society

*906. White Star Steamship Company
      exposition pavilion
      World's Columbian Exposition
      Chicago, Ill.
         condition: demolished
         begun: July, 1892   built: 1892-1893
         cost: $ 16,889
         contractor: George A. Fuller

907. Whitney, Harry Payne
     additions and alterations to existing house
     Westbury, N.Y.
        begun: July, 1905   built: 1906-1908
        cost: $ 45,362

908. Whitney, Harry Payne
     further alterations to house
     Westbury, N.Y.
        begun: February, 1910   built: 1910
        cost: $ 7,425

909. Whitney, Henry M.
     project, "for houses in Brookline, Mass."
        not built (?)
        begun: June, 1890
        cost: est. $ 50,000

*910. Whitney, Payne (for Oliver H. Payne)
      townhouse (half of a double house; see J. C. Lyons, No. 476)
      972 Fifth Avenue
      New York, N.Y.
         condition: extant
         begun: May, 1902   built: 1902-1909
         designer: White [LGW, B, K]
         cost: $ 563,629
               + 428,311
               991,940
         extant drawings: New-York Historical Society

911. Whitney, Payne
      alterations to townhouse
      972 Fifth Avenue
      New York, N.Y.
        condition: extant
        begun: 1917   built: 1917-1918
        cost: $ 2,774

912. Whitney, Payne
      further alterations to townhouse
      972 Fifth Avenue
      New York, N.Y.
        condition: extant
        begun: 1918   built: 1918-1919
        cost: $ 4,776

913. Whitney, William Collins
      additions and alterations to existing townhouse
      2 W. 57th Street
      New York, N.Y.
        condition: demolished
        begun: October, 1889   built: 1889-1890
        designer: White (?)
        cost: $ 24,850
             + 25,290
               50,140

*914. Whitney, William Collins
      additions and alterations to existing townhouse
      871 Fifth Avenue
      New York, N.Y.
        condition: demolished
        begun: September, 1897   built: 1898-1902
        designer: White [LGW, B, K]
        cost: $ 931,068
        extant drawings: New-York Historical Society

915. Whitney, William Collins
      house
      Westbury, N.Y.
        condition: demolished
        begun: March, 1900   built: 1900-1902
        cost: $ 626,535
            + 206,652
            833,187

916. Whitney, William Collins
      trainer's cottage
      Sheepshead Bay, N.Y.
        begun: September, 1900   built: 1900
        cost: $ 11,888

*917. Whittemore, Harris
       house
       Church Street
       Naugatuck, Conn.
          condition: extant
          begun: February, 1901   built: 1901-1903
          cost: $ 45,954
          extant drawings: J. H. Whittemore Company,
             Naugatuck, Conn.

*918. Whittemore, Howard, Memorial Library
       public library (for John Howard Whittemore)
       Church and Divisions Streets
       Naugatuck, Conn.
          condition: extant, enlarged
          begun: November, 1891   built: 1892-1894
          cost: $ 55,987
          contractor: Norcross Brothers

*919. Whittemore, John Howard
       house
       Church Street
       Naugatuck, Conn.
          condition: partially extant
          begun: September, 1885   built: 1887-1890
          designer: White [B]; Mead [K]
          cost: $ 48,947
                + 17,509
                  66,456

*920. Whittemore, John Howard
       house and farm
       Middlebury, Conn.
          condition: extant
          begun: October, 1894   built: 1895-1896
          designer: White [B]
          cost: $ 28,074

[Note: John Howard Whittemore was also the client for the Naugatuck
Public School, the Naugatuck High School, the fountain on the Naugatuck Green, and "The Buckingham" in Waterbury, Connecticut. He
was also instrumental in bringing to the firm the commissions for
the Congregational Church and the Naugatuck National Bank in Naugatuck, and the passenger station of the New York, New Haven, and
Hartford Railroad in Waterbury. He also had the firm prepare
designs for a second bank and a new city hall in Naugatuck which
remained unbuilt. See Nos. 169, 243, 552, 553, 554, 555, 556, 557,
and 582.]

*921. Whittier, Charles A.
       townhouse
       270 Beacon Street
       Boston, Mass.
       condition: demolished
       begun: November, 1881   built: 1881-1883
       designer: McKim [K]
       cost: $ 77,992
           + 75,186
            153,178

922.   Wight, L. Allyn
       house
       Montclair, N.J.
       begun: October, 1891   built: 1891-1892
       cost: $ 14,734

923.   Wight, L. Allyn
       addition to house
       Montclair, N.J.
       begun: April, 1894   built: 1894
       cost: $ 3,708

924.   Wilgus, W. J.
       monuments, four
       Forest Lawn Cemetery
       Buffalo, N.Y.
       begun: April, 1919
       cost: $ 2,930
       extant drawings: New-York Historical Society

*925. Willard, Joseph E.
       house
       Monument Avenue
       Richmond, Va.
       begun: July, 1906   built: 1907-1910
       designer: supervised by Noland & Baskerville,
                 associate architects, Richmond
       cost: c. $ 71,400
       extant drawings: New-York Historical Society

926.   *William the Silent*
       project, base for figure by Daniel Chester French
       New York, N.Y.
       not built
       begun: January, 1895

*927.   Williams, Charles H.
        house
        690 Delaware Avenue
        Buffalo, N.Y.
            condition: extant
            begun: February, 1895   built: 1895-1896
            designer: White [B]
            cost: $ 66,700
                  + 18,294
                    84,994

*928.   Williams, George L.
        house
        672 Delaware Avenue
        Buffalo, N.Y.
            condition: extant
            begun: June, 1895   built: 1896-1899
            designer: White [B, K]
            cost: $ 127,859
                  + 44,018
                   171,877
            contractor: C. A. Rup

 929.   Williams, R. A.
        "on wall and gates"
        Philadelphia (Germantown), Penna.
            begun: November, 1880   built: 1880
            cost: flat fee, $ 50

*930.   Williams College
        Delta Psi Fraternity, Lamda Chapter
        Williamstown, Mass.
            condition: extant
            begun: January, 1884   built: 1884-1886
            designer: McKim (?)
            cost: $ 18,299

*931.   Winans, Ross R.
        house
        1217 St. Paul Street
        Baltimore, Md.
            condition: extant
            begun: February, 1882   built: 1882-1883
            designer: White [B, K]
            cost: $ 87,905
                  + 76,281
                   164,186
            decorative frieze by Thomas W. Dewing

932. Winans, Ross R.
    alterations to house
    1217 St. Paul Street
    Baltimore, Md.
       condition: extant
       begun: March, 1900   built: 1900
       cost: $ 1,465

933. Winslow, Edward
    house
    Great Neck, N.Y.
       begun: August, 1887   built: 1887-1889
       cost: $ 26,940
            +   4,399
              31,339

934. Winthrop, Robert Dudley
    house
    Westbury, N.Y.
       begun: July, 1897   built: 1897-1902
       cost: $ 69,558
            + 10,075
              79,633

*935. Wolfe, Catherine
    project, house
    Ochre Point
    Newport, R.I.
       not built
       begun: c. 1880-1881
       extant drawing: New-York Historical Society

    "Wolf's Head" Fraternity
    see Phelps Association, No. 658

*936. Womens' City Club
    alterations in the former P. H. Butler house, No. 176
    22 Park Avenue
    New York, N.Y.
       condition: demolished
       begun: 1904   built: 1905
       cost: unrecorded

937. Wood, John D.
    house
    Elberon, N.J.
       condition: demolished
       begun: August, 1880   built: 1880-1881
       designer: White
       cost: $ 16,825

938. Woodward, Colonel C. A.
       alterations to existing house
       Philadelphia (Germantown), Penna.
           begun: January, 1881   built: 1881
           cost: flat fee, $ 175

*939. World's Columbian Exposition
       Agriculture Building
       Chicago, Ill.
           condition: demolished
           begun: January, 1891   built: 1892-1893
           designer: McKim [K]
           cost: flat fee, $ 10,000
           extant drawings: New-York Historical Society
               sculpture by Philip Martiny
               pediment group, *Legend of Ceres*, by Larkin G. Mead
               Diana (original 18-foot version, atop dome) by
                   Augustus Saint-Gaudens

*940. Wylls, Ruth, Chapter, Daughters of the American Revolution
       fence and gate, John Haynes `Memorial
       Center Church
       Hartford, Conn.
           condition: extant
           begun: January, 1901   built: 1901-1902
           cost: $ 9,098
           extant drawings: New-York Historical Society

xYz

*941. Yandell, Charles R., & Company
       alterations to furniture and antique gallery
       140 Fifth Avenue
       New York, N.Y.
           condition: demolished
           begun: January, 1886   built: 1886-1887
           cost: $ 15,000

       "The Yosemite"
       see the New York Life Insurance Company, No. 581

942. *Young Faun with Heron* (*Boy with Heron*)
       fountain with bronze figure by Frederick MacMonnies
       on the grounds of the Joseph H. Choate house, "Naumkeag,"
       Stockbridge, Mass., No. 199.
           condition: extant
           begun: 1887   built: 1887
           designer: White [LGW, B] with Frederick MacMonnies
           cost: unrecorded

*943. Young Men's Christian Association
          Newburgh, N.Y.
               condition: demolished
               begun: November, 1882   built: 1883-1884
               cost: $ 15,000

*944. Young Men's Christian Association of the Oranges
          125 Main Street
          Orange, N.J.
               condition: extant, remodeled
               begun: May, 1901   built: 1901-1902
               cost: $ 54,077

ADDENDA

945. Chicago Public Library
          competition entry (invited but may not have entered)
          Chicago, Ill.
               not built
               begun (invited to enter): September, 1891

Boston Public Library

     Of all the buildings by McKim, Mead & White, perhaps the Boston
Public Library most fully embodies the union of the arts advocated by
the École des Beaux-Arts. McKim encouraged the Trustees and city of-
ficials to engage the best European and American artists, and while
the murals and sculpture are clearly subservient to the architecture,
each work is highly individualized and indicative of its creator.
This combination of individual expressions, with the classic sobriety
of the building itself, makes the Boston Public Library the high point
of the so-called American "Renaissance" of the public arts.

     Murals and wall decoration:

          Edwin Austin Abbey. *The Quest and Achievement of the Holy
          Grail*, mural in the Delivery Room; 1890-1902. Oil on can-
          vas, applied to the wall.

          John Elliott. *Triumph of Time*, ceiling mural in the Patent
          Room; 1892-1901. Oil on canvas, applied to the ceiling.

          Elmer E. Garnsey. Decoration of the Pompeiian Lobby; 1894.
          Fresco secco.

          John La Farge. Mural, project, for Bates Hall; studied c.
          1889-1893, but contract was cancelled.

171

Pierre-Cécile Puvis de Chavannes. *Les muses inspiratrices acclament le genie, messager de lumière*, main panel, with eight supplementary panels: *Pastoral Poetry, Dramatic Poetry, Epic Poetry, History, Astronomy, Philosophy, Chemistry*, and *Physics*; Grant Staircase; 1891/1893-1897. Oil on canvas, applied to the wall.

John Singer Sargent. *Judaism and Christianity* mural cycle, third floor hall, 1890-1916. Oil on canvas, applied to the wall.

Joseph Linden Smith. Decoration of the Venetian Lobby; 1894. Fresco secco.

James Abbott McNeill Whistler. Mural, project, "The Landing of Columbus," for Bates Hall; studied 1894-1895 but not completed.

Sculpture and ironwork:

Daniel Chester French. *Music, Poetry, Knowledge, Wisdom, Truth*, and *Romance*, door valves; 1894-1904. Solid castings, bronze relief.

Frederick MacMonnies. *Bacchante* (Julia Amory Appleton McKim Memorial), figure with marble base and fountain, courtyard; 1893-1896. Removed in 1896 and donated to the Metropolitan Museum of Art, New York, by McKim. Bronze.

Frederick MacMonnies. *Sir Henry Vane*, foyer; 1893. Bronze.

Domingo Mora. Spandrel rondels showing printers' insignias, exterior walls; c. 1890-1893. Granite relief.

Augustus Saint-Gaudens. Allegorical figures, project, at the Dartmouth Street entrance; 1888-1907, but not completed. Bronze castings now in the Freer Gallery of Art, Washington, D.C.

Augustus Saint-Gaudens. *Robert Charles Billings*, courtyard; 1901. Bronze relief.

Augustus Saint-Gaudens. Seals of the Commonwealth, the City, and the Library, over the Dartmouth Street entrance; 1894. Marble relief.

Louis Saint-Gaudens. Lions (Second and Twentieth Massachusetts Infantry Memorials), Grand Staircase; 1888-1892. Marble.

Snead & Company, Louisville, Ky. Lamps and iron gates at the Dartmouth Street entrance; c. 1893-1894. Iron and glass.

ID STANFORD WHITE
1879 – 1906

Stanford White designed a large number of picture frames, book covers, *objets d'art*, and other items which may be mentioned here but which need not be catalogued in the same way as the firm's buildings and designs have been. Since much of this material was never adequately recorded and has gone into private collections, a complete list cannot yet be properly assembled. This selective list, expanded from a similar list in Charles C. Baldwin, *Stanford White* (New York, 1931), is offered to suggest the wide range of White's work.

Book Covers

A Book of the Tile Club (Boston: Houghton, Mifflin and company, 1886).

The Century Dictionary, 24 vols. (New York, The Century Company, 1889-1891).

Eugene Field, *Field Flowers* (Chicago: A. L. Swift and Company, 1896), with marginal and full-page illustrations by White and others.

Oliver Goldsmith, *She Stoops to Conquer* (New York: Harper and brothers, 1887), with illustrations by Edwin Austin Abbey.

Robert Herrick, *Hesperides*, 2 vols. (Boston: Houghton, Mifflin and company, 1882).

John Keats, *Lamia* (Philadelphia: J. B. Lippincott Company, 1888), with illustrative designs by Will H. Low.

Old Songs (New York: Harper and brothers, 1889) with drawings by Edwin Austin Abbey and Alfred Parsons.

The Quiet Life (New York: Harper and brothers, 1890), certain verses by various hands; the motive set forth in a prologue and epilogue by Austin Dobson; the whole adorned with numerous drawings by Edwin Austin Abbey and Alfred Parsons.

Francis Hopkinson Smith, *Well Worn Roads of Spain, Holland & Italy* (Boston: Houghton, Mifflin and company, 1887).

Magazine Covers

    The Century Magazine, 1893

    Cosmopolitan, 1887

    The National Democratic Review, project, c. 1895

    Scribner's Magazine, 1887

Program and Booklet Covers

    Battles and Leaders of the Civil War (New York: The Century Company, c. 1893).

    The History of the Centennial Celebration of the Inauguration of George Washington as First President of the United States, ed. Clarence W. Bowen (New York: D. Appleton and Company, 1892).

    Program for the Dedication of the General Ulysses S. Grant Tomb, New York, N.Y., 1897.

Frames for Paintings, Selected

    for Thomas Wilmer Dewing:

    Mrs. Devereaux Emmett, c. 1885. Private collection.

    Elizabeth Freer with Kitten, c. 1892. Freer Gallery of Art.

    Hyman, 1885. Private collection.

    The Mandolin, n.d. National Collection of Fine Arts.

    Moonrise, c. 1893. Detroit Institute of Arts.

    The Necklace, c. 1907. National Collection of Fine Arts.

    The Recitation, 1891. Detroit Institute of Arts.

    Reclining Nude Figure of a Girl, n.d. National Collection of Fine Arts.

    for Abbott Handerson Thayer:

    The Virgin, 1893. Freer Gallery of Art.

for Dwight William Tryon

> *Autumn*, 1893. Detroit Institute of Arts, Frank J.
> Hecker Collection. [See Frank J. Hecker, No. 390.]

> *Springtime*, 1893. Detroit Institute of Arts, Frank J.
> Hecker Collection.

as well as other frames for George deForrest Brush,
William Merritt Chase, and Edward Simmons.

Frames for Relief Sculpture by Augustus Saint-Gaudens

> *Charles Stewart and Lawrence Smith Butler* (the children
> of Prescott Hall Butler), 1880-1881. Bronze.
> Private Collection.

> Robert Louis Stevenson Memorial, 1900-1905. Bronze.
> St. Giles Cathedral, Edinburgh, Scotland.

> *Bessie Smith (Mrs. Stanford) White*, 1884. Marble.
> Private Collection.

Miscellaneous

> Georgiana May Stowe Allen Memorial Tablet, 1890. Marble.
> St. Paul's Church, Stockbridge, Mass. Carved by
> Attilio Piccirilli.

fountains in collaboration with Janet Scudder.

jewelry for members of the White and Smith families.

Tarrytown drinking fountain, Tarrytown, N.Y., c. 1895.

yachting cups for Tiffany & Company.

collaborated in the design for the Veterans' Room and Library
of the Seventh Regiment Armory, Park Avenue and 67th Street,
New York, 1879-1880, executed by Louis Comfort Tiffany and
the Associated Artists. White's particular contribution is
said to have been the balcony of the Library.

II SUMMARY OF CONTRACTS

The figures for contracts, drawings, and commissions given here are reproduced from a table compiled by McKim, Mead & White auditors over a period of years and now preserved by Walker O. Cain and Associates, New York. The totals may not agree absolutely with the fragmentary information regarding contracts and commissions found throughout the Bill Books.

There are no comparable figures for the years 1878, 1879, or for 1919 or 1920.

Dollar values are not constant; rough comparisons may be made by using the indices in Part III.

The figures are grouped corresponding to the major periods into which the firm's work can be divided according to stylistic changes and development: early work, 1879-1886; synthesis, 1887-1893; economic depression and war, 1894-1899; maturity, 1900-1909; transition as the younger partners take over, 1910-1919.

	CONTRACTS	DRAWINGS	COMMISSIONS
1880	$ 176,533.62	$ 3,531.15	$ 8,014.22
1881	372,809.06	9,529.61	20,188.88
1882	313,547.05	11,126.62	29,241.55
1883	826,566.98	20,240.52	71,534.65
1884	758,914.29	15,626.12	41,554.12
1885	1,618,389.17	29,548.21	99,725.97
1886	406,244.36	6,542.48	22,755.35
1887	821,028.58	16,237.25	38,378.69
1888	913,161.61	21,208.12	56,905.60
1889	789,655.35	21,657.25	45,773.75
1890	5,604,615.28	75,505.52	257,438.12
1891	3,929,052.79	67,358.75	195,026.55
1892	1,349,878.63	25,480.08	47,203.70
1893	1,598,071.18	39,658.64	94,213.97
1894	3,616,612.52	74,755.29	191,937.36
1895	1,626,821.98	34,660.80	90,893.21
1896	3,641,471.04	71,473.27	154,758.16
1897	3,535,552.12	58,030.71	180,288.74
1898	7,935,126.90	213,124.30	397,342.30
1899	1,432,164.02	43,893.62	76,300.43

	CONTRACTS	DRAWINGS	COMMISSIONS
1900	$ 3,248,269.75	$ 97,160.02	$ 220,846.58
1901	2,502,051.52	63,580.02	138,447.50
1902	3,345,479.62	91,068.38	201,025.85
1903	4,457,900.00	120,449.76	262,141.76
1904	2,480,424.01	54,959.39	127,451.96
1905	2,875,390.59	78,732.02	150,364.77
1906	6,518,271.68	139,370.36	399,577.18
1907	3,115,949.79	78,359.05	174,583.35
1908	2,725,594.71	48,652.33	117,036.75
1909	5,110,433.59	145,504.08	371,199.00
1910	5,885,595.84	246,370.53	321,204.99
1911	11,907,392.25	311,599.55	616,247.07
1912	3,684,369.75	155,327.62	305,828.19
1913	12,233,289.15	373,266.28	698,037.75
1914	10,472,730.54	481,193.33	648,720.68
1915	2,446,033.92	73,729.94	141,403.63
1916	1,512,298.95	43,164.03	80,784.39
1917	5,816,281.83	123,849.44	331,504.73
1918	1,935,831.33	59,220.15	94,772.99

TOTALS
1880-1918 $133,539,605.35 $3,647,743.59 $7,522,653.56

III BUILDING COST INDEX

1870 — 1977

The cost index figures given here are meant solely for making comparisons between years; they do not reflect actual replacement or restoration costs of late nineteenth-century construction. They do reveal clearly, however, how much building costs have risen in the past century. Because of this sharp economic change, as well as other factors, it is now largely impossible to match the uniformly high quality of workmanship and material found in the work of McKim, Mead & White.

The index figures are derived from two sources:

1870-1902: from Miles L. Colean and Robinson Newcomb, *Stabliz-ing Construction* (New York, 1952), Appendix N, Table 4, 238-240, based on original indexes prepared by Riggleman.

1903-1977: from *Engineering News-Record* 188 (March 23, 1972), 56-57. For a detailed explanation of this index see "News Record Indexes: History and Use," *Engineering News Record* 143 (September 1, 1949), 398-431. The index is based on wages for unskilled labor and prices of lumber, cement, and steel.

Because the index was started in 1921 to study the rise in construction costs during the First World War, the base year was fixed as 1913 (1913 = 100), but the figures given here have been recomputed according to a new base (1885 = 100) on the assumption that this was the best year for McKim, Mead & White before the slump of the late 1880s and the depression of the 1890s. 1885 may well have been their bench mark. The new figures were determined by this formula:

$$\text{Index}_{new} = \frac{\text{Index}_{old}}{73.1_{\text{index for 1885 on old base}} \div 100} = \text{Index}_{old} \cdot 1.3680$$

181

BUILDING CONSTRUCTION COST INDEX, 1870 - 1977

(Base Year, 1885 = 100)

1870 130.67	1895 95.49	1920 343.75
1871 135.98	1896 93.43	
1872 135.71	1897 90.97	1927 282.14
1873 132.70	1898 92.34	
1874 123.39	1899 101.78	1932 214.73
1875 112.18	1900 109.30	1941 352.73
1876 108.07	1901 114.36	
1877 100.68	1902 114.64	1946 473.38
1878 95.35	1903 128.46	
1879 92.07	1904 119.56	1950 697.16
1880 100.14	1905 123.87	1955 902.50
1881 106.16	1906 130.10	
1882 111.49	1907 137.55	1960 1126.62
1883 112.04	1908 132.97	
1884 100.27	1909 124.38	1965 1328.63
1885 100.00	1910 131.78	1970 1896.54
1886 106.84	1911 127.81	
1887 106.43	1912 124.08	1975 3150.23
1888 102.87	1913 136.79	
1889 103.01	1914 121.15	1977 3625.75 September
1890 100.27	1915 126.65	
1891 96.99	1916 177.27	
1892 96.99	1917 247.94	
1893 97.26	1918 258.83	
1894 94.67	1919 271.44	

BIBLIOGRAPHY

Archives

New-York Historical Society.

The most important source of information is the McKim,
Mead & White Archive deposited in the Map and Print Collection,
New-York Historical Society, New York. This consists of various financial records, journals, photographic albums, scrapbooks, over 1000 file boxes of correspondence, and more than
500 tubes of drawings. This mass of material covers the years
1879 through 1948. The most important items include:

Bill Books, 1878-1947, 17 volumes.

Cash Books, 1894-1944, 10 volumes.

Contract Books, 1903-1930, 8 volumes.

Journals, 1882-1942, 9 volumes.

Payments to Engineers, 1917-1931, 1 volume.

Scrapbook, Clippings and Newspaper Notices, 1875-1888,
1 volume.

Scrapbook, Bank of Montreal, photographs, 1 volume.

Scrapbook, E. D. Adams house, "Rohallion," photographs,
1 volume.

Scrapbook, H. B. Hollins house, photographs, 1 volume.

Scrapbook, H. W. Poor house, photographs, 1 volume.

Scrapbook, H. Villard house, photographs, 1 volume.

Scrapbook, S. White house, photographs, 1 volume.

Scrapbook, miscellaneous residences, buildings, photographs,
1 volume.

Scrapbook, Senate Park Commission, photographs of models
and drawings, 1 volume.

Amherst College. Rare Book Room, William R. Mead Collection, consisting of about forty letters. A small portion of the firm's
original library was donated to Amherst and is now dispersed
in the Amherst College Library.

Art Institute of Chicago. Burnham Architectural Library. Burnham
Collection: letterbook containing correspondence regarding
the World's Columbian Exposition; microfilmed drawings of the
Lathrop and Blair houses; Tallmadge Holograph Collection.

Boston Public Library. Trustees' Records: Trustees' files and
records; minutes of Trustees' meetings; Annual Reports.

Columbia University. Avery Architectural Library. McKim, Mead &
White Collection. (Gift of James Kellum Smith and Amherst
College, 1963): Scrapbook 1, Brooklyn Institute (Brooklyn Museum); Scrapbook 2, World's Columbian Exposition; Scrapbook 3,
Municipal Building; Scrapbook 4, Office Work, clippings; Scrap-
book 5, Office Work, clippings; Scrapbook 6, Photographs of
Renderings; Scrapbook 7, Eastman School of Music, 1922; Scrap-
book 8, Senate Park Commission; Scrapbook 9, William C. Whitney
house; Scrapbook 10, World's Columbian Exposition; Scrapbook 11,
Arlington Memorial Bridge; Scrapbooks 12 through 14, Miscella-
neous office work, 1927-1934. (Gift of Walker O. Cain, 1974):
Album I, Hotel Pennsylvania; Album II, Pennsylvania Station;
Album III, University Club; Album IV, The White House; Album V,
University of Virginia, Bank of Montreal, New York Public Library
Branches; Album VI, Bank of Buffalo; Album VII, Charles T. Bar-
ney house; Album VIII, John Innes Hane house; Album IX, Payne
Whitney house; Album X, Miscellaneous; Album XI, Urban houses;
Album XII and XIII, Photographs of Renderings; Album XIV, McKim's
European photographs; Album XV, Greek architecture; Album XVI
and XVII, Italian Gardens; Album XVIII, Miscellaneous photographs.
Miscellaneous: McKim sketches; Photographs; Birch Burdette Long
renderings of White's major designs. See complete catalogue
at the Avery Library.

Harvard University. Houghton Library. Correspondence of James Miller
McKim, Henry Villard, and between C. F. McKim and Charles Eliot.

Library of Congress. Manuscript Division. Charles F. McKim Collection: 14 file boxes containing diary, original and typescript
copies of correspondence, 1863-1870; McKim's office letterbooks,
1891-1909; Reports of Clerk of the Works, Boston Public Library.

Library of Congress. Manuscript Division. Charles Moore Collection: drafts of *The Life and Times of Charles Follen McKim*, with extracts from Bill Books and McKim letterbooks; other miscellaneous material.

Library of Congress. Manuscript Division. Frederick Law Olmsted Collection.

Museum of the City of New York. Photographic Archives: major collection of photographs, c. 1000 negatives, largely post-1892.

Newport Historical Society. Library and Archives: miscellaneous material relating to early work, 1874-1890.

New-York Historical Society. Library; Manuscript Division. Richard Grant White and Stanford White Collections: varied personal correspondence; S. White's correspondence largely confined to letters to and from artists (S. White correspondence available on microfilm).

New York Public Library. Manuscript Room. Charles F. McKim and Margaret McKim Maloney Collection: c. 150 letters between McKim and his family, 1860-1880; miscellaneous letters relating to office business and personal life.

Walker O. Cain and Associates, New York. Various scrapbooks of buildings types, with finished buildings and projects, c. 1890-1930; portions of the original firm library; financial records and personnel records.

White family. St. James, Smithtown, and New York, N.Y.
Laura Chanler White (Mrs. Lawrence Grant White): various memorabilia, personal photographs.
Frederick Lawrence Peter White: various renderings and published materials.
Robert White: watercolors by Stanford White, scrapbooks of White's letters form Europe, 1878-1879.
Ann White Buttrick: published material, scrapbooks, a small portion of the original firm library.

Adams, Adeline. *Daniel Chester French, Sculptor.* Boston, 1932.

Adams, Adeline. *The Spirit of American Sculpture.* New York, 1929.

Armstrong, David Maitland. *Day Before Yesterday, Reminiscences of a Varied Life.* New York, 1920.

Cortissoz, Royal. *American Artists.* New York, 1923.

Cortissoz, Royal. "An American Sculptor, Frederick MacMonnies." *The Studio* 6 (October, 1895), 17-26.

Cortissoz, Royal. *Art and Common Sense.* New York, 1913.

Cortissoz, Royal. *Augustus Saint-Gaudens.* Boston, 1907.

Cortissoz, Royal. *John LaFarge, A Memoir and a Study.* Boston, 1911.

Cortissoz, Royal. *The Painter's Craft.* New York, 1930.

Craven, Wayne. *Sculpture in America.* New York, 1968.

Cresson, Margaret French. *Journey Into Fame: The Life of Daniel Chester French.* Cambridge, Mass., 1947.

Dorr, Charles H. "A Sculptor of Monumental Architecture." *Architectural Record* 33 (June, 1913), 518-532.

Dryfhout, John. *Augustus Saint-Gaudens; The Portrait Reliefs.* Washington, D.C., 1969.

Fairman, Charles. *Art and Artists of the Capitol.* Washington, D.C., 1917.

French, Mrs. Daniel Chester. *Memories of a Sculptor's Wife.* Boston, 1928.

Low, Will H. *A Chronicle of Friendships.* New York, 1908.

McSpadden, J. Walker. *Famous Sculptors of America.* New York, 1924.

Robbins, Daniel. "Statues to Sculpture: From the Nineties to the Thirties." *200 Years of American Sculpture.* New York, 1976.

Saint-Gaudens, Augustus. *The Reminiscences of Augustus Saint-Gaudens.* 2 vols. New York, 1913.

Strother, French. "Frederick MacMonnies, Sculptor." *The World's Work* 11 (December, 1905), 6965-6981.

Taft, Loredo. *The History of American Sculpture*. rev. ed. New York, 1924.

Tharp, Louise Hall. *Saint-Gaudens and the Gilded Era*. Boston, 1969.

Planning and Landscape Architecture

Baker, John Cordis. *American Country Homes and Their Gardens*. Philadelphia, 1906.

Fabos, Julius G., Gordon T. Milde, and V. Michael Weinmayr. *Frederick Law Olmsted, sr., Founder of Landscape Architecture in America*. Amherst, Mass., 1968.

Fein, Albert. *Frederick Law Olmsted and the American Environmental Tradition*. New York, 1972.

Ferree, Barr. *American Estates and Gardens*. New York, 1904.

Newton, Norman. *Design on the Land: The Development of Landscape Architecture*. Cambridge, Mass., 1971.

Olmsted, Frederick Law, jr., and Theodora Kimball. *Frederick Law Olmsted, Landscape Architect, 1822-1903*. 2 vols. New York, 1922.

Reps, John W. *The Making of Urban America*. Princeton, 1965.

Roper, Laura Wood. *FLO, A Biography of Frederick Law Olmsted*. Baltimore, 1973.

Tunnard, Christopher, and Henry Hope Reed. *American Skyline*. Boston, 1955.

Tunnard, Christopher. *The City of Man*. rev. ed. New York, 1970.

Tunnard, Christopher. *The Modern American City*. New York, 1968.

American Architecture

Andrews, Wayne. *Architecture in New York: A Photographic History.* New York, 1969.

Andrews, Wayne. *Architecture in America: A Photographic History.* New York, 1960.

Andrews, Wayne. *Architecture, Ambitions, and Americans: A Social History of American Architecture.* New York, 1964.

Blackshaw, Randall. "The New New York." *Century Magazine* 64 (August, 1902), 493-513.

Brown, Glenn. *1860-1930: Memories; A Winning Crusade to Revive George Washington's Vision of a Capitol City.* Washington, D.C., 1931.

Burchard, John, and Albert Bush-Brown. *The Architecture of America; A Social and Cultural History.* Boston, 1961.

Bush-Brown, Harold. *Beaux-Arts to Bauhaus and Beyond.* New York, 1976.

Cook, Clarence. "Architecture in America." *North American Review* 135 (September, 1882), 243-252.

Cram, Ralph Adams. *My Life in Architecture.* Boston, 1936.

Downing, Antoinette F., and Vincent Scully. *The Architectural Heritage of Newport, Rhode Island.* 2nd ed. New York, 1967.

Eaton, Leonard K. *American Architecture Comes of Age.* Cambridge, Mass., 1972.

Edgell, G. H. *The American Architecture of To-Day.* New York, 1928.

Hamlin, A. D. F. "Twenty-five Years of American Architecture." *Architectural Record* 40 (July, 1916), 1-14.

Hamlin, A. D. F. "The Influence of the École des Beaux-Arts on our Architectural Education." *Architectural Record* 23 (April, 1908), 241-247.

Hamlin, Talbot. *The American Spirit in Architecture.* New Haven, 1926.

Hines, Thomas S. *Burnham of Chicago.* New York, 1974.

Hitchcock, Henry-Russell. *Architecture: Nineteenth and Twentieth Centuries.* 3rd ed. Baltimore, 1968.

Hitchcock, Henry-Russell. *The Architecture of H. H. Richardson and His Times*. rev. ed. Cambridge, Mass., 1966.

Hitchcock, Henry-Russell. "Frank Lloyd Wright and the Academic Tradition of the Early Eighteen-Nineties." *Warburg and Courtauld Institute Journal* 7 (1944), 46-63.

Kaufmann, Edgar, jr., ed. *The Rise of an American Architecture*. New York, 1970.

Kimball, S. Fiske. *American Architecture*. Indianapolis, 1928.

Kidney, Walter C. "Another Look at Eclecticism." *Progressive Architecture* 48 (September, 1967), 122 ff.

Kidney, Walter C. *The Architecture of Choice; Eclecticism in America, 1880-1930*. New York, 1974.

Lancaster, Clay. *The Japanese Influence in America*. New York, 1963.

Lewis, Dudley Arnold. "Evaluations of American Architecture by European Critics, 1875-1900." Doctoral dissertation, University of Wisconsin, 1962.

Longfellow, W. P. P. "The Course of American Architecture." *New Princeton Review* 3 (March, 1887), 200-211.

Magonigle, H. Van Buren. "A Half Century of Architecture." *Pencil Points* 14 and 15 (November, 1933, through November, 1934), a series of seven articles.

Meeks, Carroll L. V. "Creative Eclecticism." *Journal, Society of Architectural Historians* 11 (December, 1953), 15-18.

Meeks, Carroll L. V. "Picturesque Eclecticism." *Art Bulletin* 32 (September, 1950), 226-235.

Meeks, Carroll L. V. *The Railroad Station*. New Haven, 1956.

Meeks, Carroll L. V. "Wright's Eastern Seaboard Contemporaries: Creative Eclecticism in the United States around 1900." *Problems of the 19th & the 20th Centuries; Studies in Western Art*. Acts of the Twentieth International Congress of the History of Art. 4 vols. Princeton, 1963. 4:64-77.

Moore, Charles. *Daniel H. Burnham, Architect, Planner of Cities*. 2 vols. Boston, 1921.

O'Gorman, James F. *The Architecture of Frank Furness*. Philadelphia, 1973.

O'Gorman, James F. *Henry Hobson Richardson and His Office: Selected Drawings*. Cambridge, Mass., 1974.

Platt, Frederick. *America's Gilded Age: Its Architecture and Decoration*. Cranbury, N.J., 1976.

Schuyler, Montgomery. *American Architecture and Other Writings*. W. H. Jordy and R. Coe, eds. 2 vols. Cambridge, Mass., 1961.

Schuyler, Montgomery. "Schools of Architecture and the Paris School." *Scribner's Magazine* 24 (December, 1898), 765-766.

Schuyler, Montgomery. "The Work of Charles C. Haight." *Architectural Record,* Great American Architects Series, July, 1899.

Schuyler, Montgomery. "The Works of Cram, Goodhue and Ferguson: A Record of the Firm's Representative Structures, 1892-1910." *Architectural Record* 29 (January, 1911), 1-112.

Sturgis, Russell. "Building of the Modern City House." *Harper's Magazine* 98 (March, 1899), 579-594, and (April, 1899), 810-822.

Sturgis, Russell. "A Critique of the Works of Bruce Price." *Architectural Record,* Great American Architects Series, June, 1899.

Sturgis, Russell. "A Critique of the Works of Shepley, Rutan & Coolidge and Peabody & Stearns." *Architectural Record,* Great American Architects Series, June, 1896.

Sturgis, Russell. "Good Things in Modern Architecture." *Architectural Record* 8 (July-September, 1898), 92-110.

Sturgis, Russell. "How to Beautify the City." *Scribner's Magazine* 33 (April, 1903), 509-512.

Sturgis, Russell. "Modern Architecture." *North American Review* 112 (January, 1871), 160-177, and (April, 1871), 370-391.

Sturgis, Russell. "A Review of the Work of George B. Post." *Architectural Record,* Great American Architects Series, June, 1898.

Sturgis, Russell. "Schools of Architecture and the Paris School." *Scribner's Magazine* 24 (December, 1898), 767-768.

Sturgis, Russell. "The Warehouse and Factory in Architecture." *Architectural Record* 15 (January, 1904), 1-17, and (February, 1904), 122-133.

Sturgis, Russell. "The True Education of an Architect."
Atlantic Monthly 81 (February, 1898), 246-255.

Scully, Vincent. *American Architecture and Urbanism.* New
York, 1969.

Scully, Vincent. *The Shingle Style.* New Haven, 1955.

Scully, Vincent. *The Shingle Style Today or The Historian's
Revenge.* New York, 1974.

Tallmadge, Thomas E. *The Story of Architecture in America.*
New York, 1927.

Valentine, Lucia and Alan. *The American Academy in Rome,
1894-1969.* Charlottesville, Va., 1973.

Van Brunt, Henry. *Architecture and Society: Selected Essays
of Henry Van Brunt.* William Coles, ed. Cambridge, Mass.,
1969.

Van Rensselaer, Mariana Griswold. "Recent Architecture in
America." *Century Magazine* 28 through 32 (May, 1884, through
July, 1886), a series of nine articles on contemporary
American architecture of various types.

Wharton, Edith, and Ogden Codman. *The Decoration of Houses.*
New York, 1897.

Wight, Peter Bonnett. "Reminiscences of Russell Sturgis."
Architectural Record 26 (August, 1909), 123-131.

"The Works of Messrs. Carrère & Hastings." *Architectural
Record* 27 (January, 1910), 1-121, 122-128.

Charles Follen McKim

Honors:

    M.A., Harvard, 1890

    M.A., Bowdoin, 1894

    LL.D., University of Pennsylvania, 1909

    Gold Medal, Paris Exposition, 1900

    Royal Gold Medal, Royal Institute of British Architects, 1903

    Gold Medal, American Institute of Architects, 1909

    Fellow, American Institute of Architects, 1877

    President, American Institute of Architects, 1902-1903

Academician, American Academy of Arts and Letters

Academician, National Academy of Design

Academia de San Luca, Rome

Obituary Notices:

American Architect and Building News 96 (September 22, 1909) 115.

Quarterly Bulletin, American Institute of Architects 10 (October, 1909), 222-224.

Architects' and Builders' Magazine 10 (November, 1909), 41-48.

Architectural Record 26 (November, 1909), 381-382.

Architecture 20 (December, 1909), 189.

Current Literature 47 (November, 1909), 522-527.

Harper's Weekly 53 (October 2, 1909), 31.

Nation 89 (September 23, 1909), 287-288.

New York Architect 3 (September, 1909), 113-118.

New York Times, September 15, 1909, 1; September 17, 5; October 2, 2.

Outlook 93 (September 25, 1909), 142-144.

World's Work 19 (November, 1909), 12185, 12206-12207

"The American Institute of Architects Pays Tribute to the Memory of Charles Follen McKim." *American Architect and Building News* 96 (December 29, 1909), 280-281.

"American Memorials in Rome." *American Magazine of Art* 20 (March, 1929), 172-173.

Bacon, Henry. "Charles Follen McKim—A Character Sketch." *Brickbuilder* 19 (February, 1910), 38-47.

Charles Follen McKim Memorial Meeting, American Institute of Architects, The Corcoran Gallery of Art, Washington, D.C., Dec. 15, 1909. Washington, D.C., 1910.

Cortissoz, Royal. "The Basis of American Taste." *Creative Art* 12 (January, 1933), 20-28.

Cortissoz, Royal. "Some Critical Reflections on the Architectural Genius of Charles F. McKim." *Brickbuilder* 19 (February, 1910), 23-37.

Cortissoz, Royal. *The Painter's Craft*. New York, 1930, 427-437.

Cortissoz, Royal. "The Secret of the American Academy in Rome." *American Magazine of Art* 13 (November, 1922), 459-462.

Exhibition of the Work of Charles Follen McKim, The Art Institute of Chicago, Jan. 18 to Feb. 6, 1910. Chicago, 1910.

Granger, Alfred Hoyt. *Charles Follen McKim; a study of his life and work.* Boston, 1913.
    Reviews: *Architectural Record* 35 (May, 1914), 463-465; *The Dial*, May 1, 1914, 384-385.

Hill, Frederick P. *Charles F. McKim: the Man.* Francestown, N.H., 1950.

Memorial Meeting in Honor of the Late Charles Follen McKim held in the New Theater, New York, November 23, 1909. New York, 1909?

Moore, Charles. *The Life and Times of Charles Follen McKim.* Boston, 1929.
    Reviews: *American Magazine of Art* 21 (March, 1930), 178; *Apollo* 12 (July, 1930), 60; *International Studio* 95 (April, 1930), 70.

Partridge, William T. "Recollections Concerning Charles Follen McKim." Unpublished typescript, Avery Library, Columbia University.

Peabody, Robert S. "A Tribute." *Brickbuilder* 19 (February, 1910), 55-56.

Schuyler, Montgomery. "Charles Follen McKim." *Architectural Record* 26 (November, 1909), 381-382.

"Saint-Gaudens-McKim bronzes given to the New York Public Library." *New York Public Library Bulletin* 43 (September, 1939), 643-644.

Swales, Francis S. "Charles Follen McKim." *Architectural Review (London)* 26 (October, 1909), 183-191.

Tallmadge, Thomas E. "Holographs of Famous Architects." *American Architect* 143 (March, 1934), 11.

"Tribute of the American Institute of Architects to the memory of Charles F. McKim." *Ohio Architect and Builder* 15 (January, 1910).

Walker, C. Howard. "The Influence of McKim." *Brickbuilder* 19 (February, 1910), 48-53.

William Rutherford Mead

Honors:

LL.D., Amherst, 1902

M.S., Norwich University, 1909

D.F.A., University of Pennsylvania, 1921

Knight Commander, Order of the Crown of Italy, 1922

President of the New York Chapter, American Institute of
Architects, 1907-1908

Gold Medal, American Academy of Arts and Letters, 1913

President, American Academy in Rome, 1909-1928

Obituary Notices:

American Architect and Building News 134 (July 5, 1928), 12.

American Art Journal 25 (1928), 371.

Architectural Forum 49 (July, 1928), 37.

Architectural Record 64 (September, 1928), 254.

Journal, American Institute of Architects 16 (July, 1928),
280.

New York *Herald-Tribune*, June 21, 22, 1928.

New York Times, November 27, 1928, 14; December 5, 1928, 20.

Pencil Points 9 (August, 1928), 470, 529.

"As He Is Known, being brief sketches of contemporary members
of the architectural profession." *Brickbuilder* 24 (December, 1915), 315.

Cabot, M. R. *Annals of Brattleboro, 1681-1895.* Brattleboro,
1922.

Country Life in America 39 (April, 1921), 43.

Stanford White

Honors:

M.A., New York University, 1881

Obituary Notices:

American Architecture and Building News 89 (June 30, 1906),
213; 90 (August 18, 1906), 54.

Quarterly Bulletin, American Institute of Architects 7
(July, 1906), 100-108.

Architectural Review 13 (July, 1906), 101.

The Critic 49 (August, 1906), 105.

Nation 83 (July 5, 1906), 5-6.

New York Times, June 27, 1906, 2-3; June 28, 1906, 6; June 29, 1906, 2.

Baldwin, Charles C. *Stanford White.* New York, 1931.
Reviews: *Architectural Forum* 55 (December, 1931), sup. 8.

Davis, Richard Harding. "Stanford White." *Collier's Magazine* 37 (August 4, 1906), 17.

"Exhibition at Davis Gallery." *Art News* 62 (April, 1963), 13.
[Similar notice in *Art Quarterly* 25 (Winter, 1962), 420.]

"Exhibition at Davis Gallery." [second exhibition] *Art News* 64 (April, 1965), 56.

"Exhibition at Davis Gallery." *Arts* 39 (May, 1965), 71.

Hewlett, J, Monroe. "Stanford White as those trained in his office knew him." *Brickbuilder* 15 (December, 1906), 245.

Hewlett, J. Monroe. "Stanford White, Decorator." *Good Furniture* 9 (September, 1917), 160-179. Partially reprinted in subsequent edition of *Good Furniture* 11 (October, 1918), 198-206.

McQuade, Walter. "Stanford White and the wherewithall." *Architectural Forum* 123 (November, 1965), 70.

Memorial Meeting in honor of the late Stanford White held at the library of New York University for the dedication of the Stanford White Memorial doors, December 10, 1921. New York, 1921?

Ross, Albert Randolph. "Stanford White as those trained in his office knew him." *Brickbuilder* 15 (December, 1906), 246.

Saarinen, Aline. "The Splendid World of Stanford White." *Life* 61 (September 16, 1966), 87-108.

Saint-Gaudens, Homer. "Intimate Letters of Stanford White, correspondence with his friend & co-worker, Augustus Saint-Gaudens." *Architectural Record* 30 (August, 1911), 107-116; (September, 1911), 283-298; (October, 1911), 399-406.

Sawyer, Philip. "Stanford White as those trained in his office knew him." *Brickbuilder* 15 (December, 1906), 247.

Scudder, Janet. *Modeling My Life.* New York, 1925.

"Sentimental approach to antiques: Stanford White Collection."
Arts and Decoration 41 (May, 1934), 58-60.

Simmons, Edward W. *From Seven to Seventy; Memories of a
Painter and Yankee.* (New York, 1922). "Stanford White,"
pp. 237-255.

"Stanford White items are notable feature of March dispersal."
Art News 32 (March 17, 1934), 14.

"Stanford White again; exhibition, Museum of the City of New
York." *Architectural Forum* 76 (April, 1942), sup. 8.

Swales, Francis S. "Master Draftsmen, Part I. Stanford White."
Pencil Points 5 (April, 1924), 59-64.

Tallmadge, Thomas E. "Holographs of Famous Architects."
American Architect 143 (March, 1933), 11.

Walker, C. Howard. "Stanford White—His Work." *Brickbuilder*
15 (December, 1906), 243-244.

World's Work 9 (November, 1904), 5439.

Young, Mahonri Sharp. "Stanford White, the Palace and the
Club." *Apollo* 93 (March, 1971), 210-215.

McKim, Mead & White

[Entries here pertain to interpretive and critical essays
or reviews of groups of the firm's buildings. It is not
possible to cite here the many hundreds of articles on
individual buildings.]

Andrews, Wayne. "McKim, Mead and White: New York's Own Architects." *New-York Historical Society Quarterly* 35 (January, 1951), 87-96.

Andrews, Wayne. "McKim, Mead & White: their mark remains."
New York Times Magazine, January 7, 1951, 18-21.

Atlantic Terra Cotta 9 (June, 1927), entire issue.

Barber, Donn. "The Work of McKim, Mead and White." *Architectural Record* 40 (October, 1916), 393-396.

Bowles, J. M. "Business Buildings Made Beautiful." *World's
Work* 9 (November, 1904), 5499-5508.

Black, Mary. *Old New York in Early Photographs, 1853-1901.*
New York, 1973. Good visual background material.

Brown, Glenn. "Personal Reminiscences of Charles Follen McKim." *Architectural Record* 38 (November, 1915), 575-582, "McKim and the American Institute of Architects"; (December, 1915), 681-689, "McKim and the Park Commission"; 39 (January, 1916), 84-88, "McKim and the White House"; (February, 1916), 178-185, "McKim's Way."

Butler, Alexander R. "McKim's Renaissance: A Study of the American Architectural Profession." Doctoral dissertation, Johns Hopkins University, 1953.

Chapman, John Jay. "McKim, Mead and White." *Vanity Fair* 13 (September, 1919), 37, 102, 104.

Cortissoz, Royal. "Architectural Ideas, Old and New." New York *Herald-Tribune*, March 17, 1940.

Cortissoz, Royal. "Ghosts in New York." *Architectural Forum* 53 (July, 1930), 87-90.

David, A. C. "An Architectural Oasis." *Architectural Record* 19 (February, 1906), 135-144. Essay on the firm's work in Naugatuck, Conn.

Desmond, Henry W., and Herbert Croly. "The Work of Messrs. McKim, Mead & White." *Architectural Record* 20 (September, 1906), 153-246. Entire issue; a major study of the firm's work.

Goldsmith, Goldwin. "I remember McKim, Mead and White." *Journal, American Institute of Architects* 13 (April, 1950), 168-172.

"Historical Society Exhibits Works." *Architectural Record* 109 (January, 1951), 214.

A Monograph of the Work of McKim, Mead & White, 1879-1915. 400 plates in 4 vols. New York, 1914-1920.

A Monograph of the Work of McKim, Mead & White. Students' Edition. 2 vols. New York, 1925.

Moses, Lionel. "McKim, Mead and White; a history." *American Architect and Building News* 121 (May 24, 1922), 413-424.

Myer, John Walden. "The New York Work of Stanford White." *Museum of the City of New York Bulletin* 5 (March, 1942), 46-52.

"One firm and many styles in architecture; exhibition at the New York Historical Society." *Art Digest* 25 (January 15, 1951), 16.

197

Parker, Gurdon S. "The Work of Three Great Architects."
World's Work 12 (May-October, 1906), 8051-8066.

Ramsey, Stanley C. "The Work of McKim, Mead and White."
Journal, Royal Institute of British Architects 25 (November 5, 1917), 25-29.

*Recent Buildings Designed for Educational Institutions by
McKim, Mead & White.* Philadelphia, 1936.

*Recent Work by the Present Partners of McKim, Mead & White,
Architects.* New York, 1952.

Reilly, Charles Herbert. *McKim, Mead & White.* London, 1924.

Roth, Leland M. "McKim, Mead & White Reappraised." Introductory essay and notes on the plates for *A Monograph of the
Works of McKim, Mead & White, 1879-1915.* new ed.
New York, 1973.

Sawyer, Philip. *Edward Palmer York: Personal Reminiscences.*
Stonington, Conn., 1951.

Schroeder, Francis de N. "Stanford White and the second blossoming of the Renaissance." *Interiors* 110 (February, 1951),
106-109.

Silver, Nathan. *Lost New York.* Boston, 1967.

Some Recent Buildings Designed by McKim, Mead & White.
Privately printed, 1941.

Smith, Eugenia B. "Rhode Island Resort Architecture of McKim,
Mead & White." Master's thesis, University of Wisconsin,
1964.

Sturgis, R. Clipston. "Voice from the past." *Journal, American Institute of Architects* 16 (July, 1951), 23-28.

Sturgis, Russell. "The Works of McKim, Mead & White." *Architectural Record,* Great American Architects Series, May,
1895. A major study of the firm's earlier work.

Swartwout, Egerton. "An Architectural Decade." Unpublished
typescript, n.d., c. 1935. Office of Walker O. Cain and
Associates, New York.

Walker, C. Howard. "Joseph Wells, architect, 1853-1890."
Architectural Record 66 (July, 1929), 14-18.

White, Lawrence Grant. *Sketches and Designs by Stanford White*. New York, 1920.

Wilson, Richard Guy. "Charles F. McKim and the Development of the American Renaissance: A Study in Architecture and Culture." Doctoral dissertation, University of Michigan, 1972.

INDEX

The index gives geographical locations for all those commissions where known, but because of their number the many hundreds of buildings in New York City (all five boroughs) are not repeated here. Interspersed in the single alphabetical listing are references to the muralists and sculptors with whom the firm worked, and the architects with whom they associated for distant commissions.

(Boston) No. 245; Emmons, Nathaniel H., monument, No. 278; New England Trust Co., No. 561; Nickerson, George A., house, No. 614; Olney, Richard, house, No. 628; Parkman, Francis, Memorial, No. 648; Shaw, Col. Robert Gould, Memorial, No. 771; State Street Exchange, project, No. 796; Swift, Edwin F., house, No. 811; Whittier, Charles A., house, No. 921
Brainerd, Minn., Northern Pacific RR hospital, No. 616
Brandtford, Ont., Can., Bank of Montreal, No. 94
Bratenahl, Ohio, Hanna, Howard M., house, No. 352
Brattleboro, Vt., Estey, Julius, J. monument, No. 280; school house, No. 142
Breck, George W., Reid, Whitelaw, house, No. 716; Cabell Hall, University of Virginia, No. 877
Bridgeport, Conn., Bridgeport City Hall project, No. 145
Bristol, R.I., Low, William G., house, No. 474
Broadalbin, N.Y., Husted, Miss M. E., house, No. 422
Brookline, Mass., Whitney, Henry M., house, project, No. 909
Brunswick, Maine, Bowdoin College, Walker Art Gallery, No. 137; Walker Memorial Gates, No. 138
Buffalo, N.Y., Bank of Buffalo, No. 89; Metcalf, Mrs. E. F., house, No. 499; Root, Robert K., house, No. 737; Tracy, Francis H., monument, No. 831; Wilgus, W. J., monuments, No. 924; Williams, Charles H., house, No. 927; Williams, George L., house, No. 928
Burlington, Vt., Cannon, LeGrand B., house, No. 181

Calder, A. Stirling, *Nations of the East* (Panama-Pacific Exposition), No. 639; *Washington in Peace* (Washington Memorial Arch), No. 890
Cambridge, Mass., Booth, Edwin, monument, No. 130; First Unitarian Church, project, No. 294; Flagler, John H., monument, No. 299; Harvard University, Bradley Memorial, No. 363; Harvard Stadium (Allston, Mass.), No. 361; Harvard Union, No. 362; Johnston Memorial Gate, No. 365; Lowell Memorial, No. 364; Memorial Class Gates, Nos. 368-380; Meyer Memorial Gate, No. 366; Robinson Hall, No. 360; Radcliffe College, No. 704; Radcliffe Gymnasium, No. 705
Carles, Antonin Jean, bell ringers (*New York Herald* Building), No. 572
Cazenovia, N.Y., Barklay, Sackett M., house, No. 96; Park, William G., house, No. 641
Champaign-Urbana, Ill., University of Illinois, Women's Building, No. 423
Charlottesville, Va., University of Virginia, plan, No. 875; boiler house, No. 876; Cabell Hall, No. 877; Cocke Hall, No. 878; Garrett Hall, No. 879; law library, project, No. 880; President's house, No. 881; Rotunda, restoration, No. 882; Rouss Hall, No. 883
Chattanooga, Tenn., First Presbyterian Church, No. 293
Chicago, Ill., Blair, Edward T., house, No. 128; Chicago Public Library, project, No. 945; Honore, A. C., monument, No. 406; Kimball, William W., monument, No. 441; Lathrop, Bryan, house, No. 463; *Lincoln* (Seated), No. 470; *Lincoln* (Standing), No. 471; *Logan, General John A.*, No. 472; New York State Building, No. 597; Palmer, Potter, art gallery, No. 636; Patterson, Robert W., house, No. 651; Puck Building, No. 693; White Star Steamship Co. pavilion, No. 906; World's Columbian Exposition, Agriculture Building, No. 939
Cincinnati, Ohio, University of Cincinnati, plan, No. 205

Cleveland, Ohio, Hanna, Howard M., house, No. 351; Hanna, Leonard C., house, No. 352; Harkness, Mrs. S. V., monument, No. 353; Pack, Charles L., mausoleum, No. 633; Strong et al., project, No. 808
Clinton, N.Y., Root, Elihu, house, No. 736
Codman, Ogden, Vanderbilt, Frederick W., house, No. 864
Colorado Springs, Colo., Baldwin, Charles A., house, project, No. 86
Cornwall, Penna., Alden, Percy R., house, No. 58
Cornwall-on-Hudson, N.Y., Stillman, James, house, No. 801
Cox, Kenyon, *Venice* (Walker Art Gallery, Bowdoin College), No. 137

Dayton, Ohio, National Cash Register Co., No. 548
de Wolfe, Elsie, Colony Club, No. 211
Detroit, Mich., Bicentennial Memorial Column, project, No. 262; Freer, Charles L., house, project, No. 304; Hecker, Frank J., monument, No. 390; State Savings Bank, No. 795
Dewing, Thomas W., *Dawn* (Hotel Imperial), No. 411; *The Days* (Anne W. Cheney house), No. 194; Osborn, Charles J., house, No. 631; State Savings Bank, No. 795; Winans, Ross R., house, No. 931
District of Columbia, Adams Memorial, No. 52; Hearst School for Girls, project, No. 389; King, David H., jr., house, project, No. 443; Library of Congress, consultation, No. 469; Munsey Building (first), Nos. 541, 542; Munsey Building (second), No. 543; Page, Thomas N., house, No. 634; Patterson, Robert W., house, No. 652; St. John's Church, No. 748; Selfridge, Thomas O., jr., house, No. 769; Senate Park Commission, No. 770; Truesdell, George, project, No. 834; U. S. Army War College, Nos. 847-849; Warder, Benjamin H., monument, No. 886; The White House, Nos. 904, 905
Dobbs Ferry, N.Y., Villard, Henry, house, Nos. 870-872
Donaldson & Meier, associate architects, No. 794
Duluth, Minn., St. Luke's Hospital, No. 749

East Orange, N.J., Chubb, Mrs. Victoria, house, No. 200
Easton, Penna., Eyerman, John, house, No. 281
El Paso, Texas, Bronson & King Bank, No. 149
Elberon, N.J., Brokaw, Isaac V., house, No. 147; Cook, Charles T., house, No. 244; Elberon Hotel and cottages, Nos. 6, 7; Fahnestock, Harris C., house, No. 283; Francklyn, Charles G., house, No. 10; Garland, James A., house, No. 313; Newcomb, H. Victor, house, No. 607; Packer, C. M., house, No. 41; Stuyvesant, A. Van Horne, house, No. 810; Talbot, Richmond, house, No. 43; Taylor, H. A. C., house, No. 44; Taylor, Moses, house, No. 22; White, Horace, house, No. 900; Wood, John D., house, No. 937
Elizabeth, N.J., Elizabeth General Hospital, Nurses Home, No. 274
Elliott, John, Boston Public Library, p. 171
Enfield, Conn., Abbey, Captain Thomas, monument, No. 51
Englewood, N.J., Jones, Dwight A., house, No. 431
Evans, Allen (Furness, Evans & Co.), associate architect, No. 321

Fairfield, Conn., Bronson, Mrs. Frederick, monument, No. 148; Iselin, Mrs. Adrian, monument, No. 425
Fanwood (see also Scotch Plains), N.J., Shepard, Augustus D., house, No. 773
Farmington, Conn., Pope, Alfred A., house, No. 674

French, Daniel Chester, Boston Public Library, doors, p. 172; *Alma Mater* (Columbia University), No. 231; Parkman, Francis, Memorial, No. 648; St. Bartholomew's Church, portals, No. 745; *Washington, George*, No. 891; *William the Silent*, project, No. 926

Galveston, Texas, Sealy, George, house, No. 765; Sealy, George, monument, No. 766
Garden City, N.Y., Garden City Hotel, Nos. 308, 309; Garden City houses, No. 310
Garnsey, Elmer E., Boston Public Library, p. 171
Garrison-on-Hudson, N.Y., Fish, Hamilton, monument, No. 296
Germantown, Penna., see Philadelphia, Penna.
Gilbert, Cass, see Nos. 616, 618
Glaenser, Georges A., Vanderbilt, Frederick W., house, No. 864
Gould's Island, N.Y., Homans, Edward C., house, No. 403
Great Barrington, Mass., Hopkins, Mrs. Mark, house, No. 410
Great Neck, N.Y., Winslow, Edward, house, No. 933
Greenpoint, N.Y., Havemeyer Sugar Co., project, No. 384
Greenwich, Conn., Brigham, William, house, No. 146; Hooker, Mrs. Blanche Ferry, house, Nos. 408, 409; Rowland, George, house, No. 738
Guerin, Jules, Pennsylvania Station, No. 656

Hanover, N.H., Church of Christ at Dartmouth, No. 201
Hartford, Conn., Hunt Memorial Building, No. 421; Morgan, Edwin Dennison, sr., mausoleum, No. 14; Olmsted, A. H., house, No. 627; Wylls, Ruth, Chapter, DAR, memorial, No. 940
Holabird & Roche, supervisory architects, No. 463
Hunter's Island, N.Y., Iselin, Charles O., house, No. 426
Huntington, N.Y., *Hale, Nathan*, No. 348
Hyde Park, N.Y., Vanderbilt, Frederick W., house, No. 864

Interlaken, N.Y., Cayuga Lake Hotel, No. 2
Irvington-on-Hudson, N.Y., *Cosmopolitan Magazine* Offices, No. 252

Jamestown, N.C., Mackay, Clarence H., hunting lodge, No. 481

Kansas City, Mo., Kansas City Casino, No. 438; Mastin, Thomas H., house, Nos. 494, 495; New York Life Insurance Company Building, No. 576
Konti, Isidore, Column of Progress (Panama-Pacific Exposition), No. 639

La Farge, John, *The Ascension of Our Lord* (Church of the Ascension), No. 202; *Athens* (Walker Art Gallery, Bowdoin College), No. 137; Boston Public Library, project, p. 171; Judson Memorial Church, No. 434; Reid, Whitelaw, house, No. 716
Lathrop, Francis, Osborn, Charles J., house, No. 631
Lenox, Mass., Appleton, the Misses, house, No. 75; Casey et al., house, No. 30; Furniss, C., house, No. 36; Lenox Episcopal Church, project, No. 467; Ward, Samuel G., house, No. 23; White, J. M., house, No. 49
Lentelli, Leo, sculpture, Panama-Pacific Exposition, No. 639

Lewiston, Maine, Munsey, Frank A., house, No. 540
Lexington, Ky., Fayette National Bank, No. 289; Hagin, Louis L., house, No. 346
Lincoln, Neb., Nebraska State Capitol, project, No. 558
Litchfield, Conn., FitzGerald, W. J., monument, No. 298
Lloyd's Neck, Long Island, N.Y., Alden, Mrs. Anna C., house, No. 25
London, Eng., Penn, William, memorial tablet, No. 654; Sherry hotel project, No. 779
Long Branch (Elberon), N.J., Brokaw, Isaac V., house, No. 147
Low, Will H., *Lamia*, p. 173
Lynn, Mass., Keene brothers buildings, No. 439

MacMonnies, Frederick W., Bowery Savings Bank (pediments), No. 139; *Boy and Duck* fountain, No. 140; Cataract Construction Co., flagstaff base, No. 183; Church of St. Paul the Apostle (angels), No. 751; *Hale, Nathan*, Nos. 347, 348; *The Horse Tamers (The Triumph of Mind over Brute Force)*, No. 686; *Pan of Rohallion*, No. 638; *Slocum, General Henry W.*, No. 791; *Vane, Sir Henry* (Boston Public Library), p. 172; *Victory* (West Point Battle Monument), No. 854; Washington Memorial Arch (spandrels), No. 890; *Young Faun with Heron*, No. 942
MacNeil, Hermon A., *Adventurous Archer* (Panama-Pacific Exposition), No. 639; *Washington in War* (Washington Memorial Arch), No. 890
Madison, N.J., Twombly, Hamilton M., house, Nos. 839-842
Mamaroneck, N.Y., Osborn, Charles J., house, No. 631
Manchester-by-the-Sea (and Pride's Crossing), Mass., Coolidge, Thomas Jefferson, house, No. 246; Manchester Public Library, No. 488
Mandan, N.D., Northern Pacific RR station, No. 617
Massapequa, N.Y., railroad station and park, No. 493
Marion, Mass., Gilder, Richard W., house, No. 320
Martiny, Philip, Church of St. Paul the Apostle, No. 751; St. Bartholomew's Church, No. 745; World's Columbian Exposition, Agriculture Building, No. 939
Mead, Larkin G., World's Columbian Exposition, Agriculture Building, No. 939
Middlebury, Conn., Whittemore, John H., house and farm, No. 920
Milton, Mass., Bowditch, Ernest W., house, No. 135
Minneapolis, Minn., Minneapolis Museum of Fine Art (Minneapolis Institute of Arts), No. 519; Washburn, W. D., house, project, No. 888
Monmouth Beach, N.J., Cornell, J. M., house, No. 33
Montauk Point, N.Y., Agnew, Dr. Cornelius R., house, No. 57; Andrews, William L., house, No. 74; Benson, A. W., house, No. 125; deForest, Henry G., house, No. 261; Hoyt, Alfred M., house, No. 417; Montauk Point Association hall, Nos. 522, 523; Orr, Alexander E., house, No. 630; Sanger, Henry, house, No. 762
Montclair, N.J., Livermore, John, house, No. 13; Montclair Presbyterian Church, chapel, No. 525; Wight, L. Allyn, house, Nos. 922, 923
Montreal, Que., Can., Bank of Montreal, Nos. 90, 91; Mount Royal Club, No. 538; Royal Trust Co., No. 739
Montrose, N.J., Page, Henry A., house, No. 15
Mora, Domingo, Boston Public Library, rondels, p. 172
Moriches, N.Y., Taylor, George C., house and cottage, No. 812

Morristown, N.J., Ballantine, Mrs. Isabella, house, No. 87; Freling-
huysen, Peter H. B., house, No. 305; Haydock, Mrs. Hannah W.,
house, No. 386; Morris County Savings Bank, project, No. 531;
Pyle, James T., house, No. 700; St. Peter's Church, Nos. 754-756;
St. Peter's Church, baptismal font, No. 458; St. Peter's Rectory,
No. 757; Thurston, William R., house, No. 823; Turnbull, Robert
L., house, No. 838; Vanderpoel, the Rev. Wynant, house, No. 867
Mount Kisco, N.Y., Van Cortlandt, Robert B., house, No. 861
Mount Morris, N.Y., Mount Morris Bank and Safe Deposit Co., project,
No. 537
Mount Vernon, N.Y., Howe, Dr. Robert T., house, No. 416
Mowbray, H. Siddons, Madison Square Presbyterian Church (pediment),
No. 487; Morgan, John P., library (Morgan Library, murals),
No. 530; University Club (murals), No. 859

Narragansett Pier, R.I., Cresson, George V., house, No. 254; McLane,
Allan, house, No. 483; Maconochie hotel project, No. 484; Nar-
ragansett Pier Casino, No. 547; Sherry, Louis, cottages, casino,
and restaurant, Nos. 778-780, 783; U.S. Coast Guard life-saving
station, No. 850
Naugatuck, Conn., bank, project, No. 553; Congregational Church, No.
243; fountain, No. 552; Naugatuck City Hall, project, No. 554;
Naugatuck National Bank, No. 555; Naugatuck Public Grammar School
(Salem School), No. 556; Naugatuck Public High School (Hillside
School), No. 557; Whittemore, Harris, house, No. 917; Whittemore,
Howard, Memorial Library, No. 918; Whittemore, John H., house,
No. 919
Neponsit (New York City), N.Y., Bellevue Neponsit Hospital, No. 111
New Britain, Conn., Corbin, P. and F., Co., offices, No. 248; New
Britain City Hall, No. 560; Russell, H. E., and C. B. Erwin,
hotel, No. 743
New Brunswick, N.J., Halstead, Bryan D., memorial tablets, No. 349
New Haven, Conn., Bennett, Mrs. Hannah J., house, No. 118; New Haven
Public Library, project, No. 562; Phelps Association ("Wolf's
Head" Fraternity), Yale, No. 658; Saunders, Emmett A., house,
No. 764; United Society of New Haven (United Church), memorial
tablets, No. 846
New Orleans, La., Tulane University, project, No. 837
New Rochelle, N.Y., Ayers, Mrs. Henrietta, houses, No. 83; Odell,
Edward V., house, No. 624; Wells, Dr. William L., house, No. 895
New Rochelle, Premium Point (Larchmont), N.Y., Holt, Henry, house,
No. 402; King, David H., jr., house, project, Nos. 444, 445
Newark, N.J., Cumming, Robert W., house, No. 257; Freeman, Mrs. Alden,
monument, No. 303; Newark Memorial Building, project, No. 605;
Prudential Insurance Co., project, No. 692
Newburgh, N.Y., Young Men's Christian Association, No. 943
Newport, R.I., Astor, Mrs. William, house, No. 80; Bell, Isaac, jr.,
house, No. 105; Bennett, James G., jr., houses, No. 119; Bradley,
Arthur C., house, No. 141; Bull, Charles M., house, No. 170;
Child, William S., school, No. 3; Colman, Samuel, house, No. 210;
Dennis house (St. John's Rectory), No. 4; Dunn, Thomas, house,
project, No. 5; Edgar, Commodore William, house, No. 273; Fair-
child, Charles F., stable, No. 8; Glover, John H., house, No. 322;
Goelet, Robert, house, No. 323; Havemeyer, Theodore, house, No. 383;

Potter, Edward C., Morgan, John P., library (Morgan Library, lion-
nesses), No. 530; *Washington, George*, No. 891
Poughkeepsie, N.Y., Vassar College, Vassar Auditorium, No. 868
Premium Point, N.Y., see New Rochelle, Premium Point (Larchmont), N.Y.
Pride's Crossing, Mass., see Manchester-by-the-Sea, Mass.
Princeton, N.J., Princeton University, Athletic Field fence and gate,
No. 676; Cottage Club, Nos. 677-678; FitzRandolph Memorial Gate,
No. 679; Olden Street gate, No. 680
Providence, R.I., Brown University, Rockefeller Hall, No. 167; Cha-
pin, William C., house, No. 191; Providence City Hall, project,
No. 16; Rhode Island State Capitol, No. 721
Purchase, N.Y., Reid, Whitelaw, house, Nos. 719, 720
Puvis de Chavannes, Pierre-Cécile, Boston Public Library (murals),
p. 172

Quogue, N.Y., Colgate, Robert, jr., house, No. 208; Quogue Episcopal
Church, No. 702

Reno, Nev., University of Nevada, Mackay School of Mines and campus
plan, No. 559
Rhinebeck, N.Y., Astor, John J., house, No. 77; Astor, John J., ten-
nis court, No. 78; Miller, George N., stable, No. 513
Richfield Springs, N.Y., McCormick, Cyrus H., house, No. 477
Richmond, Va., Confederate Memorial, project, No. 242; Willard, Joseph
E., house, No. 925
Riverdale, and Riverdale-on-Hudson, N.Y., Bend, George H., house, No.
117; Riverdale Country School, No. 722
Roanoke Rapids, N.C., Roanoke Rapids Power Company, plant and hous-
ing, Nos. 724, 725, 726
Rochester, N.Y., Eastman, George, house, No. 270; Eastman Kodak Co.,
offices, No. 272
Rockaway, and Far Rockaway (New York City), N.Y., Beaman, Charles C.,
house, No. 102; Cheever, John H., house, No. 193; New York Asso-
ciation for Improving the Condition of the Blind, Nos. 565, 566
Rome, Italy, American Academy in Rome, No. 62
Roslyn, N.Y., Mackay, Clarence H., house, Nos. 479, 480; Trinity
Church and Parish House, No. 832
Rye, N.Y., Christ Church Rectory, No. 31; Towle, Stevenson, house,
No. 830

Saint-Gaudens, Augustus, Adams Memorial, No. 52; *Billings, Robert
Charles* (Boston Public Library), p. 172; Boston Public Library,
entrance figures, project, p. 172; Boston Public Library, Seals,
p. 172; Brooks, Phillips, Memorial, No. 163; Chapin, Chester W.,
memorial, *The Puritan*, No. 190; Cooper, Peter, Memorial, No. 247;
Diana, No. 485; Farragut, Admiral David Glasgow, Memorial, No. 9;
Fish, Hamilton, monument, No. 296; frames for relief sculpture,
p. 175; Garfield Memorial, No. 311; *Lincoln* (Seated), No. 470;
Lincoln (Standing), No. 471; *Logan, General John A.*, No. 472; Mor-
gan, Edwin D., sr., mausoleum, No. 14; *The Pilgrim*, No. 660; *The
Puritan*, No. 190; Randall, Robert Richard, Memorial, No. 17; Shaw,
Colonel Robert Gould, Memorial, No. 769; Sherman, General William
Tecumseh, Memorial, No. 744; Smith, Ann Marie, monument, No. 791

(Stratton, Stratton & Ellingwood)   Charles O., house, No. 426;
    Quogue Episcopal Church, No. 702; Roosevelt, Elliott, house, No.
    733; Waterbury, James M., house, No. 894

Tacoma, Wash., Northern Pacific RR terminal station and hotel, No.
    622
Tarrytown, N.Y., Tarrytown Drinking Fountain, p. 175
Tarrytown Heights, N.Y., see Pocantico Hills, N.Y.
Taylor, Andrew T., associate architect, Nos. 90, 91
Thayer, Abbott H., *Florence* (Walker Art Gallery, Bowdoin College),
    No. 137
Tiffany, Louis C., windows, Manchester Public Library, No. 488;
    St. Paul's Church, No. 753; St. Peter's Church, No. 754
Tivoli, N.Y., Redmond, Geraldyn, mausoleum, No. 709; Villars, the
    Countess de Laugier, garage, No. 873
Tremont, N.Y., Bush, John S., house, No. 172
Trenton, N.J., New Jersey State House, project, No. 564
Tryon, Dwight W., frames for paintings by White, p. 175
Tuxedo Park, N.Y., Lorillard, Pierre, jr., house, No. 473

Urbana, Ill., see Champaign-Urbana, Ill.

Vedder, Elihu, *Rome*, or *The Art Idea* (Walker Art Gallery, Bowdoin
    College), No. 137

Wading River, N.Y., Mitchell, Roland G., house, No. 520
Wakefield, R.I., Robinson, Jeremiah P., jr., house, No. 731
Ward, J. Q. A., Beecher Memorial, Amherst College, No. 104
Warner, Olin L., New York State Building, No. 597
Warren, Whitney, U.S. Immigration Station, Ellis Island, project,
    No. 852
Washington, D.C., see District of Columbia
Washington, Penna., Smith, W. W., project, No. 793; Trinity School,
    No. 833
Waterbury, Conn., "The Buckingham" building, No. 169; New York, New
    Haven & Hartford RR, passenger station, No. 582
Weinman, Adolph A., *Fountain of the Rising Sun* (Panama-Pacific Expo-
    sition), No. 639; Madison Square Presbyterian Church (pediment),
    No. 487; Municipal Building, No. 539; Pennsylvania Station, No.
    656; Prison Ship Martyrs' Monument, No. 681
Westbury, N.Y., Canfield, A. Cass, house, Nos. 179, 180; Park, Wil-
    liam G., house, No. 643; Whitney, Henry P., house, Nos. 907, 908;
    Whitney, William C., house, No. 915; Winthrop, Robert D., house,
    No. 934
West Point, N.Y., U.S. Military Academy, Battle Monument, No. 854;
    Cullum Memorial Hall, No. 855; Officers' Mess Hall, No. 856
Wheatley, N.Y., Morgan, Edwin D., jr., house, Nos. 528, 529
Whidden & Lewis, see "Portland House" hotel, No. 619
Whistler, James Abbott McNeill, Boston Public Library, mural project,
    p. 172
White Plains, N.Y., Brown, William R., stable, No. 166; Burke Relief
    Foundation hospital, No. 171;
Williamstown, Mass., Williams College, Delta Psi Fraternity, No. 930

Winnipeg, Man., Can., Bank of Montreal, No. 92
Worcester, Mass., Bancroft monument, No. 88; Sargent, Joseph, house,
   No. 19

yachts, interiors, *Invincible*, No. 100; *Naumona*, No. 124; *Polyana*,
   No. 123
York County, N.C., King's Mountain Battlefield Memorial, No. 457
Youngstown, Ohio, Butler, Joseph G., jr. (Butler Institute of Ameri-
   can Art), No. 173

PLATES

The buildings are illustrated in the order in which they are given in the Building List; each appears with the Building List number and a brief identifying caption. Although efforts have been made to illustrate as many buildings and projects as practicable, there are inevitable gaps so that there are breaks in the numerical run. Except for the prints supplied by Richard Wilson, the photographs were prepared by the author from negatives in his collection. The source for each is noted in the captions, but for convenience the following abbreviations are used:

AABN = *American Architecture and Building News*.

Avery Library = from the Scrapbooks and Albums of clippings and photographs deposited by the firm (see the Bibliography).

MM&W Archive, NYHS = McKim, Mead & White Archive, New-York Historical Society.

Monograph = *A Monograph of the Wo. : of McKim, Mead & White, 1879-1915*. 4 vols. (New York, 1914-1920).

NYSB = *New York Sketch Book of Architecture*.

Sturgis, 1895 = Russell Sturgis, "The Works of McKim, Mead & White," *Architectural Record*, Great American Architects Series, May 1895.

1. Francis Blake, jr., house, 1875. C. F. McKim.
   NYSB 2 (July, 1875).

3. William S. Child school, 1875. C. F. McKim.
    Courtesy of Richard Guy Wilson (Photo: Wilson).

View of tower
at north-east angle.

2. Cayuga Lake Hotel, 1875. W. R. Mead.
NYSB 2 (April, 1875).

4. John Dennis house, hall, 1876. C. F. McKim.
From A. Downing and V. Scully, *The Architectural Heritage of Newport, Rhode Island*.

5. Thomas Dunn house, project, 1877. C. F. McKim.
AABN 2 (July 28, 1877).

6. Elberon Hotel, 1876-1877. C. F. McKim.
    MM&W Archive, NYHS.

7. Elberon Hotel cottages, 1877-1880. McKim et al.
    (Photo: Roth)

7. Elberon Hotel cottage, 1877-1880.
   (Photo: Roth)

8. Charles F. Fairchild stable, 1876. C. F. McKim.
   Courtesy of Henry-Russell Hitchcock.

9. Admiral David Glasgow Farragut Memorial, 1876-1881.
   Augustus Saint-Gaudens and Stanford White.
   AABN 10 (September 10, 1881).

10. Charles G. Francklyn house, 1876. C. F. McKim.
    NYSB 3 (December, 1876).

11. Dwight S. Herrick house, 1877. W. R. Mead.
    AABN 2 (June 30, 1877).

12. William Dean Howells house, "Redtop," 1877-1878.
McKim and Mead.
Courtesy of Richard Guy Wilson (Photo: Wilson).

13. John Livermore house, stairwell, 1874. C. F. McKim.
NYSB 1 (July, 1874).

15. Henry A. Page house, library, 1875-1876. C. F. McKim. *NYSB* 3 (April, 1876).

18. Thomas Robinson house, hall, 1874. C. F. McKim. Courtesy of Henry-Russell Hitchcock.

16. Providence City Hall, project, 1874. McKim and Mead.
NYSB 1 (November, 1874).

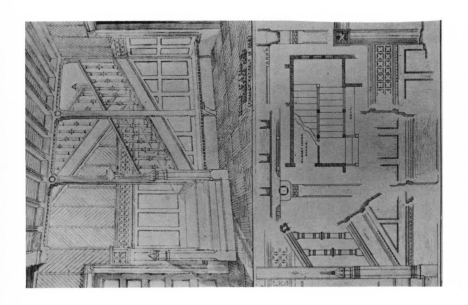

19. Joseph Sargent house, stairwell, 1872. C. F. McKim.
Architectural Sketch Book (Boston) 1 (January, 1874).

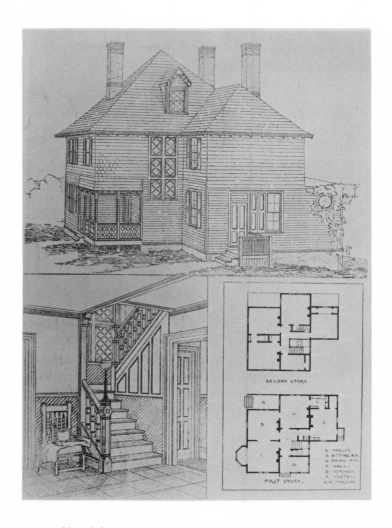

20. John Simpson house, 1873-1874. W. R. Mead.
NYSB 1 (March, 1874).

21. School house, project, 1873-1874. C. F. McKim.
     NYSB 1 (January, 1874).

22. Moses Taylor house, 1876-1877. C. F. McKim.
     (Photo: Roth)

23. Samuel Gray Ward house, "Oakswood," 1877-1878. McKim et al.
From E. A. Morley, *Lenox*, courtesy of Richard Guy Wilson.

24. Katherine P. Wormley house, 1876-1877. C. F. McKim.
(Photo: Roth)

25. Mrs. Anna C. Alden house, "Fort Hill" ("Tower Hill"), 1879-1880.
AABN 6 (August 30, 1879).

29. Prescott Hall Butler house, "Bytharbor," 1878-1880.
Rendering, water color on paper, by Stanford White (?), c. 1884.
Collection of Kyril Schabert. (Photo: Roth)

31. Christ Church Rectory, 1877?-1879.
AABN 2 (November 10, 1877).

33. J. M. Cornell house, 1879.
From G. W. Sheldon, *Artistic Country Seats*.

34. Edward N. Dickerson house, 1877-1879.
(Photo: Roth)

37. Stewart Hartshorn, model house, 1879-1880.
    (Photo: Roth)

48. Union League Club, project, 1879.
    AABN 5 (June 7, 1879).

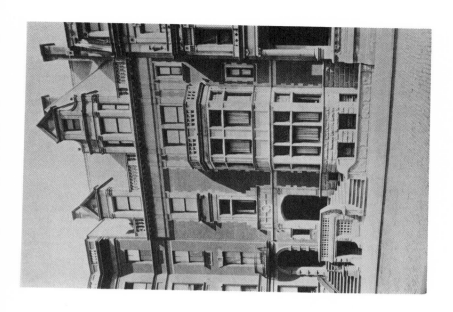

45. Frederick F. Thompson house, 1879-1881.
Museum of the City of New York.

47. "The Benedict" for Lucius Tuckerman, 1879-1882.
(Photo: Roth)

50. Clement W. Williams, double house, 1878-1879.
Sturgis, 1895.

52. Adams Memorial, 1886-1892, entire ensemble.
(Photo: Roth)

52. Adams Memorial, bronze figure by Saint-Gaudens.
(Photo: Roth)

54. Edward Dean Adams house, "Rohallion," 1886-1888. MM&W Archive, NYHS.

55. Edward Dean Adams house, "Rohallion," additions, 1890. MM&W Archive, NYHS.

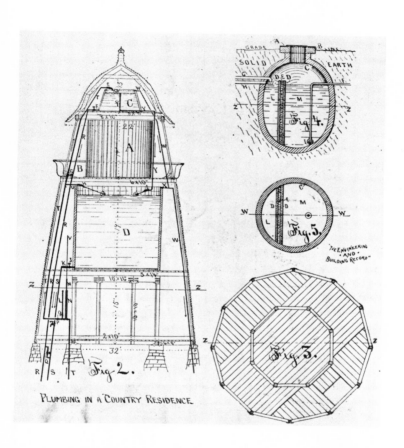

PLUMBING IN A COUNTRY RESIDENCE

55. Edward Dean Adams house, "Rohallion," windmill and water system, 1890.
Section through windmill tower showing vertical vane windmill
and storage tank.
MM&W Archive, NYHS.

58. Robert Percy Alden house, 1880-1884.
     (Photo: Roth)

62. American Academy in Rome, 1910-1914.
     (From A. and L. Valentine, *The American Academy in Rome, 1894-1969*).

60. Algonquin Club, 1886-1889.
(Photo: Roth)

63. American Safe Deposit Company and Columbia Bank, 1882-1884.
AABN 19 (January 30, 1886).

64. American Surety Company, project, 1893.
     Avery Library.

65. American Tobacco Company (Havana Tobacco Company), 1902-1903. From L. G. White, *Sketches and Designs of Stanford White.*

66. and 67. Biology and Geology Building, Amherst College, 1906-1909 and 1912. (Photo: Roth)

68. Converse Memorial Library, Amherst College, 1915-1917.
From S. King, *"The Consecrated Eminence," The Story of the
Campus and Buildings of Amherst College.*

69. Fayerweather Hall, Amherst College, 1892-1894.
(Photo: Roth)

70. Observatory, Amherst College, 1902-1904.
     (Photo: Roth)

71 and 628.   Francis I. Amory house (right half) and Richard Olney
house (left half), 1890-1892.
MM&W Archive, NYHS.

73.   John F. Andrew house, 1883-1886.
(Photo: Roth)

72. Andover Free Christian Church, 1907-1908. Perspective rendering by Jules Crow.
MM&W Archive, NYHS.

74. William L. Andrews house, 1882-1883.
Courtesy of Richard Guy Wilson (Photo: Wilson).

74, 125, and 417. William L. Andrews house (foreground) with A. W. Benson house (in the distance on the left) and the Alfred M. Hoyt house (on the right). (Photo: Roth)

75. Julia and Marian Alice Appleton house, "Homestead," 1883-1885. MM&W Archive, NYHS.

76. Benjamin W. Arnold house, 1901-1905.
    AABN 91 (March 16, 1907).

78. John Jacob Astor IV, tennis court addition to "Ferncliff,"
    1902-1904.
    AABN 92 (November 9, 1907).

78. Astor tennis court, interior, showing light steel frame filled
with glass and Guastavino vault shells.
AABN 92 (November 9, 1907).

81 and 192. Charles L. Atterbury house, converted to a studio for
William Merritt Chase, 1888 and c. 1895.
Avery Library.

90. Bank of Montreal, First Phase, Craig Street Building, 1900-1904.
MM&W Archive, NYHS.

90. Bank of Montreal, First Phase, new banking room.
MM&W Archive, NYHS.

91. Bank of Montreal, Second Phase, renovation of the original
building, 1903-1905.
MM&W Archive, NYHS.

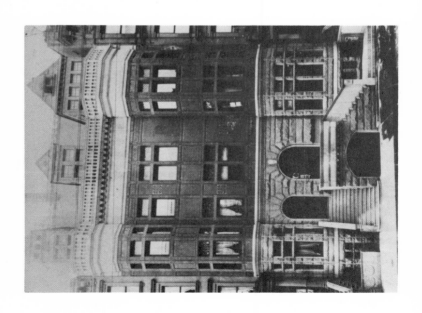

97. Charles T. Barney house, 1880-1882.
Avery Library.

92. Bank of Montreal, Winnipeg Branch, 1909-1912.
    MM&W Archive, NYHS.

94. Bank of Montreal, Brandtford Branch, 1913-1914.
    (Photo: Roth)

99. Charles T. Barney house, 1895, 1901-1902. Dining room. Avery Library.

101. Joseph Battell Memorial Fountain, 1888-1889. (Photo: Roth)

103. J. Arthur Beebe house, 1888-1889.
(Photo: Roth)

104. Henry Ward Beecher Memorial (base), 1915.
(Photo: Roth)

105. Isaac Bell, jr., house, 1881-1883.
     Wayne Andrews.

106. Bellevue Hospital, initial plan, 1903.
     Rendering, water color and ink on paper, by Jules Crow.
     (Photo: Roth)

106. Bellevue Hospital, final plan, 1905-1906.
      MM&W Archive, NYHS.

113. Bellevue Hospital, Pathological Wing, 1907-1911.
      Monograph.

116. Bellevue Hospital, Pavilions L and M, 1911-1913.
Monograph.

MAIN SALOON OF THE "NAMOUNA."

124. Interior of main saloon of *Namouna*, for James Gordon Bennett,
1885.
Century Magazine 24 (August, 1882).

125. A. W. Benson house, 1882.
     Courtesy of Richard Guy Wilson. (Photo: Wilson)

128. Edward T. Blair house, 1912-1914.
      Monograph.

130. Edwin Booth Memorial, 1895.
      From L. G. White, *Sketches and Designs of Stanford White.*

133. Boston Public Library. Rendering of design, 1888.
AABN 23 (May 26, 1888).

133. Boston Public Library, 1887-1895.
(Photo: Roth)

134. Boston Symphony Hall, 1892-1901.
(Photo: Roth)

135. Ernest W. Bowditch house, 1898.
Brickbuilder 1 (January, 1900).

137. Walker Art Gallery, Bowdoin College, 1891-1894.
(Photo: Roth)

139. Bowery Savings Bank, 1893-1895.
(Photo: Roth)

139. Bowery Savings Bank, main banking room.
(Photo: Roth)

141.   Arthur C. Bradley house, 1891-1893.
       (Photo: Roth)

144.   James L. Breese house, "The Orchard," 1898-1907.
       Monograph.

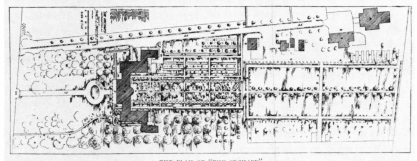

THE PLAN OF "THE ORCHARD"

144. James L. Breese house, "The Orchard," plan of the grounds
and gardens.
From J. C. Baker, *American Country Homes and Their Gardens*.

145. Bridgeport City Hall, project, 1900.
MM&W Archive, NYHS.

150. The Brook Club, 1904-1905.
Avery Library.

151. Administration Building, Brooklyn Botanic Garden, 1913-1916.
Monograph.

152. Brooklyn Institute of Arts and Sciences (Brooklyn Museum),
initial comprehensive design, 1893.
Sturgis, 1895.

154 through 159. Brooklyn Institute of Arts and Sciences, completed
pavilions, 1895-1915.
Monograph.

161. Brooklyn Municipal Building, c. 1909?
Avery Library.

163. Phillips Brooks Memorial, 1904-1910.
(Photo: Roth)

164. Mrs. George B. Brown house, 1893-1894.
Avery Library.

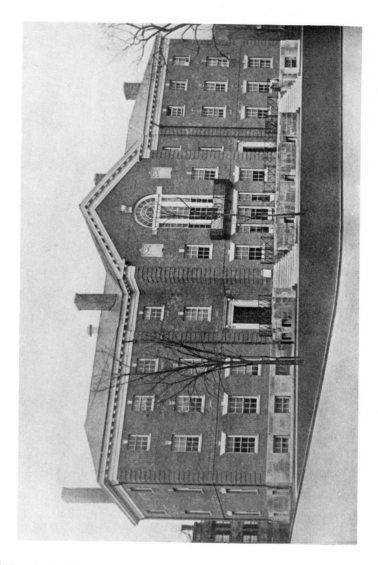

167. Rockefeller Hall (Faunce Hall), Brown University, 1902-1904.
Brickbuilder 13 (February, 1904).

168. Browne and Meredith Apartment Building, for T. O. Browne and
     J. M. Meredith, 1890-1891.
     (Photo: Roth)

171. Winnifred Masterson Burke Foundation Hospital for Convalescents,
     plan of the hospital complex, 1912.
     Avery Library.

169. "The Buckingham" for John Howard Whittemore, 1903-1906.
      (Photo: Roth)

173. Joseph G. Butler, jr., art gallery (Butler Institute of Ameri-
      can Art), 1917-1920.
      (Photo: Roth)

174 and 175.　Additions to the Prescott Hall Butler house, "Bytharbor,"
1884, 1894.
(Photo: Roth)

176 and 345.　Prescott Hall Butler house (to the front) and William D.
Guthrie house (behind and to the right), 1895-1897.
MM&W Archive, NYHS.

177. Cable Building, 1892-1894.
(Photo: Roth)

179. A. Cass Canfield house, 1902-1903.
(From F. Platt, *America's Gilded Age*).

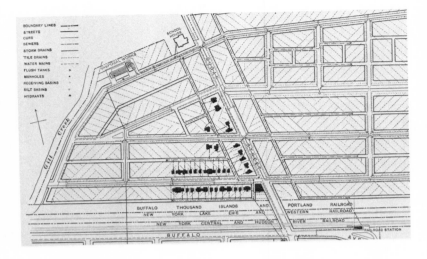

182. "Echota," housing village for employees of the Niagara Falls Power Company, built by the Cataract Construction Company. Plan of the village, 1893-1895. From J. Bogart, "The Industrial Village of Echota at Niagara," *Cassier's Magazine* 8 (July, 1895).

182. "Echota," view of the houses along A Street, c. 1895. (From E. D. Adams, *Niagara Power*).

182. "Echota," view of the houses along B Street, c. 1905.
Courtesy of the Niagara-Mohawk Company.

182. "Echota," houses on Hyde Park Street (formerly Sugar Street).
(Photo: Roth)

183.   Flagstaff in front of Niagara Falls Power Company, Adams
        Station No. 1.
        AABN 49 (September 28, 1895).

184 and 185. Niagara Falls Power Company, Adams Station No. 1, on
the right (built by the Cataract Construction Company);
Transformer Building, on the left; 1892-1894.
Courtesy of the Niagara-Mohawk Company.

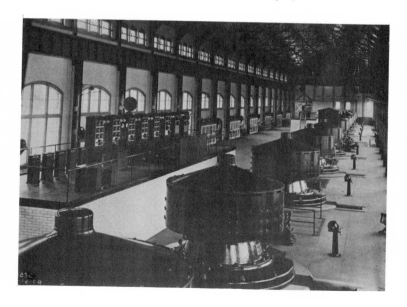

184. Niagara Falls Power Company, Adams Station No. 1, interior.
Courtesy of the Earl Brydges Public Library, Niagara Falls.

185. Niagara Falls Power Company, Transformer Building, 1893-1894.
      (Photo: Roth)

186. Century Club, 1889-1891.
      Monograph.

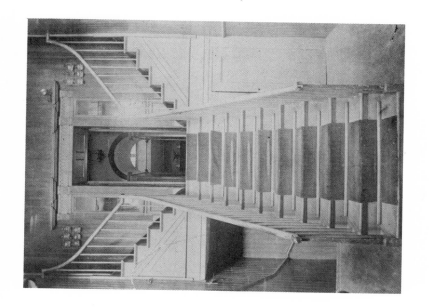

187. The Misses Chanler house, "Rokeby," 1894-1896.
Avery Library.

188. Commercial building for John Armstrong Chanler, 1899 (on the left).
(Photo: Roth)

190.   Chester William Chapin Memorial, *The Puritan*, 1884-1887.
(From L. G. White, *Sketches and Designs of Stanford White*).

193.   John H. Cheever house, "Wave Crest," 1885-1886.
(From G. W. Sheldon, *Artistic Country Seats*).

194 and 195.   Anne W. Cheney house, 1887-1888, 1902-1903.
MM&W Archive, NYHS.

198.   Rush Cheney house, 1881-1886.   Hall.
MM&W Archive, NYHS.

199. Joseph H. Choate house, "Naumkeag," 1884-1887.
AABN 24 (December 29, 1888).

199 and 942. Joseph H. Choate house, "Naumkeag," with Frederick
MacMonnies' *Young Faun with Heron* in the foreground.
Wayne Andrews.

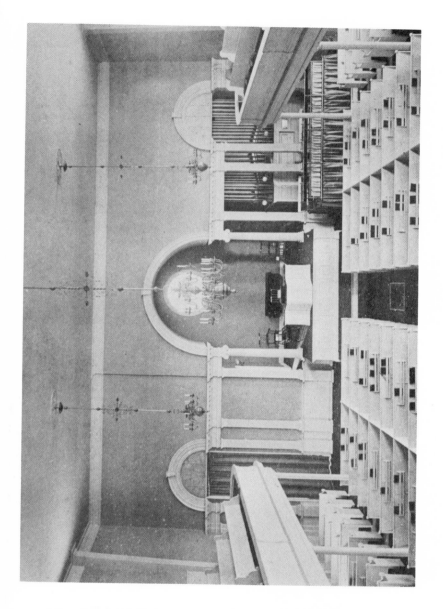

201. Church of Christ at Dartmouth, chancel alteration, 1889.
Courtesy of Frederick Lawrence Peter White.

202. Church of the Ascension, chancel alteration incorporating
The Ascension of Our Lord by John La Farge, sculpture by
Louis Saint-Gaudens, and mosaics by David Maitland Armstrong.
(From L. G. White, *Sketches and Designs of Stanford White*).

204. Church of the Ascension Parish House, 1888-1889.
(Photo: Roth)

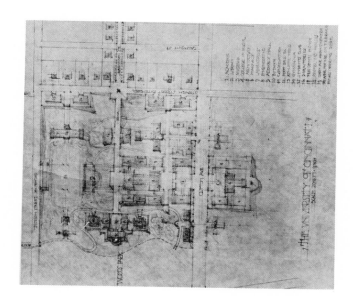

205. University of Cincinnati, comprehensive plan, sketch, 1902.
MM&W Archive, NYHS.

206. Thomas B. Clarke house, 1902.
(Photo: Roth)

207. Alexander Cochrane house, 1886-1888.
(Photo: Roth)

211. Colony Club, 1904-1908.
Avery Library.

210. Samuel Colman house, 1882-1883.
      (Photo: Roth)

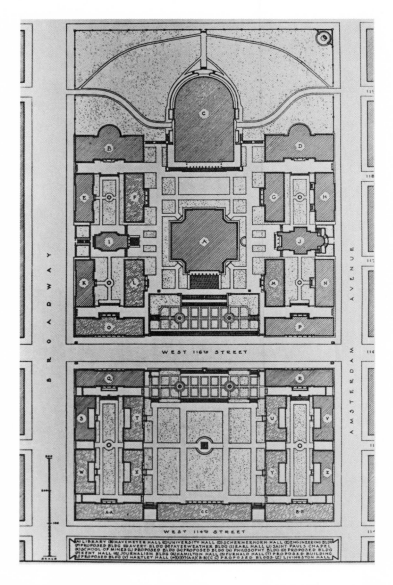

212 and 213.   Columbia University, comprehensive plan showing original
campus group (north of 116th Street), expanded campus
plan extending to 114th Street, and projected buildings.
Monograph.

212. Columbia University, view of the first buildings constructed
(Nos. 216, 217, 221, 224 and 227), c. 1898.
AABN 62 (November 5, 1898).

213. Columbia University, aerial view of completed campus complex,
c. 1930. (Compare to plan drawing).
Courtesy of Columbiana Collection, Columbia University.

214, 227, 217.   (left to right) Avery Hall, Schermerhorn Hall, and
Fayerweather Hall, Columbia University.
(Photo: Roth)

215.   Earl Hall, Columbia University.
(Photo: Roth)

219, 220, 223. (left to right) Hamilton Hall, Hartley Hall, and
Livingston Hall, Columbia University. The small
dome of the Van Amringe Memorial (No. 240) is visible between Hartley and Livingston Halls.
(Photo: Roth)

221. Havemeyer Hall, Columbia University.
(Photo: Roth)

222. Kent Hall, Columbia University.
(Photo: Roth)

224. Low Library, Columbia University, including (left to right)
     No. 231, *Alma Mater*, No. 234, fountains, and No. 239, Low
     Library forecourt landscaping and terraces.
     MM&W Archive, NYHS.

226. President's House, Columbia University, 1911-1912.
     (Photo: Roth)

233. Columbia University, exedra setting for *Pan* by George Gray Barnard, 1907-1908.
Courtesy of Columbiana Collection, Columbia University.

238. Columbia University, Memorial Sundial, Class of 1885, 1914.
Courtesy of Columbiana Collection, Columbia University.

242. Confederate Memorial, project, 1911.
MM&W Archive, NYHS.

243. Congregational Church (Congregational Society of Naugatuck),
1901-1903.
Courtesy of the Congregational Church of Naugatuck.

246. Thomas Jefferson Coolidge house, 1902-1904.
Monograph.

244. Charles T. Cook house, 1884-1885.
MM&W Archive, NYHS.

246. Thomas Jefferson Coolidge house.
MM&W Archive, NYHS.

247. Peter Cooper Memorial, 1891-1897.
       Monograph.

248. P. F. Corbin Company, office addition, 1891-1893.
(Photo: Roth)

250. Cornell Medical School, 1898-1901.
Monograph.

254. George V. Cresson house, 1883-1884.
(From G. W. Sheldon, *Artistic Country Seats*).

257. Robert W. Cumming house, 1894-1896.
Monograph.

260. Theodore R. Davis house, 1881-1885.
MM&W Archive, NYHS.

261. Henry G. deForest house, 1882.
(Photo: Roth)

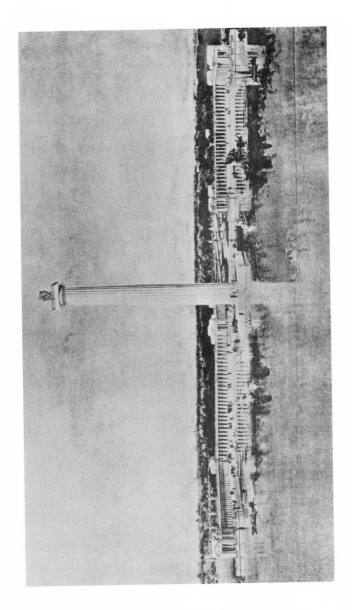

262. Detroit Memorial Column, project, 1899.
AABN 68 (June 16, 1900).

263. Deutscher Verein, club, 1889-1891.
     Sturgis, 1895.

266 and 267. "Downtown Building" of the Knickerbocker Trust Company,
              1906-1907, 1909-1911.
              Monograph.

268. J. Coleman Drayton house, 1882-1883.
Avery Library.

271. Eastman Kodak Company, offices, 1906-1907.
(Photo: Roth)

273. Commodore William Edgar house, 1884-1886.
MM&W Archive, NYHS.

277. Devereaux Emmett house, addition, 1895.
(From J. C. Baker, *American Country Homes and Their Gardens*).

280. Julius J. Estey monument, 1892.
(Photo: Roth)

288. Fanwood School, 1889-1890.
Courtesy of the Scotch Plains School System (Photo: Roth).

282. Gibson Fahnestock house, 1886-1889.
(Photo: Roth)

289. Fayette National Bank, 1912-1914.
Avery Library.

291. First Methodist Episcopal Church (Lovely Lane United Methodist
      Church), 1883-1887.
      AABN 21 (March 26, 1887).

291. First Methodist Episcopal Church, rear of sanctuary and Sunday
School wing.
Avery Library.

292. First Presbyterian Church Parish House, 1893-1894.
Avery Library.

293. First Presbyterian Church, Chattanooga, 1909-1911.
MM&W Archive, NYHS.

297. Stuyvesant Fish house, 1897-1900.
(Photo: Roth)

296. Hamilton Fish monument, 1892.
(From L. G. White, *Sketches and Designs of Stanford White*).

302. Franklin National Bank, 1915-1917.
Monograph.

305. Peter H. B. Frelinghuysen house, 1909-1913.
Monograph.

306. Freundschaft˙ Society, 1885-1889.
Sturgis, 1895.

308. Garden City Hotel, original building, 1894-1896.
Avery Library.

309. Garden City Hotel, reconstruction, 1899-1901.
     (Photo: Roth)

318. Charles Dana Gibson house, 1902-1903.
     (Photo: Roth)

314. John W. Garrett house, 1882-1886.
(Photo: Roth)

317. Germantown Cricket Club, 1889-1891.
Wayne Andrews.

321. Girard Trust Company, 1905-1909.
(Photo: Roth)

323. Robert Goelet house, "Southside," 1882-1884. Entrance front.
AABN 22 (July 2, 1887).

321. Girard Trust Company.
(Photo: Roth)

323. Robert Goelet house, "Southside." Ocean front.
(From G. W. Sheldon, *Artistic Country Seats*).

327. "Goelet Building," for Robert and Ogden Goelet, 1886-1887. Avery Library.

328. Robert and Ogden Goelet offices, 1885-1886. Sturgis, 1895.

329. "The Judge Building" for Robert and Ogden Goelet, 1888-1889.
Sturgis, 1895.

330. Robert and Ogden Goelet mausoleum, 1899.
Monograph.

331.   James J. Goodwin, double house, 1896-1898.
Monograph.

332.   Gorham Company, 1903-1906.
Monograph.

335. The Reverend John F. Goucher house, 1890-1892.
Inland Architect 23 (May, 1894).

338. Girl's Latin School, Goucher College, 1891.
Inland Architect 23 (April, 1894).

339. Gymnasium, Goucher College (right, foreground), 1887-1888;
in the distance (left to right), First Methodist Episcopal
Church, No. 291, and Goucher Hall, c. 1885, by Charles L.
Carson (?) *Brickbuilder* 15 (March, 1906).

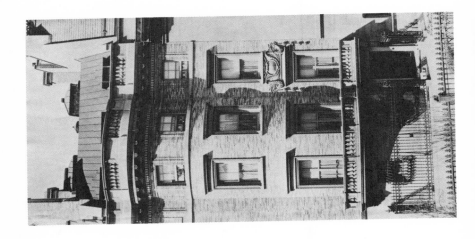

345. William D. Guthrie house, 1895-1897.
(See No. 176, Prescott Hall Butler house).
MM&W Archive, NYHS.

347. *Nathan Hale*, base, 1889.
(Photo: Roth)

346. Louis L. Hagin house, project, 1917.
Avery Library.

351. Howard M. Hanna house, 1908-1912.
(Photo: Roth)

352.   Leonard C. Hanna house, central hall, 1902-1905.
MM&W Archive, NYHS.

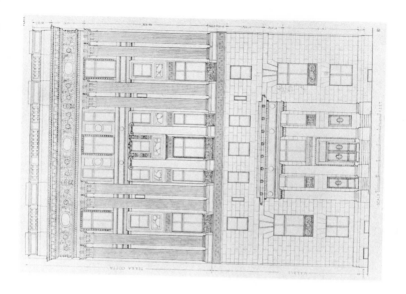

354. Harmonie Club, 1904-1907.
       Monograph.

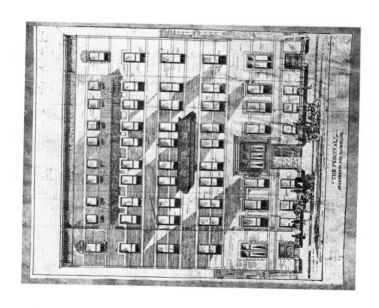

356. "The Percival" Apartment Building for O. F. Harrison,
       1882-1883.
       MM&W Archive, NYHS.

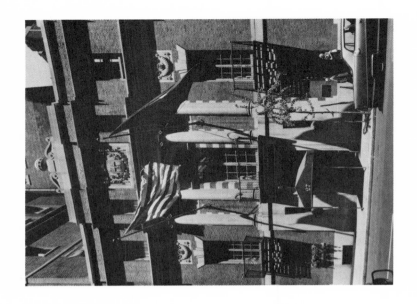

357. Harvard Club of New York, original section, 1893-1894.
(Photo: Roth)

358 and 359. Harvard Club of New York, additions to the rear
of 1900-1905 (to the left) and of 1913-1916 (to
the right).
MM&W Archive, NYHS.

359. Harvard Club of New York, addition of 1913-1916 to the front (on the left, next to the original building). *Monograph*.

360. Robinson Hall, Harvard University, 1899-1902.
Monograph.

361. Harvard Stadium, Harvard University, 1899-1903 et seq.
(From C. Moore, *The Life and Times of Charles Follen McKim*).

362. Harvard Union, Harvard University, 1899-1901.
MM&W Archive, NYHS.

363. Robert S. Bradley Memorial, Harvard University, 1910.
(Photo: Roth)

365. Samuel Johnston Memorial Gate, Harvard University, 1889-1890.
      (Photo: Roth)

366. Meyer Gate (Class of 1879), Harvard University, 1890-1891.
      (Photo: Roth)

367. Porcellian (McKean) Gate, Harvard University, 1890-1901.
(Photo: Roth)

368. Class of 1857, Memorial Gate, Harvard University, 1901-1902.
(Photo: Roth)

369. Class of 1870, Memorial Gate, Harvard University, 1899-1901.
(Photo: Roth)

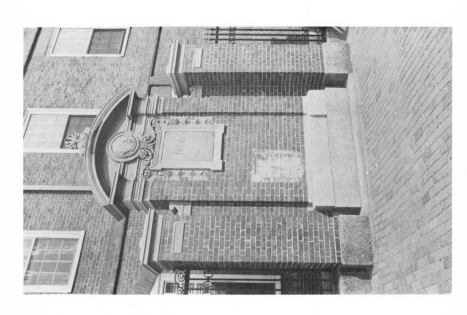

370. Class of 1873, Memorial, Harvard University, 1899-1901.
(Photo: Roth)

372. Class of 1875, Memorial Gate, Harvard University, 1899-1901. (Photo: Roth)

373. Class of 1876, Memorial Gate, Harvard University, 1899-1901. (Photo: Roth)

374. Class of 1877, Memorial Gate, Harvard University, 1899-1901.
(Photo: Roth)

375. Class of 1880, Memorial Gate, Harvard University, 1901-1902.
(Photo: Roth)

376. Class of 1885, Memorial Gate, Harvard University, 1901-1904.
(Photo: Roth)

377. Class of 1886, Memorial Gate, Harvard University, 1899-1901.
(Photo: Roth)

378. Classes of 1887 and 1888, Memorial Gate, Harvard University, 1905-1906.
(Photo: Roth)

379. Class of 1889, Memorial Gate, Harvard University, 1899-1901.
(Photo: Roth)

380. Class of 1890, Memorial Gate, Harvard University, 1899-1901. (Photo: Roth)

394. Charles W. Henry house, 1887-
AABN 48 (June 8, 1895).

399. Henry B. Hollins house, 1899-1901.
Avery Library.

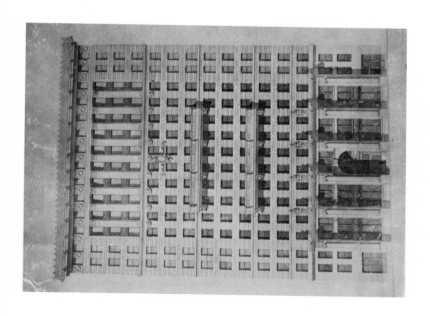

405. Home Life Insurance Company, project, 1892. Side elevation.
Avery Library.

406. A. C. Honore mausoleum, 1905.
(Photo: Roth)

407. Mrs. Blanche F. Hooker, additions to house, 1907-1908.
Monograph.

410. Mrs. Mark Hopkins house, 1885-1886.
MM&W Archive, NYHS.

411. Hotel Imperial, 1889-1891.
AABN 30 (October 25, 1890).

412. Hotel Imperial, with addition of 1891-1894 (to the left).
MM&W Archive, NYHS.

414. Hotel Pennsylvania, 1915-1920.
Atlantic Terra Cotta 9 (June, 1927).

416. Dr. Robert T. Howe house, 1886-1887.
Courtesy of Richard Guy Wilson (Photo: Wilson).

417. Alfred M. Hoyt house, Montauk Point, 1882-1883.
Courtesy of Richard Guy Wilson (Photo: Wilson).

421. Hunt Memorial Building, Hartford Medical College, 1897-1898.
Brickbuilder 13 (February, 1904).

423. Women's Building, University of Illinois, 1903-1905.
(Photo: Roth)

418. Alfred M. Hoyt house, New York, 1883-1885.
Avery Library.

436. John Innes Kane house, 1904-1908.
MM&W Archive, NYHS.

424. Interborough Rapid Transit Company powerhouse.
MM&W Archive, NYHS.

424. Interborough Rapid Transit Company powerhouse, 1901-1904.
(Photo: Roth)

434 and 435. Judson Memorial Church, tower, and Judson Hall
               (to the right), 1888-1893, 1895-1896.
               AABN 40 (May 13, 1893).

441.   William W. Kimball monument, 1907-1908.
       (Photo: Roth)

442. Dining room addition to "Kingscote," the David H. King, jr.,
      house, 1880-1881.
      (From A. Downing and V. Scully, *The Architectural Heritage of
      Newport, Rhode Island*).

447. Townhouse group built by David H. King, jr., 1885-1886.
      Brickbuilder 7 (March, 1898).

448. "King Model Houses" ("Striver's Row"), built by David H. King, jr., 1891-1892.
(Photo: Roth)

450, 451, and 452. George Gordon King house, "Edgehill," 1887-1888, 1902-1904, 1906-1907.
(Photo: Roth)

448. "King Model Houses," 259 139th Street.
(Photo: Roth)

454. LeRoy King house, 1884-1886.
MM&W Archive, NYHS.

457. King's Mountain Battlefield Memorial, 1910.
Avery Library.

458. George G. Kip memorial, Baptismal Font, 1893.
      (Photo: Roth)

461. The Lambs Club, 1903-1905.
      Monograph.

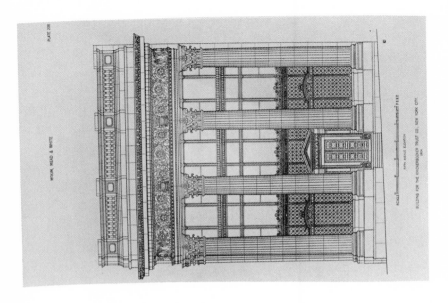

460. Knickerbocker Trust. Elevation drawing. *Monograph.*

460. Knickerbocker Trust and Safe Deposit Company, 1901-1904. MM&W Archive, NYHS.

462. Dining room wing addition to the Woodbury Langdon house (center and left), 1905-1906.
(Photo: Roth)

463. Bryan Lathrop house, 1891-1893.
(Photo: Roth)

470. *Lincoln* (Seated), 1902-1920.
(Photo: Roth)

471. *Lincoln* (Standing), 1884-1887.
(Photo: Roth)

474. William G. Low house, 1886-1887.
Library of Congress, HABS Photo by Cerwin Robinson, 1962.

475. Philip M. Lydig house, living room, 1903-1905.
Good Furniture 9 (1917).

477. Cyrus Hall McCormick house, "Clayton Lodge," 1880-1882.
      MM&W Archive, NYHS.

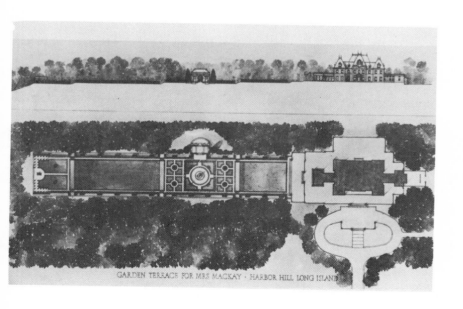

GARDEN TERRACE FOR MRS MACKAY · HARBOR HILL LONG ISLAND

479. Clarence H. Mackay house, "Harbor Hill," plan of grounds
      adjacent to the house, 1899-1902.
      Avery Library.

479. Clarence H. Mackay house, "Harbor Hill."
MM&W Archive, NYHS.

481. Study for hunting lodge for Clarence H. Mackay, 1903.
Avery Library.

482. McKinley Birthplace National Memorial, 1915-1918.
(Photo: Roth)

485. Madison Square Garden, 1887-1891.
Avery Library.

486. Madison Square Presbyterian Church, 1903-1906.
Monograph.

487. Pediment sculpture, Madison Square Presbyterian Church,
     installed 1910.
     Atlantic Terra Cotta 9 (June, 1927).

488. Manchester Public Library, 1886-1887.
     Courtesy of the Manchester Public Library.

491. Maryland Society Battle Monument, Prospect Park, 1892.
(From *King's Views of Brooklyn*).

493.   Massapequa Land Company, station and park project, 1908.
        MM&W Archive, NYHS.

495.   Thomas H. Mastin house, 1888-1889.
        Avery Library.

499. Edwin D. Metcalf house, 1882-1884.
Photograph Collection of the Division of the History of Art,
Ohio State University.

500. Metropolitan Club, 1891-1894.
MM&W Archive, NYHS.

500. Lounge, Metropolitan Club.
      AABN 55 (February 13, 1897).

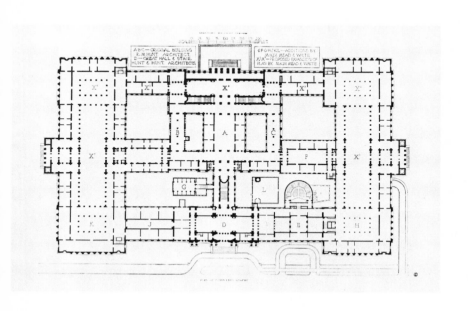

502. Metropolitan Museum of Art, comprehensive plan, 1904-1906.
      Monograph.

507, 510, and 511. Metropolitan Museum of Art, east front. Sections
                    J and K in the foreground; Sections E and H in the
                    distance.
                    (Photo: Roth)

518. Ogden Mills house, 1894-1897.
      Avery Library.

515. Tenement apartment building for James C. Miller, 1886-1887.
(Photo: Roth)

519. Minneapolis Museum of Fine Arts (Minneapolis Institute of Arts),
1911-1914.
Monograph.

521. Helena Modjeska house, 1888 et seq.
Sturgis, 1895.

524. Montclair High School project.
Avery Library.

526. William H. Moore house, 1900.
(Photo: Roth)

527. Edwin D. Morgan house, "Beacon Rock," 1888-1891.
Sturgis, 1895.

527. Edwin D. Morgan house, "Beacon Rock."
Wayne Andrews.

528. Edwin D. Morgan house, "Wheatley Hills," first section, 1890-1891.
MM&W Archive, NYHS.

529. Edwin D. Morgan house, "Wheatley Hills," additions, 1898-1900.
MM&W Archive, NYHS.

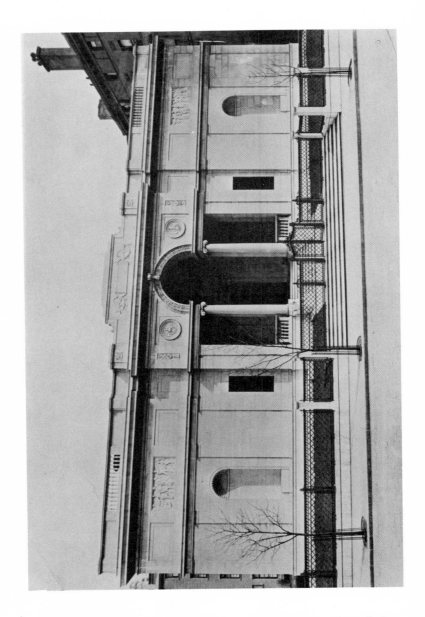

530. John Pierpont Morgan Library, 1902-1907 (a portion of the
Herbert L. Satterlee house, No. 763, is visible at the far
right).
MM&W Archive, NYHS.

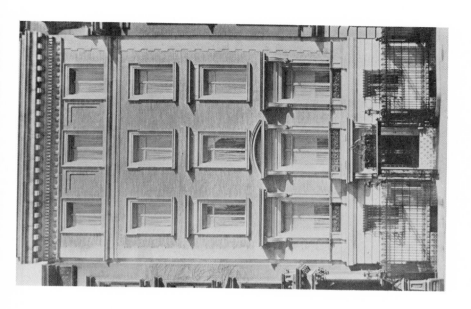

533.   Levi P. Morton house, 1896-1898.
Brickbuilder 11 (January, 1902).

539.   Municipal Building, City of New York, 1907-1916.
MM&W Archive, NYHS.

541. Munsey Building ("Times Building"), first section, 1905-1907. *AABN* 89 (May 12, 1906).

542 and 543. Munsey Building. First section enlarged and refaced (right side); new second section to the left; 1912-1918. (Photo: Roth).

544. Munsey Building, Baltimore, 1908-1913.
Avery Library.

547. Narragansett Pier Casino, 1883-1886.
MM&W Archive, NYHS.

548. National Cash Register Company, auditorium, 1911-1914.
Avery Library.

549. National City Bank, new bank offices in upper half (lower
half by Isaiah Rogers, 1836-1842), 1904-1910.
Avery Library.

549. National City Bank, renovated banking room.
Monograph.

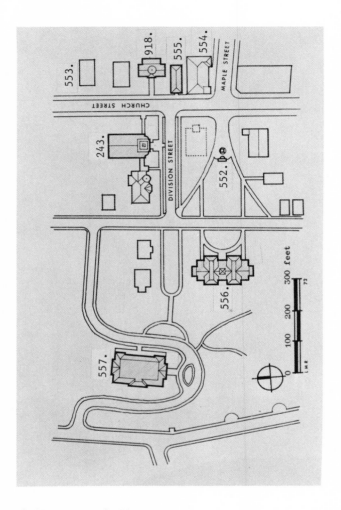

552 through 557, 243, and 918.
      Plan of Naugatuck, Connecticut, showing location of buildings
      commissioned by John Howard Whittemore and built through his
      influence.
      552. Relandscaped town green and new fountain.
      553. Approximate location of projected bank.
      554. Location of new city hall, replacing existing building.
      555. Naugatuck National Bank, 1892-1893.
      556. Naugatuck Public Grammar School, "Salem School," 1892-1894.
      557. Naugatuck Public High School, "Hillside School," 1901-1905.
      243. Congregational Church of Naugatuck, 1901-1903.
      918. Howard Whittemore Memorial Library.

      (Photo: Roth)

552, 555, 556, 243, and 918.
    View of the Naugatuck town green and surrounding buildings,
    c. 1915. (Clockwise from the Congregational Church) 243, Con-
    gregational Church; 918, Howard Whittemore Memorial Library;
    555, Naugatuck National Bank; city hall; 552, town green with
    fountain at the center; 556, Naugatuck Public Grammar School,
    "Salem School." Courtesy Howard Whittemore Memorial Library.

552. Fountain, Naugatuck green, 1894-1895.
MM&W Archive, NYHS.

553. "Naugatuck Bank," project, 1906.
Avery Library.

554. Naugatuck City Hall, project, 1906.
Avery Library.

555. Naugatuck National Bank, 1892-1893.
MM&W Archive, NYHS.

556. Naugatuck Public Grammar School, "Salem School," 1892-1894.
(Photo: Roth)

557. Naugatuck Public High School, "Hillside School," 1901-1905.
(Photo: Roth)

559. Comprehensive plan, University of Nevada, 1906.
Mackay School of Mines at the left end of the quadrangle.
Avery Library.

559. Mackay School of Mines, study.
Avery Library.

561. New England Trust Company, 1904-1907.
(Photo: Roth)

567. "Grand Central Station," project, for the New York Central
and Hudson River Railroad, 1903. View from the southwest.
MM&W Archive, NYHS.

567. "Grand Central Station," project. View from the north. MM&W Archive, NYHS.

569. New York City Board of Education Building, project, 1892. Sturgis, 1895.

570. New York City Hospital, project, 1911.
Avery Library.

572. *New York Herald* Building, 1890-1895. General view.
MM&W Archive, NYHS.

571. New York Clearing House Association, project, 1894.
Avery Library.

572. *New York Herald* Building.   34th Street entrance.
MM&W Archive, NYHS.

576. New York Life Insurance Company Building, Kansas City, 1887-1890.
Inland Architect 14 (December, 1889).

577. New York Life Insurance Company Building, Omaha, 1887-1890.
Sturgis, 1895 (misidentified there as the Kansas City building).

578-579. New York Life Insurance Company, Main Offices, 1893-1899.
(Photo: Roth)

580. Directors' Room, New York Life Insurance Company, 1896-1899.
Monograph.

581. "The Yosemite" Apartment Building, for the New York Life
Insurance Company, 1887-1890.
AABN 31 (February 21, 1891).

582. Waterbury Station, New York, New Haven, and Hartford Railroad, 1906-1909.
      Avery Library.

583. New York Post Graduate Hospital and Medical School, 1910-1912.
      Monograph.

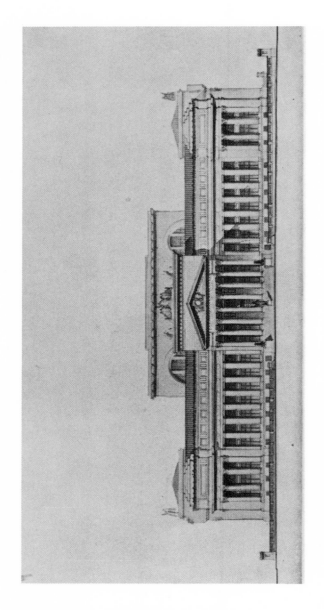

585. New York Public Library, project, 1897.
(From C. Moore, *The Life and Times of Charles Follen McKim*).

586. Chatham Square Branch, New York Public Library No. 2, 1902-1903. (Photo: Roth)

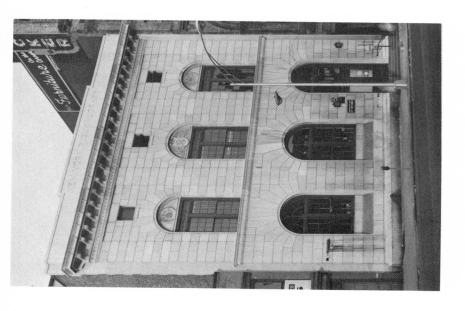

587. 125th Street Branch, New York Public Library No. 6, 1902-1903. (Photo: Roth)

588. 135th Street Branch, New York Public Library No. 10, 1903-1905. (Photo: Roth)

589. Rivington Street Branch, New York Public Library, No. 11, 1904-1905. (Photo: Roth)

590. Thompkins Square Branch, New York Public Library No. 14,
1903-1905.
(Photo: Roth)

591. Kingsbridge Branch, New York Public Library No. 23, 1904-1905.
(Photo: Roth)

592. St. Gabriel's Branch, New York Public Library No. 29, 1906-1908.
Monograph.

593. 115th Street Branch, New York Public Library No. 32, 1907-1909.
(Photo: Roth)

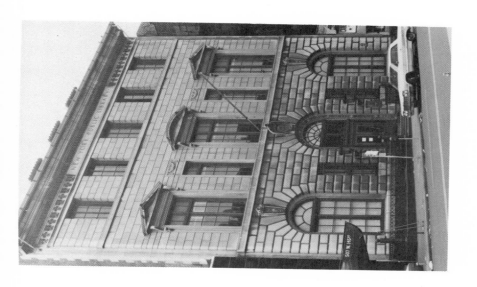

594. Hamilton Grange Branch, New York Public Library No. 35,
1905-1906.
(Photo: Roth)

595. Mt. Morris Branch, New York Public Library No. 37, 1907-1909.
(Photo: Roth)

596. Woodstock Branch, New York Public Library No. 42, 1912-1914.
Monograph.

597. New York State Building, World's Columbian Exposition, 1892-1893.
Monograph.

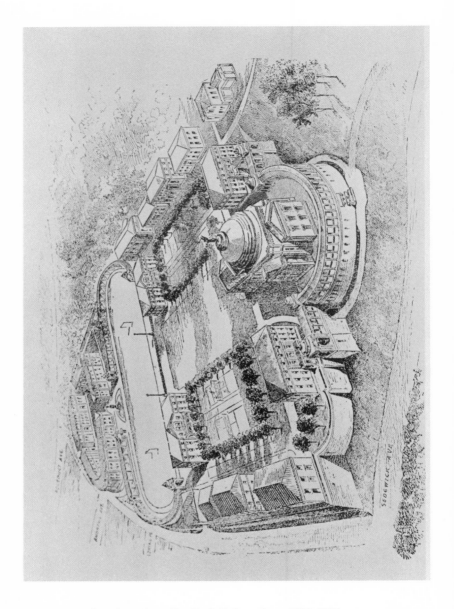

598. Comprehensive plan, New York University, 1892-1893.
The Gould Library, No. 601, is in the center foreground, with
the Hall of Languages, No. 602, to its right, and the "museum,"
No. 603, diagonally across and perpendicular to the Hall of
Languages. The Dormitory, No. 600, is at the far end of the
campus on the center axis of the library.
(From J. L. Chamberlain, *New York University*).

599. "Hall of Fame" Ambulatory around the Gould Library, 1900-1901.
MM&W Archive, NYHS.

600. Dormitory, New York University, 1896-1897.
AABN 73 (September 14, 1901).

601 and 602.   Gould Library and Administrative Offices (right), 1896-1903.
Hall of Languages (left), 1894, New York University.
AABN 73 (September 14, 1901).

603.   "Museum," New York University, 1896-1898.
(Photo: Roth)

606. Thomas Newbold house, 1916-1918.
(Photo: Roth)

607. H. Victor Newcomb house, 1880.
(From G. W. Sheldon, *Artistic Country Seats*).

610. Daniel S. Newhall house, 1886.
(Photo: Roth)

612. Newport Casino, 1879-1880.
      (Photo: Roth)

614. George A. Nickerson house, 1895-1897.
(Photo: Roth)

615. 998 Fifth Avenue Apartment Building, 1910-1914.
(Photo: Roth)

617. Mandan Station, Northern Pacific Railroad, 1884.
MM&W Archive, NYHS.

619. "Portland House," Hotel, Northern Pacific Railroad, 1882-1885.
As originally designed.
West Shore (April, 1882), Courtesy of the Oregon Historical Society.

620. Portland Terminal Station, Northern Pacific Railroad, 1882.
      West Shore (April, 1882), Courtesy of the Oregon Historical Society.

622. Tacoma Terminal Hotel, Northern Pacific Railroad, 1884.
      Courtesy of the Tacoma Public Library.

623. Oakland City Hall, project, 1910. Elevation.
Avery Library.

626. Herman Oelrichs house, "Rosecliff," 1897-1902.
Wayne Andrews.

627. A. H. Olmsted house, 1884-1887.
Inland Architect 15 (May, 1890).

629. Orange Free Library (Stickler Memorial), 1900-1901.
(Photo: Roth)

630. Alexander E. Orr house, 1882.
(Photo: Roth)

631. Charles J. Osborn house, 1883-1885.
MM&W Archive, NYHS.

634. Thomas Nelson Page house, 1896-1897.
(Photo: Roth)

631. Charles J. Osborn house. Hall.
Magazine of Art (May, 1885).

632. Charles J. Osborn mausoleum, 1909.
Monograph.

637. Potter Palmer mausoleum, 1904-1906.
      (Photo: Roth)

639. Court of the Universe, Panama-Pacific Exposition, 1912-1915.
Monograph.

639. Court of the Universe, Panama-Pacific Exposition, 1912-1915.
Monograph.

644. Park & Tilford store and offices, 1892-1893.
(Photo: Roth)

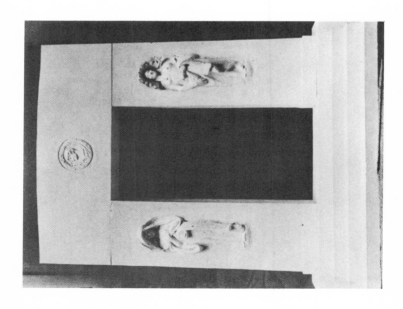

648. Francis Parkman Memorial, first design, c. 1901.
(From M. Richman, *Daniel Chester French: An American Sculptor*).

651. Robert W. Patterson house, Chicago, 1892-1895.
(Photo: Roth)

652. Robert W. Patterson house, Washington, D.C., 1900-1903.
(Photo: Roth)

656. Penn Station, Pennsylvania Railroad Company, 1902-1911.
      Aerial view, March, 1910.
      Avery Library (Dreyer Photo).

656. Penn Station. Concourse, October, 1909.
      Avery Library (Dreyer Photo).

656. Penn Station. Waiting Room, c. 1912.
MM&W Archive, NYHS.

657.   Power Station, Penn Station, Pennsylvania Railroad Company,
        1905-1908.
        (Photo: Roth)

658.   Phelps Association, "Wolf's Head," Yale University, 1884-1885.
        (Photo: Roth)

659.   Phillips and Lloyd Phoenix house, 1882-1884.
       Avery Library.

659.   Phillips and Lloyd Phoenix house.
       AABN 87 (February 4, 1905).

663. New portico, addition to the Players' Club, 1888-1889.
      Avery Library.

665. Plaza Hotel, completed from designs begun by Fife & Campbell,
      1888-1891.
      (From M. Black, *Old New York in Early Photographs*).

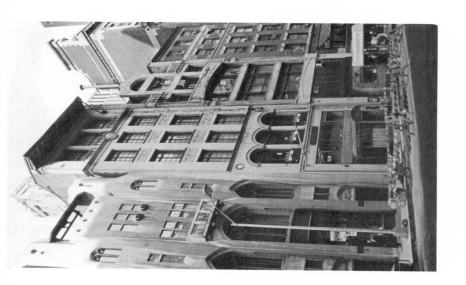

670. A. C. Polifeme Building, 1911.
(Photo: Roth)

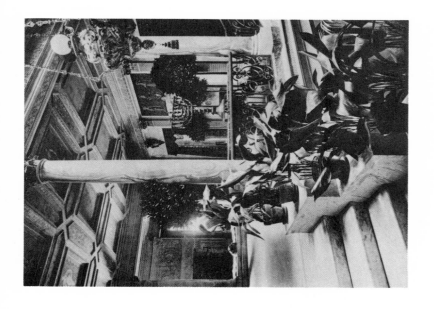

671. Henry W. Poor house, 1899-1901. Stairhall.
Monograph.

673. Alfred A. Pope house, "Hill-Stead," 1898-1901.
Monograph.

676. Athletic Field fence and gate, Princeton University, 1910-1911.
Monograph.

677. Cottage Club, Princeton University, 1904-1908.
(Photo: Roth)

679. FitzRandolph Memorial Gates, Princeton University, 1903-1905.
Monograph.

681. Prison Ship Martyrs' Monument, 1906-1909.
Avery Library.

684. Croquet Shelter, Prospect Park, 1904.
Brickbuilder 13 (December, 1904).

682 and 691. Grand Army Plaza entrance to Prospect Park, showing
original placement of the James Stranahan Memorial,
No. 691, in the foreground. Sculpture on Doric columns
by Frederick MacMonnies.
(From *King's Views of Brooklyn*).

685. Ninth Avenue and 15th Street entrance, Prospect Park, 1907-1908.
Monograph.

686. Park Circle entrance, Prospect Park (Parkside and Ocean Avenues),
1890. *The Horse Tamers (The Triumph of Mind over Brute Force)*,
by Frederick MacMonnies.
AABN 65 (September 16, 1899).

686. *The Horse Tamers* by Frederick MacMonnies.
Monograph.

688. Pavilion, Park Circle entrance, Prospect Park, 1890.
Monograph.

693. Puck Building, World's Columbian Exposition, 1892-1893.
Avery Library.

697. Joseph Pulitzer house, 1900-1903.
(Photo: Roth)

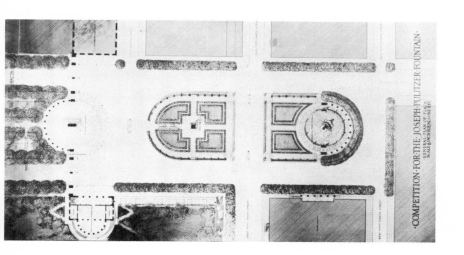

698. Pulitzer Fountain, project, 1913.
Avery Library.

701.   Percy R. Pyne house, 1906-1912.
       (Photo: Roth)

702.   Quogue Episcopal Church, 1884.
       (Photo: Roth)

703. Racquet and Tennis Club, 1916-1919.
(Photo: Roth)

705. Radcliffe College Gymnasium, 1897-1899.
Monograph.

704. Radcliffe College, study for library, 1897.
MM&W Archive, NYHS.

706. Ramona Industrial School for Indian Girls, 1887-1888 (?)
MM&W Archive, NYHS.

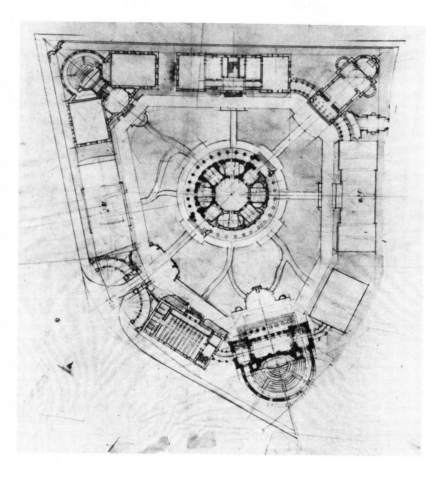

704. Radcliffe College, comprehensive plan, study, 1897.
MM&W Archive, NYHS.

708 and 874. Geraldyn Redmond house (right half) and Countess de Laugier Villars house (left half), 1912-1915.
Monograph.

718. Library addition to the Villard house for Whitelaw Reid,
1909-1913.
Monograph.

721. Rhode Island State Capitol, 1891-1903.
(Photo: Roth)

725. "Turtle Top" houses for Roanoke Rapids Power Company, 1895.
Courtesy of the North Carolina Department of Cultural Resources.

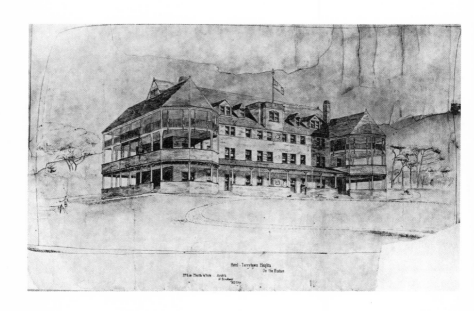

730. "The Pocantico" Hotel and cottages for Lewis Roberts, 1882-1883.
MM&W Archive, NYHS.

727. J. Hampden Robb house, 1889-1891.
(Photo: Roth)

734. Philip A. Rollins house, 1899-1902.
AABN 89 (May 12, 1906).

743. Russell and Erwin Building (RussWin Hotel) for H. E. Russell and C. B. Erwin, 1883-1885. Remodeled for New Britain City Hall (No. 560), 1907-1909. (Photo: Roth)

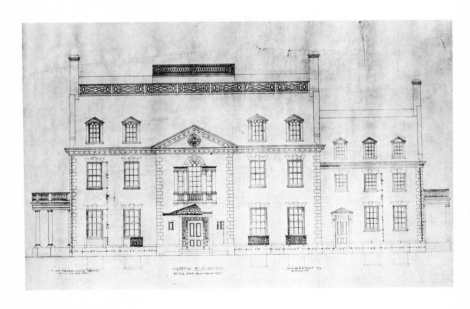

737. Robert K. Root house, 1894-1896. Drawing, ink on linen. MM&W Archive, NYHS.

739. Royal Trust Company, 1911-1914.
Monograph.

742. Henry E. Russell mausoleum, 1893-1894.
Monograph.

745. Portals (Vanderbilt Memorial), Saint Bartholomew's Church
(reinstalled in new building), 1901-1903.
(Photo: Roth)

750. Saint Marys Falls Canal Memorial Obelisk, 1905-1907.
(From C. Moore, *The Life and Times of Charles Follen McKim*).

751. Saint Paul the Apostle, High Altar, 1887-1890. Angels by
      Frederick MacMonnies, lamp by Philip Martiny.
      (From L. G. White, *Sketches and Designs of Stanford White*).

752. Saint Paul's Church, 1883-1885.
AABN 75 (February 15, 1902).

754. Saint Peter's Church, original design, 1886-1890. Elevation.
Monograph.

754. Saint Peter's Church. Chancel.
MM&W Archive, NYHS.

756 and 757. Saint Peter's Church, tower, 1905-1908; Saint Peter's
Rectory is visible next to the tree on the far right.
(Photo: Roth)

762. Henry Sanger house, 1882-1883.
Courtesy of Richard Guy Wilson (Photo: Wilson).

769. Admiral Thomas O. Selfridge, jr., house, 1897-1899.
AABN 90 (September 8, 1906).

763. Herbert L. Satterlee house, 1903-1904. Avery Library.

767. Second National Bank, 1907-1908. (Photo: Roth)

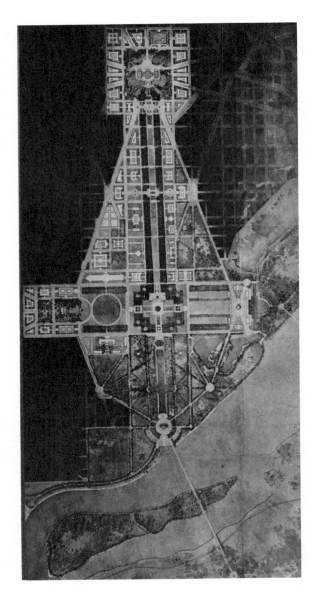

770. Plan for the restitution of the Mall, Senate Park Commission,
     1901-1902.
     MM&W Archive, NYHS.

770. Aerial view of the new Mall, Senate Park Commission.
      Library of Congress.

770. View of the proposed terraces at the Washington Monument,
Senate Park Commission (this section by McKim).
MM&W Archive, NYHS.

771. Colonel Robert Gould Shaw Memorial, 1890-1897.
AABN 57 (September 11, 1897).

774. Elliott Fitch Shepard house, "Woodlea," 1890-1895. *Monograph*.

776. General William Tecumseh Sherman Memorial, 1902-1903.
(Photo: Roth)

777. William Watts Sherman house, library renovation, 1881.
(From A. Downing and V. Scully, *The Architectural Heritage
of Newport, Rhode Island*).

778. Louis Sherry casino project (?), 1894.
MM&W Archive, NYHS.

781. Louis Sherry hotel project, London, 1902. Avery Library.

787. Shinnecock Hills Golf Club, clubhouse, 1892-1895. (Photo: Roth)

785. Ballroom, "Sherry's."
      MM&W Archive, NYHS.

785. "Sherry's" Restaurant and Hotel, 1896-1898.
      MM&W Archive, NYHS.

788.   Shore Road Commission, bridge project, 1898.
       MM&W Archives, NYHS.

789.   Short Hills Music Hall (Casino), 1879-1880.
       MM&W Archive, NYHS.

790. Mrs. Frances L. Skinner house, 1882.
(Photo: Roth)

791. *General Henry W. Slocum*, at original location on Bedford
Avenue.
(From *King's Views of New York*).

795. State Savings Bank, 1898-1900.
MM&W Archive, NYHS.

796. State Street Exchange, project, 1887.   Elevation.
AABN 22 (October 15, 1887).

796. State Street Exchange, project. Corridor.
      AABN 22 (October 15, 1887).

804. Stockbridge Casino, 1887 (removed to a new location).
      Elevation.
      MM&W Archive, NYHS.

805. William E. D. Stokes house, 1898-1900.
AABN 69 (September 1, 1900).

814. H. A. C. Taylor mausoleum, 1900-1901.
Monograph.

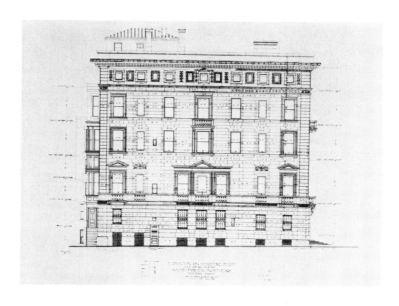

811. Edwin F. Swift house, 1898-1899.
MM&W Archive, NYHS.

813. Henry Augustus Coit Taylor house, Newport, 1882-1886.
AABN 22 (July 23, 1887).

815. H. A. C. Taylor house, New York, 1892-1896.
MM&W Archive, NYHS.

817. Double house for H. A. C. Taylor, New York, 1892-1896.
MM&W Archive, NYHS.

818. Broadcasting tower, Wardenclyffe, 1902.
Electrical World 43 (March 5, 1904).

818. Laboratory, Wardenclyffe, 1902.
      (Photo: Roth)

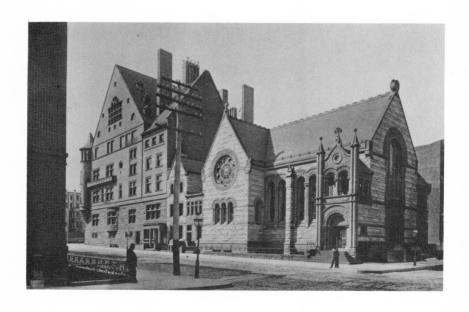

824. Charles L. Tiffany house from the north, with Saint James'
      Lutheran Church in the foreground.
      AABN 33 (July 4, 1891).

824. Charles L. Tiffany house, 1882-1885.
AABN 20 (July 17, 1886).

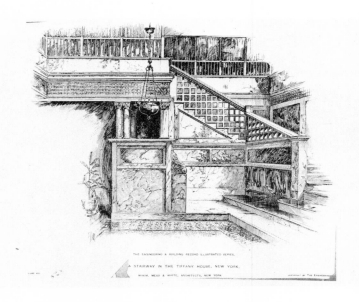

824.   Charles L. Tiffany house, stairway.
MM&W Archive, NYHS.

824.   Charles L. Tiffany house, hall.
MM&W Archive, NYHS.

826. Tiffany & Company, 1903-1906.
MM&W Archive, NYHS.

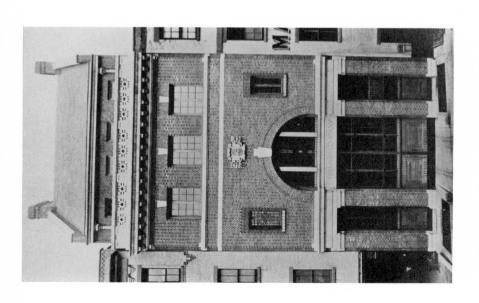

828. Tiffany & Company Stable (Garage), 1904-1905.
Brickbuilder 15 (February, 1906).

829. Samuel Tilton house, 1880-1882.
      (Photo: Roth)

829. Samuel Tilton house, hall.
      (From A. Downing and V. Scully, *The Architectural Heritage of
      Newport, Rhode Island*).

832. Trinity Church (foreground) and Parish House (in the distance
on the right), 1905-1907.
(Photo: Roth)

Coachman's Cottage for Mr. W.P. Tuckerman Oyster Bay L.I. McKim Mead and White Arch't New York City

836. Walter C. Tuckerman house, coachman's cottage, 1882.
MM&W Archive, NYHS.

847. U. S. Army War College, comprehensive plan, 1902-1908.
In the foreground is the War College building; to the
left is the Officers' Mess with Officers' houses lined
behind it to the north; to the left are more Officers'
houses; facing the quadrangle at the far north end are
Barracks; the Engineer's School, No. 848, and the Laboratory, No. 849, are at the far north end.
(Courtesy of U. S. Army).

847. U. S. Army War College.
Monograph.

850. U. S. Coast Guard, life-saving station, 1889.
Sturgis, 1895.

851. U. S. Custom House, New York, project, 1900.
MM&W Archive, NYHS.

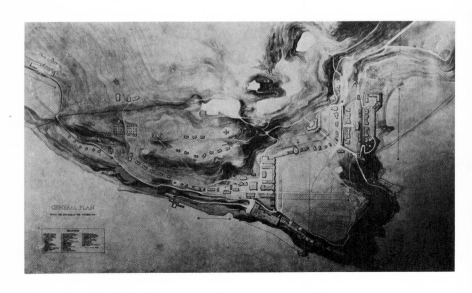

853. U. S. Military Academy at West Point, comprehensive
plan, project, 1902.
Avery Library.

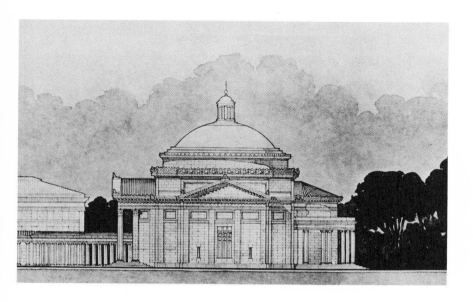

853. U. S. MIlitary Academy at West Point, comprehensive
plan, project. Chapel. Elevation.
MM&W Archive, NYHS.

854. Battle Monument, U. S. Military Academy at West Point,
1891-1896.
(Photo: Roth)

855. Cullum Memorial Hall, U. S. Military Academy at West Point, 1893-1898.
(Photo: Roth)

857. U. S. Post Office, New York City, 1908-1913.
(Photo: Roth)

859.   University Club, 1896-1900.   Photo, c. 1899, showing the
clean white surface of the Milford granite and the surrounding
balustrade at the sidewalk.
AABN 65 (August 26, 1899).

859.   University Club.   Library, showing ceiling murals by H.
Siddons Mowbray.
MM&W Archive, NYHS.

862. Office building for Cornelius and William Kissam Vanderbilt, 1892-1893.
(Photo: Roth)

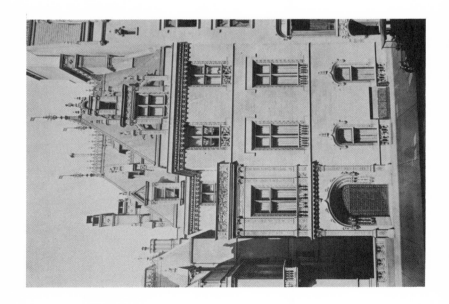

865. Mrs. William Kissam (Virginia) Vanderbilt house, 1904-1907.
MM&W Archive, NYHS.

864. Frederick William Vanderbilt house, 1895-1899.
Monograph.

865. Original William Kissam Vanderbilt house (R. M. Hunt, 1879-
1881) with the new Virginia Vanderbilt house immediately
next to it to the north.
New-York Historical Society.

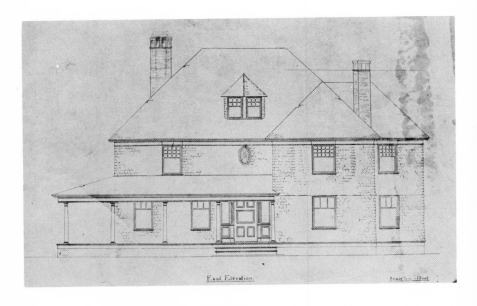

867. The Reverend Wynant Vanderpoel house, 1884-1885.
      MM&W Archive, NYHS.

868. Vassar College Auditorium, "Students' Building," 1912-1914.
      Monograph.

869. Henry Villard house group, 1882-1885.
Monograph.

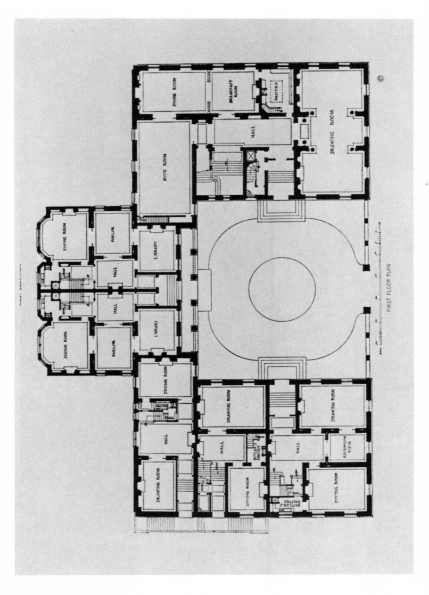

869. Henry Villard house group. Plan. The Villard house (later the
Whitelaw Reid house, No. 717) was the right or southern wing;
a portion of Whitelaw Reid's additions are just visible to the
rear in the photo. The right-hand, southern unit in the court
was the Artemas H. Holmes house, No. 401. The left-hand, northern unit in the court was the Edward Dean Adams house, No. 53.
The front of the left, northern wing, was the Harris C. Fahnestock house, No. 284. The two units behind this, which opened
unto 51st Street, were also purchased by Harris C. Fahnestock,
Nos. 285 and 286.
Monograph.

875 through 883.   University of Virginia, aerial view. In the foreground is Cabell Hall, No. 877, with its large
semicircular auditorium. Just below this is the
boiler house, No. 876, with its tall smoke stack.
To the right is Rouss Hall, No. 883; to the left
is Cocke Hall, No. 878. To the left of this
group is the Garrett Hall refectory, No. 879.
At the upper end of the Lawn is the restored
Rotunda.
Courtesy of the Alderman Library, University of
Virginia.

870. Henry Villard house, "Thorwood," Dobbs Ferry, 1880. Interior.
Century Magazine 32 (May, 1886).

877. Cabell Hall, University of Virginia, 1896-1898.
(Photo: Roth)

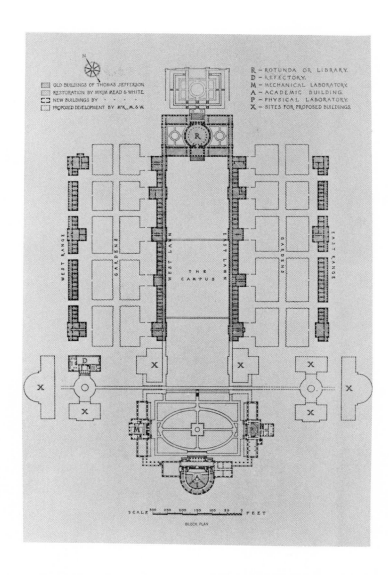

875. University of Virginia, comprehensive plan for restoration of
rotunda and new academic buildings, 1896.
Monograph.

878. Cocke Hall, University of Virginia, 1896-1898.
Courtesy of the Alderman Library, University of Virginia.

879. Garrett Hall, refectory, University of Virginia, 1906-1907.
Courtesy of the Alderman Library, University of Virginia.

879. Garrett Hall, refectory, dining hall.
Courtesy of the Alderman Library, University of Virginia.

881. President's House, "Carr's Hill," University of Virginia,
1912-1913.
(Photo: Roth)

882. Rotunda, University of Virginia (restoration of 1896-1899).
(Photo: Roth)

882. Rotunda, University of Virginia, view from the rear, showing
new porch, wings, and steps added by McKim, Mead & White,
1896-1899.
Courtesy of the Alderman Library, University of Virginia.

883. Rouss Hall, University of Virginia, 1896-1898.
Courtesy of the Alderman Library, University of Virginia.

886. Benjamin H. Warder monument, 1894.
(Photo: Roth)

887. Office building for George H. Warren, 1890-1891.
Sturgis, 1895.

900. Horace White house, Elberon, 1880-1881.
Century Magazine 32 (May, 1886).

890 and 434. Washington Memorial Arch, 1889-1892, looking toward
Judson Memorial Church across Washington Square.
(Photo: Roth)

902. Stanford White house, New York, 1884 et seq. Stairhall.
Courtesy of Frederick Lawrence Peter White.

902. Stanford White house, New York. Upper stairhall.
Courtesy of Frederick Lawrence Peter White.

902. Stanford White house, New York. Sitting room.
The frames over the mantle and to its left are very
typical of those designed by White.
Courtesy of Frederick Lawrence Peter White.

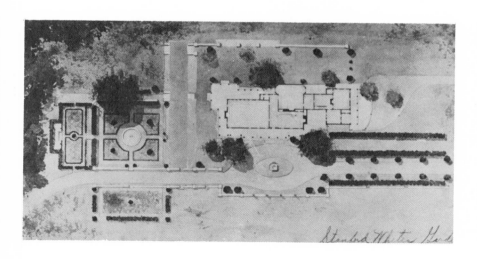

903. Stanford White house, "Box Hill," St. James, 1892 et seq.
Plan of the approaches and gardens.
Avery Library.

903. Stanford White house, "Box Hill." View from the garden.
(From J. C. Baker, *American Country Homes and Their Gardens*).

903. Stanford White house, "Box Hill." Dining room.
(From L. G. White, *Sketches and Designs of Stanford White*).

904.　The White House, renovations, 1902.
View of the East Terrace addition.
Monograph.

904.　The White House.　New public entrance and East Terrace.
Library of Congress.

906. White Star Steamship Company building, World's Columbian
Exposition, 1892-1893 (on the right). Puck building, No.
693, is on the left.
Snapshot of the exposition, author's collection.

910. Payne Whitney house. Stairhall.
Monograph.

910 and 476.   Payne Whitney house, 1902-1909 (right side; left half of the house built by the J. C. Lyons Building Company, No. 476).
(Photo: Roth)

914.   William Collins Whitney house, 1897-1902.   Stairhall.
Monograph.

917. Harris Whittemore house, 1901-1903.
      Architectural Record 19 (February, 1906).

918. Howard Whittemore Memorial Library, 1891-1894.
      Courtesy of the Howard Whittemore Memorial Library.

919.   John Howard Whittemore house, Naugatuck, 1885-1890.
(Photo: Roth)

920.   John Howard Whittemore house, Middlebury, 1894-1896.
MM&W Archive, NYHS.

921. Charles A. Whittier house, 1881-1883 (right half of double house; left half is F. L. Higginson house by H. H. Richardson, 1881-1883).
AABN 14 (November 24, 1883).

925. Joseph E. Willard house, 1906-1910.
Avery Library.

927. Charles H. Williams house, 1895-1896.
(Photo: Roth)

928. George L. Williams house, 1895-1899.
(Photo: Roth)

930. Delta Psi Fraternity, Williams College, 1884-1886.
Sturgis, 1895.

931. Ross R. Winans house, 1882-1883.
AABN 21 (April 30, 1887).

935. Catherine Wolfe house, project, c. 1880.
MM&W Archive, NYHS.

939. Agriculture Building, World's Columbian Exposition, 1891-1893.
(Photo: W. H. Jackson)

940. John Haynes Memorial fence and gate, Center Church, Hartford,
      1901-1902. Built by the Ruth Wylls Chapter, Daughters of the
      American Revolution.
      (Photo: Roth)

941. Charles R. Yandell & Company gallery, 1886-1887.
      MM&W Archive, NYHS.

THE SANITARY ENGINEER AND CONSTRUCTION RECORD ILLUSTRATED SERIES.

THE YOUNG MEN'S CHRISTIAN ASSOCIATION AND THE TURNER BUILDING, NEWBURG, N. Y.

943. Young Men's Christian Association of Newburgh, 1882-1884.
MM&W Archive, NYHS.

944. Young Men's Christian Association of the Oranges, 1901-1902. MM&W Archive, NYHS.

944. Young Men's Christian Association of the Oranges. (Photo: Roth)

DATE DUE

Demco, Inc. 38-293